P9-DNU-666

Also by Peter Irons

_____

The New Deal Lawyers

Justice at War: The Story of the Japanese American Internment Cases

*The Courage of Their Convictions: Sixteen Americans
Who Fought Their Way to the Supreme Court*

Justice Delayed: The Record of the Japanese American Internment Cases

May It Please the Court (editor and narrator)

Brennan vs. Rehnquist: The Battle for the Constitution

A People's History of the Supreme Court

Jim Crow's Children: The Broken Promise of the Brown Decision

Cases and Controversies: Civil Rights and Liberties in Context

WAR POWERS

WAR POWERS

HOW THE IMPERIAL PRESIDENCY

HIJACKED THE CONSTITUTION

PETER IRONS

METROPOLITAN BOOKS

HENRY HOLT AND COMPANY | NEW YORK

Metropolitan Books
Henry Holt and Company, LLC
Publishers since 1866
175 Fifth Avenue
New York, New York 10010
www.henryholt.com

Metropolitan Books® and m® are registered
trademarks of Henry Holt and Company, LLC.

Library of Congress Cataloging-in-Publication Data

Irons, Peter H., 1940–
    War powers : how the imperial presidency hijacked the Constitution /
Peter Irons.—1st ed.
        p. cm.
    Includes bibliographical references and index.
    ISBN-13: 978-0-8050-7593-9
    ISBN-10: 0-8050-7593-3
    1. War and emergency powers—United States—History.   I. Title.
    KF5060.I76 2005
    342.73'0412—dc22   2005041488

        Henry Holt books are available for special promotions
    and premiums. For details contact: Director, Special Markets.

                        First Edition 2005

                    Designed by Victoria Hartman

                Printed in the United States of America

                1   3   5   7   9   10   8   6   4   2

For Representative John Conyers, Jr.,
in appreciation of his steadfast defense
of congressional war powers,
and his passionate commitment
to peace and justice

CONTENTS

WAR POWERS

INTRODUCTION

War Powers examines the most fateful questions the American people have faced in the nation's history: why and how we go to war. Such issues involve the life and death of every citizen—soldier and civilian alike. More than one million Americans, in fact, have died in the dozens of wars and armed conflicts in which the United States has been engaged over the past two centuries. More than half of those deaths—almost 600,000—resulted from the tragic and bloody Civil War, in which Americans killed one another on battlefields that are now both hallowed ground and tourist attractions. Two other great conflicts, the First and Second World Wars, between them cost the lives of more than half a million American soldiers, sailors, and airmen. Another thirty thousand died in the Korean War, and more than fifty thousand died in Vietnam, the nation's longest war and its only defeat. Other hostilities, from early battles with Native American tribes to the recent invasion and occupation of Iraq, have taken thousands of additional lives. The toll of American deaths in the nation's wars is far outstripped, of course, by the millions of enemy soldiers killed by U.S. troops and by the uncounted civilians who died from disease, famine, gunfire, artillery shells, napalm, and the atomic bombs that devastated the Japanese cities of Hiroshima and Nagasaki in 1945, raising the specter of a global nuclear holocaust.

Going to war is costly in more than battlefield and civilian deaths. Another cost is the burden of paying for these wars, both in preparing for them and fighting them. The price of "defense" has risen, over the years, from millions of dollars into the trillions, saddling the American people with massive debts that future generations will struggle to pay. But an even greater cost of war, and the subject of this book, has been the gradual but increasing subversion of the U.S. Constitution. I have not chosen this loaded term lightly, and I use it with the dictionary meaning of "undermine," rather than "overthrow" or "destroy." Since the twentieth century, presidents from Theodore Roosevelt through George W. Bush have undermined the Constitution by usurping the power to "declare war" that its Framers had placed in the hands of Congress. But such subversion has not been accomplished by force or guile. Congress has been a willing, often eager accomplice in handing its constitutional war powers to presidents who have asserted their own powers as "commander in chief" to commit American military forces to combat. Federal judges, including members of the Supreme Court, have also collaborated in this process of subversion, abdicating their duty to enforce the Constitution's dictate that only Congress holds the war-declaring power. Finally, successive generations of Americans, unwilling to force their elected representatives to reclaim their powers from presidents who have ordered troops into dozens of undeclared wars, have abetted the undermining of the fundamental structure of the government. In a very real and very dangerous sense, the imperial presidency has hijacked the Constitution, to serve the interests of the American empire.

Rarely does either the press or candidates for office discuss how this process of constitutional subversion came about, and what damage it has inflicted on the American political system. The invasion of Iraq in March 2003, however, provoked an often sharp debate between the candidates in the 2004 presidential campaign, who had initially agreed that Saddam Hussein should be deposed by military force but later differed over the professed justification for that invasion. Yet neither President George W. Bush, who had ordered the "preemptive" invasion of Iraq, nor Senator John Kerry, who later accused Bush of launching "the wrong war, in the wrong place, at the wrong time," confronted the basic question of which branch of government—Congress or the presidency—should wield the ultimate decision-making power to go to war. Nor did either candidate address the issue of whether Congress had abdicated its constitutional powers by handing presidents blank-check authorizations to send troops into combat without a formal declaration of war.

These are matters the American people need to consider, particularly since the "war on terrorism" seems likely to continue for years, if not decades. To appreciate the seriousness of the issues, the public must be aware of the historical, legal, and political context in which they arose and are now of pressing concern to every citizen. This book provides that background in a relatively short, readable format— more of a survey of this crucial topic than an exhaustive treatise. Most of the issues and events we explore have been examined, often in great detail, in books and articles listed in the bibliography. Some of these works have been written for specialists in fields such as international relations and constitutional law; others are polemical in tone and partisan in approach, on both sides of the war-powers debate. This book, in contrast, is directed at concerned American citizens—and those in other countries as well—who wish to become better informed about these issues, without having to master scholarly jargon or deal with overheated rhetoric. My purpose is to facilitate understanding and to encourage readers to determine their own stands on the topics the book explores.

Let me outline the structure of this book, which proceeds, chronologically, from the Constitution's framing to the American invasion of Iraq in 2003 and its aftermath. We begin in Philadelphia in 1787, when the Framers placed the war-declaring power solely in the hands of Congress. They also limited the president's authority as commander in chief of the armed forces, in the absence of a declared war, to that of "repelling" attacks on American territory or of taking "reprisals" for attacks on its citizens or property in foreign countries or on the high seas. Without a prior declaration of war by Congress, presidents could act only in "emergencies" and for limited periods. The "original intent" of the Framers on these separate powers, both in the Constitution's text and the debates at the Constitutional Convention, was both clear and emphatic, and provides a lodestar for discussions of the shifting course of America's war-making decisions.

Over the century that followed the convention, most presidents—with one major exception—consulted with Congress and gained its approval before taking military action, from "repelling" attacks by Indians to "reprisals" against the seizure of American ships and sailors. That exception, President James K. Polk's initiation of war against Mexico in 1845–46, marked the first imperial expansion of U.S. territory by force, as troops wrested from Mexico the land that is now California, Arizona, and New Mexico. Congress did, in fact, declare war on Mexico, but only after Polk had turned a border dispute into a military conflict, with territorial aggrandizement his primary goal. The Mexican War marked the transformation of Thomas Jefferson's vision of America as the "Empire of Liberty" into an "Empire of Conquest." As the United States became an imperialist nation, it imposed its will on smaller and weaker countries to satisfy the voracious appetite of American commerce, which sought raw materials for its factories and markets for its products.

The Civil War introduces a second, and equally important, focus of this book, the impact on the Bill of Rights of presidential efforts to muzzle dissent and to punish those suspected of giving "aid and comfort" to the nation's enemies. Abraham Lincoln's efforts to defeat the Confederate rebels, which included the suspension of habeas corpus and the establishment of military tribunals to try suspected rebel sympathizers, raised profound questions of presidential power during wartime and produced judicial rebukes in cases with close parallels to those stemming from the Bush administration's treatment of "enemy combatants" in the war on terror. In later chapters we will examine cases involving free speech during World War I, the internment of Japanese Americans during World War II, and the government's powers to prosecute those suspected of giving "material aid" to America's enemies in the war on terror.

Following the Union victory in the Civil War, the "Empire of Conquest" gained momentum, as the United States used the Spanish-American War (1898) as a means to annex Puerto Rico and the Philippines. Significantly, President William McKinley resisted calls for war with Spain, but finally bowed to pressure from congressional hawks who spoke openly of "imperialist" aims in the Pacific. Early in the twentieth century, Woodrow Wilson professed his desire to keep America out of the First World War but later manipulated Congress into declaring war on Germany, supposedly as "reprisal" for its submarine attacks on American shipping. Wilson lost his postwar battle with congressional isolationists over U.S. participation in the toothless League of Nations, and his three Republican successors during the 1920s limited their dispatch of troops to interventions in Central America, to prop up friendly governments and protect American investment from radical movements.

Franklin D. Roosevelt came to office in 1933 with a mandate to mobilize an active government to lift the nation from the depths of the Great Depression. The New Deal majority in Congress promptly created agencies with sweeping powers to regulate almost every facet of business and agriculture. In presiding over this vast expansion of federal power, FDR became the first to occupy the imperial presidency (the term was coined by the historian Arthur Schlesinger, Jr.). The rapid growth of the federal bureaucracy, and the president's ability to command its operations, led to a governmental empire that far exceeded the limited resources available to Congress. Even greater expansion took place during World War II, with military and industrial mobilization establishing agencies and adding thousands of federal employees. By the war's end, not only had the presidency become an "imperial" office, but the global network of U.S. military bases, set up to protect the nation's "vital interests," enabled presidents to advance imperial political and economic interests. Between them, the crises of the Depression and World War II marked a massive acceleration in the subversion of the Constitution by the imperial presidency. The Depression allowed Roosevelt to expand—with overwhelming public support but with dubious constitutional backing—the domestic authority of the presidency, while the war gave him the opportunity to broaden his powers as commander in chief of a military force engaged in combat around the world. During the twelve years of Roosevelt's presidency, the political center of gravity shifted from Congress to the White House, and has not yet returned to the balance of powers envisioned by the Constitution's Framers.

By the end of World War II, the United States had become the world's dominant military and economic power, but several postwar developments limited the nation's ability to control events without challenge. First, the Cold War with the Soviet Union sparked an arms race—including huge arsenals of nuclear weapons on both sides—that was not only costly but potentially disastrous, should any regional conflict flare into global warfare. Second, the demand for independence by colonial states in Africa and Asia led to wars of national liberation in countries such as Vietnam, in which the United States aided the French in their losing battle with the Communist-led forces of the Vietminh. Third, the victory in 1949 of the Chinese Communists over the U.S.-backed Nationalist government produced further instability in Asia. Both singly and together, each of these developments created pressures on the presidents who succeeded Franklin Roosevelt to intervene in conflicts that supposedly threatened American interests. The first of these military interventions began when North Korean troops invaded South Korea in 1950, prompting Harry Truman to send American troops to repel the invasion; the Chinese Communists, in turn, dispatched troops into Korea. Significantly, Truman acted without a formal declaration of war by Congress, relying instead on a UN resolution that called on member states to join an international "police" force. The Korean War ended in 1953 with a shaky armistice, enforced ever since by American troops. That conflict also produced a Supreme Court rebuff to Truman's move to seize the nation's steel mills to head off a strike, an act he made without congressional sanction.

Even before the Korean War ended, the United States became embroiled in another Asian war—this time, a U.S.-backed regime in South Vietnam was battling a Communist-backed guerrilla insurgency. Four successive presidents—Dwight Eisenhower, John Kennedy, Lyndon Johnson, and Richard Nixon—dispatched increasing numbers of troops to Vietnam, and all did so without a declaration of war by Congress. In 1964, Johnson secured from Congress the so-called Tonkin Gulf Resolution, backing his power as commander in chief to respond with "all necessary force" to attacks the North Vietnamese were said to have launched on naval vessels but that probably never happened. Not until 1973, when Nixon agreed to withdraw American forces from Vietnam, did Congress attempt to reclaim its constitutional prerogatives by passing the War Powers Resolution; the measure put a sixty-day limit on presidential dispatch of troops into combat without congressional approval. As we shall see, every president since Nixon has disregarded—and in some cases flatly disobeyed—the provisions of what has become a monument to legislative futility. Congress, however, has done little to put teeth into the War Powers Resolution, and the federal courts have dismissed more than a dozen lawsuits that have sought to enforce its provisions, relying on the "political question" doctrine that allows judges to evade the issues of presidential usurpation of Congress's war-declaring power.

Shielded by a supine Congress and compliant federal judges from any effective constraints on their war-making powers, a succession of imperial presidents have sent troops to countries such as Panama and Grenada to depose leaders who were considered corrupt or radical. These were small-scale and successful wars in which few Americans died and that provoked little criticism in Congress or among the American public. Nor were there many critics of the Gulf War, launched by President George H. W. Bush in 1991, which drove the Iraqi army out of Kuwait after it had invaded its neighbor. Congress had given Bush a blank-check authorization to use military force against the Iraqis, but the president resisted pressure from hawks in Congress to take advantage of the Iraqi retreat from Kuwait to depose Saddam Hussein, who ruled Iraq with an iron fist and had killed thousands of his country's Kurdish minority with chemical weapons.

The Gulf War matched two armies on the battlefield, in what might be called a "classic" war, even though American firepower far outmatched that of the poorly equipped Iraqi troops. However, the emergence in the 1990s of a radical Islamic movement, fueled by resentment toward what was perceived as uncritical American support for Israel in its struggle with the Palestinians, unleashed a new kind of war. The bombing of the World Trade Center in New York City in 1993 gave the United States its first exposure to terrorism at home, and presaged a series of attacks on American facilities abroad, from embassies in Africa to naval vessels in the Persian Gulf.

The deadly impact of terrorism was brought home when hijacked airplanes slammed into the World Trade Center and the Pentagon on September 11, 2001. What is usually called the 9/11 attacks marked a turning point in American history—the beginning of the war on terror, whose first major demonstration was an armed response to the Islamic militants who planned and carried out the 9/11 aerial assault, and their leader, Osama bin Laden. A member of a wealthy Saudi Arabian family with close ties to the Saudi ruling elite and the monarchy, bin Laden had formed al Qaeda, the organization to which the 9/11 hijackers belonged, and had masterminded its earlier attacks on American embassies and ships. Bin Laden operated from a sanctuary in Afghanistan, whose Taliban regime shared his Islamic fundamentalism and anti-American views. George W. Bush, armed with a hastily enacted authorization from Congress, dispatched troops to Afghanistan, where they quickly routed the Taliban forces but failed to find the elusive bin Laden.

Significantly, the hawks who had failed to convince the first President Bush to carry the Gulf War into Iraq and depose Saddam Hussein, and who retreated into conservative think tanks during Bill Clinton's eight years in the White House, returned to high posts in the administration of the second President Bush. During their years of political exile, these advocates of American unilateralism had framed a long-range plan, based on preemptive military strikes against nations that posed threats to what were considered the vital interests of the United States. The primary goal of the strategists was to protect American access to Middle Eastern oil. Saudi Arabia, whose regime depended heavily on American military and economic aid, controlled the greatest oil reserves, but Iraq held the next-largest share, some 11 percent of the world's total.

Even before the 9/11 attacks, Bush administration hard-liners had prodded the president to find some pretext for invading Iraq and deposing Saddam Hussein. Following the Gulf War in 1991, the United Nations had demanded that Iraq destroy its stockpiles of weapons of mass destruction, which included chemical and biological weapons, and dismantle facilities that might produce nuclear weapons. Iraq's foot-dragging compliance with UN inspections offered such a pretext; the 9/11 attacks provided another, based on claims that Iraq harbored and supported the al Qaeda terrorist network. Early in 2002, President Bush and his top advisers made emphatic claims that Iraq possessed large stockpiles of weapons of mass destruction and had collaborated with al Qaeda terrorists. At the same time, Pentagon officials began shifting troops to Middle Eastern bases and preparing for an invasion. Congress played its supporting role by passing another blank-check authorization for Bush to use military force against Iraq.

The president set a deadline of March 20, 2003, for Iraq to comply fully with UN weapons inspections. The day before the deadline, Bush ordered a surprise attack on Iraq; missiles and bombs rained on the capital city of Baghdad, while American tanks raced across the desert from Kuwait. Faced with this onslaught, the Iraqi army quickly melted away, and Saddam Hussein fled from Baghdad, eluding capture until December. The quick military victory, as we know, was followed by an American occupation, which may last for years. As we also know, there were no Iraqi stockpiles of WMDs, nor any credible evidence of collaboration with al Qaeda. But in large measure because Congress and the media failed to challenge the Bush administration's claims, a majority of Americans supported the invasion—although many regretted their acquiescence when those claims were later exposed as spurious.

This sketch of significant events, from 1787 to the present, provides a context for the questions addressed in this book. Let me summarize these questions before we begin with the Constitutional Convention in 1787. What did the Constitution's Framers mean in giving Congress the sole power to declare war and making the president the commander in chief of the nation's military forces? How did Congress and presidents exercise their shared powers during the nineteenth century, as the United States grew rapidly in population and in economic strength? What impact have armed conflicts between the Civil War and the war on terror had on the rights of citizens to criticize the government's policies? To what extent has the emergence of the imperial presidency contributed to the subversion of the Constitution by usurping the war-declaring power that belongs solely to Congress? If the nation is engaged in a war on terror that will not end with a formal surrender or peace treaty, has the Constitution become outmoded? Should presidents be able to deploy military forces in this war without formal declarations by Congress? And does the Constitution require amendment to deal with this new situation? Although I address these questions specifically in the book's conclusion, I raise them here to stimulate thought and discussion of the broader issues the book examines: Why and how do we go to war?

1

IN THE BEGINNING:

"The Power of War and Peace"

On May 14, 1787, a dozen men gathered at the redbrick State House in Philadelphia, the seat of Pennsylvania's government. Several had attended the historic meeting, in the same building, at which the Declaration of Independence from Great Britain had been adopted, on July 4, 1776. And several had fought in the War of Independence, which ended on October 19, 1781, with the surrender of British general Charles Cornwallis at Yorktown, Virginia, to the Continental Army led by its commander in chief, General George Washington. The final treaty of peace between Great Britain and its former American colonies was not signed until 1783, but two years earlier, the thirteen states that made up the new nation had ratified the Articles of Confederation, which established a "firm league of friendship" between the "sovereign" states.

The men who gathered at the State House in 1787 had been drawn to the meeting because the "united states" of the Confederation were anything but united. During the six years since they formed a league, the states had acted in decidedly unfriendly ways toward one another. They disagreed over trade and commerce, recognition of their separate currencies, boundaries between the states, and the creation of new states in the burgeoning western territories of the vast American continent. In short, they acted more like quarreling European principalities than like states united by common purposes. The Confederation had been created in reaction to the arbitrary rule of a powerful imperial government, but the drafters of the Articles erred in the opposite direction: The government they designed was weak, divided, and unable to resolve conflicts between warring interests and regions.

The flaws in the Articles were built into the governmental structure they created. Each state retained "its sovereignty, freedom and independence, and every power, jurisdiction, and right, which is not by this Confederation expressly delegated to the United States, in Congress assembled." The only powers the drafters had delegated to the legislature were those to conduct foreign affairs, make treaties, and declare war—important duties to be sure, but not ones that the Congress, as established by the Articles of Confederation, could execute. In this ineffective governing body, no state was obligated to abide by the decisions of Congress; they were, for all practical purposes, merely advisory, and states often rejected the advice. Furthermore, the government lacked an executive body, or any person invested with executive powers, to enforce the laws passed by the Confederation Congress. Nor did the Articles provide for a national judiciary, so no institution was available to adjudicate conflicts between states or citizens of different states. In understandable reaction to the tyrannical rule against which they had revolted, the drafters of the Articles had replaced one of the strongest governments in the Western world with one of the weakest.

Between 1781 and 1785, the four states that bordered Chesapeake Bay and the Potomac River—Pennsylvania, Delaware, Maryland, and Virginia—became embroiled in disputes over fishing rights in those waters, especially over the harvesting of crabs and oysters. Among the competing fishermen, tempers flared and threatened to break out into violence. This regional conflict, which became known as the Oyster War, prompted a young Virginian, James Madison, to call a meeting of delegates from the four states in 1785, at the Mount Vernon estate of George Washington. Madison hoped to enlist Washington's prestige to persuade the contending states to agree on an informal treaty to settle their differences. Although the Mount Vernon gathering did not succeed, those who attended resolved to meet with delegates from the other nine states in Annapolis, Maryland, in September 1786. The Virginia legislature, of which Madison was a member, invited the states to send delegates to "take into consideration the trade of the states" and to draft, if possible, a "uniform system in their commercial regulations." The resolution also set a quorum of seven states to begin deliberations.

Because not enough delegates showed up in Annapolis to make up a quorum, nothing was done to end the fishing dispute. But the delegates who did attend passed a resolution, promoted by Madison and Alexander Hamilton, a wealthy lawyer from New York, calling upon all state legislatures to send delegates to another meeting to consider "the situation of the United States" and to "devise such further provisions as shall appear to them necessary to render the constitution of the federal government adequate to the exigencies of the Union." The Annapolis delegates set the meeting time for the second Monday of May 1787 and the place in Philadelphia. Whether enough states would send delegates to yet another meeting was far from certain.

Behind these efforts to bring the thirteen "sovereign" states together for discussion of the "constitution of the federal government" was the fertile mind of Madison. Born in 1751, the eldest of ten children, he grew up on a plantation whose fields were planted and plowed by slaves. Madison's father, a close friend of Washington's, sent him north for an education at the College of New Jersey, later known as Princeton. Here the young scholar read widely in political philosophy, and buried himself in the works of John Locke, an English political theorist, and other advocates of democratic rule and of separation of powers in governments. During the months before he arrived in Philadelphia in May 1787, Madison made extensive notes on the histories of republics and confederacies, from ancient Greece to the nations of Europe; he filled one notebook with a list of the "Vices of the Political System of the United States." Chief among the vices was the absence, in the Articles of Confederation, of the tripartite system of government that Locke had proposed a century earlier in his *Second Treatise of Government,* with functions divided among legislative, executive, and judicial branches. Madison agreed with Locke that the legislative branch, which directly represented the people through elections of its members, should be "first among equals" of the three branches. But he also accepted Locke's notion of checks and balances, which would—at least in theory—prevent any branch of government from usurping the powers of the other two.

The delegates who gathered in Philadelphia in May 1787 came with the ostensible purpose of revising and amending the "constitution of the federal government" to render its provisions "adequate to the exigencies of the Union." But Madison had an entirely different goal in mind. As a member of the ineffective Confederation Congress, he was aware that the Articles under which it operated were not a constitution of the federal government and that, in fact, no such government existed under a charter that recognized the sovereignty of each state. Moreover, as Madison well knew, the Articles could be amended only by unanimous vote of the thirteen states. Therefore, since Rhode Island had refused to elect members to the Confederation Congress and refused, as well, to send delegates to the Philadelphia convention, there was no chance that delegates from the other twelve states, even by unanimous vote, could devise any plan to amend the Articles. What Madison actually had in mind was to replace the Articles with a completely new constitution that established a strong national government, with three separate but coordinate branches. He and most of the other delegates to the Philadelphia meeting, which later became known as the Constitutional Convention, adopted the label Federalists, a term with a much different meaning from Confederationists. Before the Convention, Madison revealed his real intentions in a letter to Washington. His plan for a new constitution was based on "a due supremacy of the national authority," but did not "exclude the local authorities whenever they can be subordinately useful." In other words, the formerly "sovereign" states would yield to the "supremacy" of the federal government. Madison's plan, he told Washington, would invest the federal government "with positive and complete authority in all cases which require uniformity; such as the regulation of trade" between the states and with foreign nations.

The convention resolution of the Virginia legislature had set a quorum of seven states to begin deliberations on proposals to revise the Articles of Confederation, but in reality to replace them with a new constitution. The first official session began on May 25, when the quorum was finally achieved, with twenty-nine delegates from seven states in attendance. Before this session, Madison met almost daily with his fellow Virginians, whose seven members formed the largest delegation. He circulated among them copies of the fourteen points in his plan for a new government. His first, and most delicate, task was to convince Edmund Randolph, the persuasive Virginia governor, to set aside his objections to a new constitution. Madison won over Randolph by allowing him to add, to the "Virginia Plan," a fifteenth resolution, elevated to first place above Madison's fourteen. Randolph proposed, and Madison accepted, a resolution that "the Articles of Confederation ought to be so corrected and enlarged as to accomplish the objects proposed by their institution; namely, common defense, security of liberty and general welfare." This was decidedly *not* what Madison had in mind, but he viewed Randolph's resolution as harmless and his support for the other fourteen as essential.

With this concession, Randolph presented the Virginia Plan to the delegates in a lengthy speech, shortly after the unanimous election of George Washington as presiding officer of the convention. Randolph enumerated "the defects of the confederation" and of its Articles, especially the inability of the Confederation Congress to act without unanimity among the states, the lack of an executive to carry out the few decisions the states could agree on, and the absence of a judicial body to resolve conflicts between the states. To remedy the shortcomings, Madison's plan sought a strong federal government in which power would be dispersed among three branches, to avoid both the "instability" of governments based on legislative supremacy and the "monarchical" tendencies of unchecked executive power. Madison proposed, and Randolph presented to the delegates, a system that included a "National Legislature" of two houses, one "elected by the people of the several states," the other chosen by the members of the first house from "persons nominated by the individual legislatures" of each state. The Virginia Plan also called for a "National Executive" with "a general authority to execute the national laws," and a "National Judiciary," to consist of "one or more supreme tribunals, and of inferior tribunals to be chosen by the National Legislature." The scope of the judicial branch's authority extended to "piracies and felonies on the high seas, captures from an enemy, cases in which foreigners or citizens of other states applying to such jurisdictions may be interested, or which respect the collection of the National revenue; impeachments of any National officers, and questions which may involve the national peace and harmony." Although the initial enumeration of federal judicial powers, combining narrow and broad grants of jurisdiction, did not survive the final drafting process, it indicated Madison's intention of creating a judicial branch that could decide cases in the area of foreign affairs.

Despite the Virginia Plan's conception of a federal government with power dispersed among three branches, Madison and the other Federalists clearly envisioned the legislature to be, in Locke's phrase, "first among equals": The laws it enacted would be enforced by an executive, with a judiciary available to resolve conflicts between the other two branches. Not surprisingly, therefore, the debates among the delegates focused on the powers granted, under the new constitution, to the lawmaking Congress. The first debate on the subject began with a discussion of Madison's proposal that Congress should have the authority "to legislate in all cases to which the separate states were incompetent." After taking copious notes of the debates from his desk at the front of the State House chamber, Madison recorded his own words on this crucial issue. He told the delegates that he had brought with him into the convention "a strong bias in favor of an enumeration and definition of the powers necessary to be exercised by the national legislature; but also brought doubts concerning its practicability." Madison did not elaborate on his "doubts," but assured the delegates that he "should shrink from nothing which should be found essential to such a form of government as would provide for the safety, liberty, and happiness of the community."

The "safety" of the community to which Madison referred, in his first speech on the powers of Congress, depended on the national government's ability to protect the American people from the possible designs of hostile foreign nations. Although a peace treaty had been negotiated with Great Britain to acknowledge the military victory of the revolutionists and the king's recognition of the newly independent nation, many delegates still feared that conflicts in Europe might cross the Atlantic and threaten the weak confederation of states. Should the nation face military danger, the Confederation Congress was virtually powerless to protect American shipping or repel an invasion of the nation's territory. Madison and other advocates of a strong federal government were acutely conscious of the need to grant the proposed Congress adequate powers to protect the nation from foreign threats to its sovereignty or trade. The Federalists in Philadelphia were also aware that the constitution they were drafting should give the "National Executive" sufficient powers to repel any military invasion. The problem these delegates faced was to balance the powers in such a manner that neither Congress nor the executive had exclusive control of foreign relations but each could play an appropriate role in this crucial area of national government.

As they wrestled with this difficult question, the Philadelphia delegates looked to the British experience, despite the fact that the Revolution had begun with a rejection of royal power to occupy the colonies, with military forces under the king's direct command. The Declaration of Independence, in fact, had included, among its listing of "repeated injuries and usurpations," King George's unfettered ability to "render the Military independent of and superior to the Civil Power." In proposing a national government of dispersed powers, Madison and other Federalists were greatly influenced by Locke's

Second Treatise of Government, especially its advocacy of the tripartite system. But Locke had also defended what he called the "prerogative" of the king to make unilateral decisions as to war and peace, without any check from the British Parliament. According to Locke, relations between countries approached a state of international anarchy. Because of the fluidity and unpredictability of such relations, moreover, legislative bodies such as Parliament, designed for measured deliberation, were so unwieldy and slow-acting that it was unwise to hobble the king by forcing him to rely on "antecedent, standing, positive laws" in his conduct of foreign affairs. In particular, Locke said that legislative bodies should not hinder the national executive's ability to employ troops and naval forces to repel sudden invasion. Locke went so far as to argue that the executive must be free to engage in "many things . . . which the laws do not prescribe." His notion of prerogative extended to the executive's power to act *against* the law. As we shall see, American presidents have repeatedly asserted their "inherent" power to employ military force without legislative sanction and even *against* the clear declarations of Congress. In this sense, Locke's notion of executive prerogative remains alive, more than two centuries after the Philadelphia delegates rejected that notion.

In addition to Locke's works, most of the delegates were familiar with Sir William Blackstone's widely read and enormously influential *Commentaries on the Laws of England,* a four-volume treatise that covered virtually every facet of law, both private and public. Blackstone went beyond Locke in his endorsement of executive prerogative in foreign and military affairs. The king, he asserted, had absolute authority over Britain's relations with other countries, including the power to deploy and command military and naval forces and to make treaties and alliances. In practice, however, the British monarchy had yielded some of its powers in these areas to Parliament, which controlled the purse strings. During the eighteenth century, royal prerogative had weakened; by the time of the Philadelphia convention, Parliament had established that the king could act in foreign affairs only "by and with the advice and consent"

of the elected body. The one exception to this rule, which the delegates to the Constitutional Convention clearly recognized, was the
executive's right to repel any invasion of the nation's territory, a
power that Parliament had conceded to the king. As lawmakers in
both countries were aware, legislatures moved too slowly, in the
days of travel by horse and carriage, to make decisions required during an emergency.

Many delegates also brought with them to Philadelphia their personal experiences of the Revolution, as members of the Continental
Congress, which had authorized General Washington to command
the troops that fought the British. In a resolution adopted on June
19, 1775, that legislature had instructed Washington, "punctually to
observe and follow such orders and directions, from time to time, as
you shall receive from this or a future Congress." But the very next
day, the Congress had adopted a second resolution, acknowledg-
ing that "whereas all particulars cannot be foreseen, nor positive
instructions for such emergencies so beforehand given but that many
things must be left to your prudent and discreet management." Read
together, the two resolutions reflected the Continental Congress's
awareness that its control over Washington's military command
would necessarily be subject to his assessment of the steps required
in meeting the "emergencies" he faced.

These pragmatic considerations had a substantial impact on the
debates, in Philadelphia, over the proper balance between legislative
and executive powers in foreign and military affairs. The issue came
before the delegates shortly after Randolph presented the Virginia
Plan on May 29, in which he proposed a constitution with a provision "that a national Executive be instituted." At this point in the
convention, the delegates had not agreed that executive power should
be vested in a single person or how that person should be elected.
The decision to give the executive the title of "president" came much
later in the convention, after the office itself had been agreed on, but
for purposes of simplicity we will employ the term here. Even before
the delegates considered the powers of Congress under the new constitution, questions were raised about the president's role in foreign

affairs. To Charles Pinckney of South Carolina, giving the president responsibility for "peace and war . . . would render the Executive a Monarchy, of the worst kind, to wit an elective one." Another South Carolinian, John Rutledge, agreed that he "was for vesting the executive power in a single person," although he "was not for giving him the power of war and peace."

Other delegates sought to assure Pinckney and Rutledge that executive authority would not extend so far. James Wilson of Pennsylvania, perhaps the most influential delegate after Madison, referred to Blackstone in responding that "making peace and war are generally determined by writers on the Laws of Nations to be legislative powers." Wilson took pains to distance the constitution the delegates were drafting from the British model. "The prerogatives of the British Monarchy," he said, were not "a proper guide in defining the executive powers. Some of the prerogatives were of a legislative nature. Among others that of war and peace." Speaking after Wilson, Madison agreed that "executive powers . . . do not include the rights of war and peace . . . but should be confined and defined—if large we should have the evils of elected Monarchies."

The delegates had created a Committee on Detail, charged with the task of turning all the proposals for constitutional provisions into concrete language. On August 6 the committee presented the convention with a draft that included a provision—"The legislature of the United States shall have the power to make war"—that clearly excluded the "National Executive" from the war-making power and reflected the delegates' resolve to establish legislative supremacy in this crucial area. During the debate over the proposal, several delegates voiced concerns about giving Congress control over war and peace. Pinckney argued that the legislature's "proceedings were too slow" in making decisions that required dispatch rather than deliberation. On the other side, Pierce Butler, another South Carolina delegate, replied that he "was for vesting the power in the President, who will have all the requisite qualities, and will not make war but when the nation will support it." Butler put his opinion into a motion, which prompted Elbridge Gerry of Massachusetts to respond that he "never expected to hear in a republic a motion to empower the Executive alone to declare war." Gerry's words carried the day, and Butler's motion died for lack of a second among the delegates.

Although Butler stood alone in proposing to vest the war-making power in the president, many delegates questioned the Committee on Detail's proposal to place this authority in the hands of Congress. Madison and Gerry offered a motion that would substitute the verb "declare" for "make" in the committee's draft constitution on war. Their motion also provided for "leaving to the Executive the power to repel sudden attacks." During the debate that followed, almost every delegate supported the wording change proposed by Madison and Gerry. In stating that "the executive should be able to repel and not to commence war," Roger Sherman of Connecticut expressed the prevailing view. George Mason of Virginia added that he "was for clogging rather than facilitating war, but for facilitating peace." Delegates voted by states, rather than individually, and when debate over the Madison-Gerry motion ended, it was approved by a vote of eight states to one.

What may have seemed at the time a minor semantic change in the draft constitution, which became part of the first article of the final document, has provoked a continuing debate over the respective powers of Congress and the president. During the Vietnam War, for example, Senator Barry Goldwater argued that by changing the power of Congress from "making" to "declaring" war, "the Framers intended to leave the 'making of war' with the President." In Goldwater's expansive view of presidential war-making power, Congress was authorized only to "declare" an event that had already begun. But the Framers understood these words differently from the way the Arizona Republican did. The term "declare" was synonymous with "commence," and, in this context, they both referred to the initiation of hostilities, not to their subsequent acknowledgment or ratification by Congress. The Framers agreed that the president could act without a congressional declaration of war to repel an invasion but that only Congress could authorize the deployment of forces outside the nation's territory in combat against foreign troops.

Support for this reading of the Framers' intent comes from their inclusion, among the powers granted to Congress, of the issuing of "letters of marque and reprisal." Dating back to the Middle Ages, this phrase initially referred to sovereigns' employment of private military forces to conduct "reprisals" against other sovereigns for injuries to their subjects or interests. The "letters" were a form of contract between the sovereign and the private force. Over time, such reprisals were generally conducted by public armies and navies, and the phrase "letters of marque and reprisal" was considered, by the Framers, to include armed hostilities short of declared war. Sending military forces to protect American citizens in foreign countries, or to retrieve property that had been unlawfully seized, was an example of such congressional power. The Framers also understood that armed reprisals were acts of war, however limited in duration or in number of troops. Thomas Jefferson later wrote of the authority required in conducting a reprisal that "Congress must be called upon to take it; the right of reprisal being expressly lodged with them by the Constitution, and not with the executive."

In addition, the Framers gave Congress broad authority to organize, fund, and maintain the nation's armed forces. There was little debate in the Philadelphia convention over provisions setting out these powers in Article I of the Constitution, which includes five related clauses on this subject. First, Congress was authorized "to raise and support armies, but no appropriation of money to that use shall be for a longer term than two years." Second, Congress could "provide and maintain a navy" through appropriations to the executive branch. The third clause empowered Congress "to make rules for the government and regulation of the land and naval forces" of the United States. These three clauses were actually prospective, since the nation did not have, in 1787, a standing army or navy. At the time of the convention, the nation's armed forces consisted of separate state militias, and the Framers placed control of these forces in the hands of Congress, in the fourth provision, which enabled the elected body to "provide for calling forth the militia to execute the laws of the United States, suppress insurrections and repel invasions."

There was a general understanding among the delegates that this clause did not conflict with, or limit, the president's power to employ armed forces in an emergency, such as a sudden attack on American territory. The "invasions" the delegates had in mind were sustained and large scale, requiring the mobilization of the state militias. Finally, the Framers gave Congress the responsibility "to provide for organizing, arming, and disciplining the militia, and for governing such part of them as may be employed in the service of the United States." This fifth clause reserved "to the states respectively, the appointment of the officers, and the authority of training the militia according to the discipline prescribed by Congress."

Read together, as the Framers clearly intended them to be, the five clauses in Article I of the Constitution lodged the ultimate power over the nation's armed forces in Congress. That body would "make rules" for the governing of these forces, appropriate the money to organize and support them, and call them into service to "repel invasions" of the nation's territory. The president retained the inherent power of any sovereign to employ armed forces to meet a sudden attack, whether to protect the "homeland" of the United States or American citizens abroad. But this executive power was limited to the immediate situation. Should hostile forces launch "invasions" of the United States, Congress alone had the right of "declaring war" in response, and of granting the president the authority to "command" the troops through subordinate officials, both civilian and military.

During every debate in the Philadelphia convention, the delegates addressed their remarks to its presiding officer, George Washington. They all respected him as the commanding general of the Continental Army, which had secured the nation's independence through a long, bitter war. And most of the delegates anticipated that Washington would become the first president of the United States, whose charter of government they were drafting. Hardly anyone, both inside the State House chamber or outside its walls, feared that Washington would act rashly as president, certainly not as an autocrat who would drag the nation into war. But the delegates were also looking ahead, with the nation's future in mind. Conscious that the Constitution they were drafting was intended to endure for generations, even centuries, to come, they deliberately separated the duties of the legislative and executive branches of the federal government. Congress would control and exercise the war-making power, and the president would execute that power, subject to congressional authorization and oversight.

The delegates wrote this principle into Article II of the Constitution, which provided that "the executive power shall be vested in a President of the United States." They understood that "execution" followed, rather than preceded, the authorization by Congress of any power, including that of declaring war. In Section 2 of that article, the Framers provided that "the President shall be Commander in Chief of the Army and Navy of the United States, and of the militia of the several states, when called into the actual service of the United States." This provision is all the Constitution says about the president's military powers.

As we shall see, presidents have repeatedly—and increasingly—seized on this provision to claim for themselves the war-making power the Framers specifically placed in the hands of Congress. But a look at the meaning of the term "commander in chief," as the Framers understood it, clearly shows that later claims of presidential authority to send forces into combat, anywhere in the world and for any purpose, have no constitutional support.

The term itself, and the office conferred on those who hold such a title, was first employed by King Charles I in 1639, when he named the earl of Arundel as "commander in chief" of the army that battled the Scots in the First Bishops War. It soon came to refer to the highest officer in a military chain of command. During the English civil wars, both the king and Parliament named commanders in chief of several armies. In 1645, for instance, Parliament appointed Sir Thomas Fairfax as commander in chief of all the armed forces, providing that he was "subject to such orders and directions as he shall receive from both Houses or the committee" established to supervise the war effort. Over time, each British army or naval fleet was headed by a commander in chief, and with the development of the cabinet system of English government, Parliament created the post of secretary of war, and placed the military commanders in chief under his direction. The close supervision rankled many generals and admirals; the duke of Wellington complained that "the commander in chief cannot move a Corporal's Guard from one station to another, without a route signed by the Secretary of War. This is the fundamental principle of the Constitution of the British Army." And it became the fundamental principle of the U.S. Constitution as well, placing military officers under the command of a civilian president, whose orders were subject to congressional authorization.

The Framers of the federal constitution had no disagreement with the fundamental principle of control by elected bodies of the nation's military forces, headed by a civilian commander in chief whose powers were defined and supervised by Congress. Debate on this issue at the convention began on May 29, when Charles Pinckney proposed the title of "president" for the "National Executive" that Madison had included in the Virginia Plan. The South Carolinian also moved that the president "shall, by virtue of his office, be Commander in Chief of the Land Forces of U.S. and Admiral of their Navy." Although the final draft of the Constitution altered Pinckney's wording, the delegates agreed, with virtually no debate, to grant the president the titular power to act as commander in chief. But the delegates also acknowledged that the president could exercise the "command" of the nation's military forces during wartime but could not "declare" war through his command.

The debates in the convention, the later writings of delegates to that meeting, and speeches in the state conventions that voted on ratification of the Constitution leave no doubt that the president's title and role as commander in chief gave him no powers that Congress could not define or limit. Speaking at the North Carolina ratification convention, James Iredell, a future Supreme Court justice, outlined the differences between the British system and the new American government. "In almost every country," he said, "the executive has command of the military forces. From the nature of the thing, the command of armies ought to be delegated to one person only. The secrecy, dispatch, and decision, which are necessary in military operations, can only be expected from one person. The President, therefore, is to command the military forces of the United States, and this power I think a proper one; at the same time it will be found to be sufficiently guarded." Furthermore, Iredell noted, "the King of Great Britain is not only the commander-in-chief of the land and naval forces, but . . . also has the power to declare war. The President has not the power to declare war. The powers are vested in other hands. The power of declaring war is expressly given to Congress."

Alexander Hamilton, arguing for ratification of the Constitution in the newspaper essays later published as the *Federalist Papers,* wrote in number 69 that the president's powers as commander in chief "would amount to nothing more than the supreme command and direction of the military and naval forces, . . . while that of the British kings extends to the declaring of war and to the raising and regulating of fleets and armies, all which, by the Constitution under consideration, would appertain to the Legislature." According to Hamilton, the president could exercise his powers as "first General and Admiral" only "in the direction of war when authorized or begun." The context of these words makes clear that Hamilton meant wars "begun" by hostile nations through attacks on the United States or their own declarations of war.

Perhaps the most authoritative statement on the primacy of legislative over executive powers in this field comes from Madison, who initiated the effort to draft a new Constitution and who insisted on the separation of powers among the branches of the federal government. Madison argued that "those who are to *conduct a war* cannot in the nature of things, be proper or safe judges, whether *a war ought* to be *commenced, continued,* or *concluded.* They are barred from the latter functions by a great principle in free government, analogous to that which separate the sword from the purse, or the power of executing from the power of enacting laws."

Madison's emphatic statement, and the entire record of the Constitutional Convention, leaves no doubt that the Framers agreed that Congress, the body elected by the people, should hold the awesome power to commit the nation to war. The president, and the military forces under his command, could employ troops and ships only in cases of emergency, to repel foreign invasion as a defensive measure or to protect American citizens and property abroad.

Having completed their labors on September 17, 1787, after four hard, hot months of debate and deliberation, thirty-nine delegates from twelve states put their signatures on the new Constitution. Nine months later, on June 21, 1788, New Hampshire became the ninth state to ratify the document, bringing into existence the new nation whose struggle for independence had begun with the first shots at Concord and Lexington in 1775. Given the military weakness of this fledgling country, and the imperial designs of the European nations that coveted the vast territories between the thirteen "united states" and the Pacific Ocean, it seemed inevitable that more shots would be fired, as the Americans themselves continued moving west, into territories occupied or claimed by Indians and foreign traders and settlers. Whether the Constitution's Framers had wisely provided for further wars remained to be seen as the first Congress and the first president assumed their duties in April 1789.

2

"NOT ONLY WAR BUT PUBLIC WAR":

Congressional Authority in the New Nation

The nation that had won its independence from the British Empire through a protracted war had no imperial ambitions or warlike designs. The United States was, in fact, a relatively small country in population, with some four million inhabitants—one-quarter of them slaves—thinly spread along the Atlantic coast. The imperial powers of Europe, dominated by England, France, and Spain, vastly outnumbered the United States in population, controlled the commerce of the globe, and possessed large standing armies and naval fleets to protect and expand their empires. Among its aims, the Constitution's preamble included the Framers' desire to "provide for the common defense" of the formerly sovereign and independent states. But no army or navy stood ready to defend the nation against the imperial powers of Europe, which occupied and laid claim to vast tracts of the North American continent, to the north, south, and west of the thirteen states. Nor were there military or naval forces to protect American merchant ships carrying goods such as timber, tobacco, and cotton along the Atlantic coast and across the ocean, as a thriving commerce began to increase the wealth and well-being of the American people.

The greatest danger to the United States, and the greatest challenge to its new government, lay in two areas. The first, and most hazardous, resulted from foreign interference with U.S. maritime commerce. With no navy to protect it, the nation's merchant fleet offered tempting targets for pirates who flew no country's flag. American ships were also defenseless against foreign governments who demanded "tribute" for the privilege of entering their ports. Another source of danger lay in the prospect of U.S. ships and their goods becoming entangled in the cross fire of the episodic wars between European powers, not only on that continent but also on the oceans surrounding the United States.

The challenge of dealing with the perils fell, initially, on the shoulders of George Washington, elected by acclamation in 1789 as the nation's first president. Like several of his successors, Washington came to the presidency as a military hero; he had served as commander in chief of the Continental Army during the Revolution. As noted in chapter 1, Washington had accepted and followed, with no reservations, the directives of the Continental Congress during the war for independence; he was not given to Napoleonic behavior. Furthermore, Washington had presided over the Philadelphia convention, whose delegates had drafted the Constitution, which vested the war-making power solely in Congress. During his two presidential terms, between 1789 and 1797, Washington confronted both dangers to the nation. Each of the episodes reveals that the first serious tests of the constitutional balance between Congress and the president followed the Framers' design and intentions.

The initial foreign policy and military crisis that faced the United States began two years before the Constitution was drafted and stemmed from piracy in the Mediterranean. What became known as the Algiers Affair started on July 25, 1785, with the boarding and seizure of the U.S. schooner *Maria* off the northern coast of Africa by an "Algerine corsair," as Washington's secretary of state, Thomas

Jefferson, later described the event. Five days later, the U.S. ship *Dauphine* was seized by "another Algerine" in the Atlantic, some fifty miles west of Lisbon, Portugal. Both corsairs belonged to the fleet of the Ottoman Empire, based in what is now Turkey. At the time, Algiers, Tunis, and Tripoli were autonomous regencies under the control of Turkish officials, and were loosely allied with the independent nation of Morocco. Known as the Barbary Powers, the four states conducted a campaign of piracy against foreign shipping, in which they would declare war on other countries, seize their ships, make slaves of captive sailors, and then offer peace and the return of the captives, exacting tribute in exchange for allowing the ships to ply the Atlantic and Mediterranean unhindered.

The year before the seizure of the American ships, the Continental Congress had resolved to negotiate treaties with the Barbary Powers to prevent such piracy, but these efforts failed. Congress then commissioned a prestigious group—John Adams, Benjamin Franklin, and Thomas Jefferson—to conduct further treaty negotiations. They sent an agent to Algiers, whose Turkish leader demanded a tribute of $60,000 for the twenty-one American sailors held as captives. The fee was more than fourteen times the amount the commissioners had been willing to pay, and their agent returned empty-handed, with the seamen still in Algiers. They remained in captivity for four years before Washington became president and Jefferson joined his cabinet. During that time, numerous efforts to ransom the seamen had failed, as Turkish officials refused to lower their exorbitant tribute demands.

It would take a full chapter to recount and untangle the complicated negotiations over the release of the seamen, who finally gained their freedom in July 1796, eleven years after their seizure. But the focus here is on the relations between President Washington, advised by Jefferson, and the members of both houses of Congress during the negotiations. Despite public calls for Washington to order naval and ground actions against the Barbary Powers, both men deferred to Congress to make such a move. In a report to Congress in December 1790, prepared by Jefferson and submitted by Washington, the secretary of state discussed proposals to "repel force by force" as an alternative to the fruitless negotiations over tribute to Algiers or outright ransom of the captives. "Upon the whole," Jefferson wrote, "it rests with Congress to decide between war, tribute, and ransom as the means of re-establishing our Mediterranean commerce." If Congress chose to declare war, Jefferson said, that body would consider "how far they will enable the Executive to engage" in such a war. "If tribute or ransom," he added, "it will rest with them to limit and provide the amount; and with the Executive, observing the same constitutional forms, to make arrangements for employing it to the best advantage."

Conflicts with the Barbary Powers continued into the nineteenth century, as piracy, seizure of ships and sailors, and demands for tribute escalated. In 1815 the dangers to American ships in the Atlantic and Mediterranean became so serious that President James Madison, who as the leading Framer of the Constitution had strongly backed giving the war-declaring power to Congress, asked its members for a declaration of war against Algiers. Congress responded, however, with legislation authorizing Madison to employ "such of the armed vessels of the United States as may be judged requisite." In this respect, Congress foreshadowed many later blank-check grants to presidents to deploy American forces in combat, short of a formal declaration of war; the most notable was the Tonkin Gulf Resolution in August 1964, authorizing Lyndon Johnson to commit troops against the North Vietnamese. But unlike the Vietnam War, the Algiers Affair ended on a peaceful note, in 1816, when the Algerian ruler signed a treaty that halted further acts of piracy. During a period of more than thirty years, four American presidents, from Washington through Madison, refrained from unilateral military action and worked closely with Congress to resolve the conflict peacefully.

In 1793, President Washington faced another foreign policy crisis, during the war between England and France, in which Spain and Holland became allies of the British. Partisans of the warring parties in the United States conducted both public debate and private intrigues on behalf of both England and France, and Washington rightly feared that the country might be dragged into the hostilities, with no military or naval forces to protect it. What would later be called the Citizen Genet affair caused the president great concern. Edmond-Charles-Edouard Genet was a French diplomat in the United States whose efforts to enlist political leaders to support private military adventures on behalf of France threatened to divide the country. Genet represented the revolutionary Jacobin regime in France, and after his arrival in the United States in April 1793, he encouraged American "privateers" to seize British ships off the Atlantic coast. One of the privateers brought its "prize" into the port at Philadelphia, the seat of the government at the time. After Genet had presented his ambassadorial credentials to President Washington, he attended a dinner in his honor in the Pennsylvania city; at the banquet the head of a roasted pig was named after the recently beheaded King Louis XVI of France. Genet became a celebrity, but the growing violence of the Jacobins—who dragged thousands of royalists to the guillotine—shocked many Americans who had initially supported the revolution overseas.

On April 22 President Washington responded to the growing crisis by issuing a Proclamation of Neutrality, assuring both England and France that the United States would remain "friendly and impartial toward the belligerent powers." By this act, Washington effectively abrogated the Franco-American Treaty of Alliance of 1778, which proclaimed the "perpetual alliance" of the two nations. Although the treaty had been ratified by the Continental Congress, ten years before the new Constitution was adopted, it symbolized U.S. support for France, and reliance on French military backing during the Revolutionary War.

The Citizen Genet affair raised a serious constitutional matter. Did the president have the legal right to issue a neutrality proclamation without the prior consent of Congress, or at least of the Senate, the body delegated with the power to ratify treaties and, presumably, to cancel or annul them? Washington was aware of the problem, and before he signed the proclamation, he convened a cabinet meeting, seeking advice on whether he should exercise his power to call the

Congress—which was then in recess—into a special session to debate the neutrality question and perhaps enact a resolution expressing its support of his move. When the cabinet advised the president not to call a special session, however, Washington proceeded to issue the proclamation on his own authority. But the initiative sparked a fierce public debate.

Jefferson, the secretary of state, kept his distance from the political fray, but he expressed his views in a private letter to his old friend Gouverneur Morris, who had played a key role at the Constitutional Convention as a Pennsylvania delegate. Jefferson sympathized with France, where he had served as envoy during the convention, but he was concerned that Genet's intrigues might persuade American citizens to take up arms on the French side. As Jefferson wrote to Morris: "if one citizen has a right to go to war of his own authority, every citizen has the same. If every citizen has that right, then the nation (which is composed of all its citizens) has a right to go to war, by the authority of the individual citizen. But that is not true either on the general principles of society, or by our Constitution, which gives that power to Congress alone."

On this matter, Jefferson loyally backed the president's authority to issue the neutrality proclamation as part of his constitutional duty to direct the nation's foreign affairs, short of going to war. Of course, Washington was trying to keep the United States *out* of the war between England and France and to refrain from any military intervention on either side. The central concern was not the president's war-making power but his authority to issue what might be considered treaties, in substance if not in form. The secretary of state had an unlikely ally on this question, Alexander Hamilton, and an equally unlikely adversary, James Monroe. Hamilton, who clashed repeatedly with Jefferson over political and economic affairs, also served in the cabinet as secretary of the Treasury. Writing under the pseudonym of Pacificus, Hamilton replied to attacks on Washington's proclamation with the argument that the president was vested by the Constitution with the power to manage foreign affairs. The chief executive was "the *organ* of intercourse between the nation and foreign nations," Hamilton wrote, and "the *interpreter* of national treaties." It was "entirely erroneous" to claim that Washington's neutrality proclamation constituted either a new treaty or the abrogation of an existing one, or that it was a law that only Congress was empowered to enact. In effect, Hamilton argued, the proclamation was designed to keep the nation at peace, unless and until Congress exercised its constitutional right to declare war.

Hamilton and Jefferson became unlikely allies on the question of presidential authority to issue the neutrality proclamation. It was equally surprising that Jefferson's longtime friend and political compatriot James Madison entered the debate on the other side. Madison, who was then serving in the House of Representatives, wrote a series of essays under the pseudonym Helvidius. He denounced Hamilton, an unabashed admirer of British royal prerogatives, for elevating executive powers above those of Congress. "In no part of the Constitution is more wisdom to be found," Madison argued, "than in the clause which confides the question of war and peace to the legislature, and not to the executive department."

In Madison's view, the president's neutrality proclamation, as a form of lawmaking, breached this constitutional wall. Enforcement of the proclamation against American citizens who violated its provisions, Madison asserted, required a congressional statute. In fact, when the government prosecuted Gideon Henfield for serving aboard a French privateer, he was acquitted because jurors decided that no law barred his actions. With no statute to support additional prosecutions, the government dropped charges against other defendants.

The impact of these events—including the exchanges between Jefferson, Hamilton, and Madison, and the Henfield case—was not lost on George Washington. When Congress returned to session in December 1793, the president sent a message that he sought "the wisdom of Congress to correct, improve, or enforce" the neutrality proclamation. It would be necessary to "extend the legal code" to authorize further prosecutions, he told the lawmakers. Congress responded by passing the Neutrality Act of 1794, which made unlawful the involvement of any person, within the jurisdiction of the United States, to engage in or assist "any military expedition or enterprise . . . against the territory or dominions of any foreign prince or state with whom the United States are at peace."

During the presidential administration of John Adams, who succeeded Washington in 1797, relations with France continued to bedevil the American government. Violations of the Neutrality Act led to numerous prosecutions of American citizens, most of them privateers who sought prizes by seizing foreign ships and selling their cargoes. Despite the clear wording of the law, Congress encouraged the privateers during the so-called Quasi-War with France, which took place between 1798 and 1801. It did so by enacting two laws, in 1798 and 1799, providing that the captains of ships that "rescued" other U.S. vessels from seizure by an "enemy" could be awarded a portion—up to half—of the rescued ship's value and cargo.

The two laws gave the federal courts their first opportunity to interpret the war-powers clauses of the Constitution. Three cases, decided between 1800 and 1806, illustrate the judicial branch's approach to these uncharted constitutional waters. The first case, *Bas v. Tingy,* involved the seizure of an American merchant vessel, the *Eliza,* by a French privateer. Some three weeks later, the *Eliza* was rescued by an American ship under the command of Captain Tingy, who filed a claim in federal court for a prize of half the *Eliza*'s value. But the rescued ship's owners disputed the claim, arguing that since the United States was not at war with France, the French privateer was not an enemy ship and the congressional act did not apply.

When the case reached the Supreme Court, the justices faced a new and difficult question. Was the United States at war with France? Congress had not declared war on France, but the seizure of American ships was clearly a belligerent act. Did the situation make the French privateer an enemy vessel, under the direction of the French government? At the time, the Supreme Court issued *seriatim* opinions, in which each justice expressed his views, in contrast to the later practice of issuing decisions in a single majority opinion. Two justices wrote opinions, in *Bas v. Tingy,* that addressed the question of how to define the term "war" under the Constitution.

In his opinion, Justice Bushrod Washington defined two distinct kinds of war, which he called "perfect" and "imperfect." "Every contention by force by two nations, in external matters, under the authority of their respective governments, is not only war, but public war," Washington stated. "If it be declared in form, it is called solemn, and is of the perfect kind; because one whole nation is at war with another whole nation; and *all* the members of the nation declaring war, are authorized to commit hostilities against all the members of the other, in every place, and under every circumstance."

But this definition required a congressional declaration of war, which did not exist. Justice Washington then looked to the "law of nations" for guidance. "But hostilities may subsist between two nations," he wrote, "more confined in its nature and extent; being limited as to persons, places, and things; and this is more properly termed *imperfect* war." Under this definition, the United States and France were indeed engaged in war at the time the *Eliza* had been seized by the French privateer and then rescued by Captain Tingy. Bushrod Washington described the relations between the two countries in 1799, when Congress had passed the "rescue" law under which Tingy sought his prize: "Congress had raised an army; stopped all intercourse with France; dissolved our treaty; built and equipped ships of war; and commissioned private armed ships" with authority to rescue American ships and collect a prize.

For Justice Washington, these facts showed clearly that Congress had acknowledged a state of war against France, without a formal declaration. "If they were not our enemy, I know not what constitutes an enemy," he wrote. "In fact and in law we are at war" with France. "In my judgment, it is a limited, partial war. Congress has not declared war in general terms, but Congress has authorized hostilities on the high seas by certain persons in certain cases." Washington then combined his two definitions of war into one. "So far it is, unquestionably, a partial war; but, nevertheless, it is a public war, on account of the public authority from which it emanates." In a much briefer opinion, Justice William Paterson agreed with his colleague. He described the situation as "a public war between the two nations, qualified, on our part, in the manner prescribed by the constitutional organ of our country."

The Supreme Court decision in *Bas v. Tingy* upheld the prize award to Captain Tingy. More important, the Court established a significant, far-reaching precedent, one that looked to Congress, rather than the president, as the body with sole constitutional authority to commit the nation to war, whether formally declared or not. President John Adams had asked Congress in 1798 to deal with the increasing hostility between the United States and France. The growing prospect of armed conflict with France compelled him, Adams wrote in a message to Congress, "to recommend to your consideration effectual measures of defense" against the French. The legislative branch had responded by passing several dozen bills, providing funds for naval armaments and authorizing Adams to raise a provisional army, to commission U.S. privateers to seize French shipping, and to suspend commerce with France. In granting these powers to Adams, Congress left no doubt that it considered the nation in a state of war with France, despite the lack of a formal declaration. During the congressional debates on these measures, Representative Edward Livingston said the United States was "now in a state of war; and let no man flatter himself that the vote which has been given is not a declaration of war." Whether or not Livingston correctly described the congressional defense measures as the functional equivalent of a formal declaration of war, the fact remained that Adams had asked for this legislation.

Adams did, however, become the first—although by no means the last—president whose violation of congressional directives led to judicial rebuke. The second of the three precedent-setting cases, *Little v. Barreme*, began in 1799 but was not decided by the Supreme Court until 1804, after Jefferson had succeeded Adams as president. Adams himself was not a party in the case, nor did his name appear in the opinion written by Chief Justice John Marshall, whom Adams had named in 1801 to head the Court. Although the contending parties were fighting over a relatively small amount of money, a significant principle was at stake, and this otherwise unimportant case became the vehicle for the Court to limit presidential power and to reassert congressional authority in foreign affairs.

The *Little* case stemmed from one of the laws that Adams had asked Congress to pass in 1798, during the Quasi-War with France. Known as the Non-Intercourse Act, the statute was designed to bar any ships owned by Americans from sailing "to any port or place within the territory of the French Republic," including French dependencies in the West Indies. The president was authorized to instruct "the commanders of the public armed ships of the United States" to stop and seize any such vessel, with a prize of half the value of the ship and its cargo. But it was often difficult, particularly on the high seas, for the captains of American privateers to know whether a ship they stopped was actually owned by Americans. Some of the ships that tried to evade the Non-Intercourse Act sailed under the flags of neutral countries, whose vessels were not covered by the law.

Despite the clear wording of the statute, allowing the seizure only of ships bound *to* a French port, and not *from* one, the orders issued by Adams to American privateers applied to "all intercourse, whether direct or circuitous, between the ports of the United States and those of France or her dependencies." Under this instruction, issued by the secretary of the navy, the American frigate *Boston,* commanded by Captain George Little, boarded and seized the brigantine *Flying Fish,* bound from a French port in the West Indies to the Danish island of St. Thomas. The *Flying Fish* had flown the Danish flag, but Little suspected that it was owned by Americans. Little brought his quarry to Boston, where he filed a prize claim for half the ship's value. The ship's owners, insisting they were in fact Danish, sued Little, in return, for damages. The federal judge who heard the case decided that the *Flying Fish* actually was Danish, and ordered that it be returned to its owners. But he refused to award damages against Captain Little, holding that he had "probable cause" to believe that the ship was American, despite its Danish flag. Little's appeal of this ruling to a federal circuit court turned out to be a serious mistake. Because the *Flying Fish* was bound *from* a French port, the judges held, Little had no authorization to seize it, even if it had been an

American vessel. Therefore, Little was liable to the Danish owners for damages, which the circuit court set at $8,504.

Having lost his bid to recover damages, Little now sought to avoid paying them, filing an appeal to the Supreme Court. His lawyers, trying to shift the blame for Little's mistake in seizing the Danish ship, argued that he was simply carrying out the president's orders. How was Little to know, they suggested, that Adams had either ignored, or mistakenly construed, the clear language of the Non-Intercourse Act? A military officer, they added, had to obey the orders of a superior officer—in this case, the commander in chief of the nation's armed forces. Even if the presidential order was unlawful, did not Captain Little's duty of obedience "excuse" his seizure of the Danish ship?

This last question proved difficult for Chief Justice Marshall, who wrote for the Court in the *Little* case. "I confess the first bias of my mind," he admitted, "was very strong in favor of the opinion that though the instructions of the executive could not give a right, they might yet excuse from damages." Marshall referred to the "implicit obedience which military men usually pay to the orders of their superiors, which indeed is indispensably necessary to every military system." But the arguments of his judicial colleagues had changed Marshall's mind. "I have been convinced that I was mistaken," he wrote, "and I have receded from this first opinion. I acquiesce in that of my brethren, which is, that the instructions cannot . . . legalize an act which, without those instructions, would have been a plain trespass" against the *Flying Fish*. "Captain Little, then, must be answerable in damages to the owner of this neutral vessel," Marshall concluded.

The chief justice spared Adams from any personal rebuke, but his opinion implicitly blamed the former president for disregarding the clear words of the Non-Intercourse Act. The *Little* case, although rarely cited as precedent in later Supreme Court opinions, laid down a basic principle of constitutional law: In directing the nation's foreign policy and in authorizing military action to enforce that policy, presidents must follow congressional directives. Over the past two centuries, as we shall see in later chapters, that fundamental notion has often been ignored—by presidents of both parties. But that fact does not undermine its continuing legitimacy.

In 1806 the federal courts decided a third case that raised issues of presidential war powers. In this case, Colonel William S. Smith was charged with assisting a rebellious Spanish general in planning a military expedition against the Spanish province of Caracas, in what is now Venezuela. Smith was indicted under the Neutrality Act, which made it a crime for an American citizen to engage in military action against any nation with which the United States was at peace. In his defense, Smith's lawyers secured subpoenas to force the testimony of Secretary of State James Madison and the secretary of the navy in President Jefferson's cabinet. When the two officials refused to appear in court, claiming that Jefferson had instructed them to remain at their posts, Smith's lawyers submitted an affidavit to the judge, stating the cabinet members' testimony was necessary to prove that Smith's military plans were "begun, prepared, and set on foot with the knowledge and approbation of the president of the United States," and with that of Madison as well.

The case of *United States v. Smith* came before Supreme Court Justice William Paterson, who was then "riding circuit" in the New York federal circuit court. During the first several decades of the Court's history, Supreme Court justices spent much of their time on the road, sitting with district judges at trials. Paterson had been a member of the Constitutional Convention in 1787, and played a key role in drafting the war-powers clause. Rejecting Smith's demand to compel Madison's testimony, Paterson wrote an opinion that echoed the words of Chief Justice Marshall in the *Little* case. Supposing "that every syllable of the affidavit is true," Paterson said of Smith's claim that he had acted with the "knowledge and approbation" of Jefferson and Madison, "of what avail can it be on the present occasion?" Colonel Smith could not shift the blame to the president, any more than Captain Little could. "The president of the United States cannot control the statute," Paterson wrote, "nor dispense with its execution, and still less can he authorize a person to do what the law forbids." Paterson noted that the United States and Spain were at peace. "If, then, the president knew and approved of the military expedition set forth in the indictment against a prince with whom we are at peace," he continued, "it would not justify the defendant in a court of law, nor discharge him from the binding force of the act of Congress, because the president does not possess a dispensing power."

Justice Paterson addressed the president's limited authority under the Constitution. "Does he possess the power of making war? That power is exclusively vested in Congress." Presidents did, he wrote, have power as "commander in chief of the forces by sea and land, to repel an invading foe. But to repel aggressions and invasions is one thing, and to commit them against a friendly power is another." Paterson extended this role beyond purely defensive military actions. "If, indeed, a foreign nation should invade the territories of the United States," he stated, it would "be not only lawful for the president to resist such invasion, but also to carry hostilities into the enemy's own country; and for this plain reason, that a state of complete and absolute war actually exists between the two nations." Paterson stressed the "manifest distinction between our going to war with a nation at peace, and a war being made against us by an actual invasion, or a formal declaration. In the former case, it is the exclusive province of Congress to change a state of peace into a state of war."

In his *Smith* opinion, Justice Paterson was not writing for the Supreme Court. But his words carried weight, not only because he was a member of the Court but also because, at the Constitutional Convention, he had argued for strong judicial powers. In fact, Paterson was the author of what became known as the "supremacy clause," a provision in the Constitution empowering the federal courts to enforce the document as "the supreme law of the land." Paterson made no ruling in the *Smith* case as to whether Jefferson or Madison had, as Colonel Smith claimed, given their "approbation" to his planned military expedition against Spain. But even if they had, Smith could not offer their support to "excuse" his violation of the Neutrality Act. Congress alone held the power of "authorizing the executive authority to proceed hostilely against the king of Spain," Paterson concluded. "But nothing of this kind has been done, or at least appears to have been done. Congress does not choose to go to war, and where is the individual among us who could legally do so without their permission?" Clearly not Colonel Smith, but just as clearly not President Jefferson.

It was Jefferson, however, who first cracked open the door through which later presidents barged with impunity. Early in his first term in office, Jefferson showed great deference to Congress in military actions. Responding in December 1801 to tribute demands from the pasha of Tripoli, who threatened to seize American ships in the Mediterranean, the president dispatched a small fleet of frigates to protect them against attack. Before any hostilities began, Jefferson asked Congress for permission to proceed from defensive measures to offensive responses, should that become necessary. He acknowledged that he was "unauthorized by the Constitution, without the sanction of Congress, to go beyond the line of defense." Only Congress, the president said, could authorize "measures of offense also." The lawmakers approved Jefferson's request for prior approval of any offensive naval action he might order. Faced with this expression of American resolve, the pasha backed down and dropped his tribute demands.

Six years later, Jefferson confronted the kind of military emergency that made prior consultation with Congress impossible. During a congressional recess in 1807, a British vessel fired on an American ship, the *Chesapeake*. In response, the president ordered military purchases to meet the emergency, although Congress had not appropriated funds for the supplies. Jefferson defended his actions in a report to Congress after it returned to session. "To have awaited a previous and special sanction by law," he wrote, "would have lost occasions which might not be retrieved." He had taken emergency measures without congressional sanction, and later explained why he felt compelled to act without prior legislative approval. The necessity "of saving our country when in danger," he said, justified his extralegal actions. "To lose our country by a scrupulous adherence to written law," Jefferson argued, "would be to lose the law itself, with life, liberty, property, and all those who are enjoying them with us; thus absurdly sacrificing the end to the means."

Clearly, Jefferson limited his ends-justifies-the-means argument to the kinds of emergency situations that required prompt action, especially at a time when instant communication with congressional leaders was impossible. But claims that the "law of necessity" might excuse a president from "scrupulous adherence to written law," however compelling in the crisis that Jefferson faced in 1807, have been made, by later presidents, in much less compelling situations. Jefferson acted with the aim of protecting American ships and crews from the very real threat of attack by the British. Protecting the safety and perhaps the lives of citizens during this emergency clearly justified defensive military action, such as dispatching naval forces to the danger zone. It was much less clear that purchasing military supplies to meet some future threat fell within the emergency powers of the president, without prior congressional approval. Congress later voted the funds that Jefferson had already committed for these supplies, and the potential conflict between the legislative and the executive branches of government ended without any judicial intervention and with little public debate.

In the broad scope of American history, and particularly in light of later conflicts—such as the two world wars, Vietnam, and the 2003 invasion of Iraq—the events recounted in this chapter may seem inconsequential and remote. But they represented serious challenges to the citizens of a new nation, small in population and limited in military force. The threat posed by the tribute demands of the Barbary Powers who took American sailors hostage cannot be dismissed as trivial, any more than the threat posed by present-day terrorists who have taken Americans hostage in the Middle East. How presidents and Congress responded to such early challenges, and how the federal courts resolved cases stemming from them, have continuing relevance to the later assertions of inherent presidential war-making powers. During the first decades of the nation's history, presidents and Congress generally respected the original intent of the

Constitution's Framers concerning their respective powers, and the courts established legal principles of enduring significance. But, as we shall see, the emergence of imperial ambitions—for territory and markets alike—followed the rapid growth of the nation's population and economy.

3

"A WAR UNJUST AND UNNECESSARY":

Seizing a Continental Empire

The first two decades of American independence from Great Britain, won through a long, costly war to free the colonies from the domination of the world's most powerful empire, hardly gave the new nation and its citizens any respite from conflicts with England. Although the British signed a peace treaty with the victorious revolutionaries in 1783, and the two countries both prospered from a growing trade across the Atlantic, the huge disparity in wealth and military might between the ostensible commercial partners created tensions. At the dawn of the nineteenth century, the United States became entangled in European wars, with dire consequences for American trade. In 1805, early in the second term of President Thomas Jefferson, the British revoked the orders that had allowed American ships to carry goods to both sides in England's war with France. The next year, England and France imposed new restrictions on American trade with Europe, and both countries seized and confiscated hundreds of ships for violating those orders.

Responding to the economic crisis, Jefferson asked Congress to declare an embargo on all U.S. exports, which the lawmakers approved. This move, intended to damage the trade of England and France and pressure them to settle their war, caused hardly a ripple in either country. In fact, Jefferson's plan backfired and seriously damaged the American economy, whose traders were cut off from their European markets. For any president, economic hardship creates political hardship, and Jefferson was no exception. Once lauded as the author of the Declaration of Independence, he left office in 1809 with his reputation tarnished and his influence diminished. Later generations of Americans have placed him in the nation's pantheon of great presidents, but Jefferson's foreign policy blunders left his successor in the White House, James Madison, with a weak hand in dealing with the increasingly bellicose British.

Madison, who had served in the ineffectual Continental Congress and later—after he played the primary role in drafting the Constitution—in the House of Representatives, was both schooled and skilled in the legislative arena. But he sorely lacked the skills required for effective presidential leadership. Known dismissively as "Little Jemmie," Madison had served as Jefferson's secretary of state but had little experience in diplomacy and negotiations with foreign leaders. If Jefferson left office as a weakened president, Madison began his first term even weaker, in both domestic and foreign estimation. And he took the helm of government at a time when the U.S. Navy, its funding cut sharply by Congress, was no match for the British armada, which became the undisputed "master of the oceans" after Lord Nelson's victory over the French and Spanish fleets at Trafalgar in 1805.

British leaders took full advantage of the new president's lack of experience in foreign affairs, and the weakness of both the American economy and naval forces. During the first two years of Madison's tenure, British ships prowled the Atlantic and seized American ships and sailors at will. Besieged by critics and facing a popular clamor for war with England, Madison first tried to appease the British through diplomacy and restrictions on commerce between the two nations. But the English held all the cards, and Madison had no more success than Jefferson in playing a weak hand. He lost even more leverage and credibility when, in 1811, Congress refused to renew the charter of the national bank; as a result, the credit on which the government could borrow to fund naval construction and military fortifications was cut off.

Despite these serious problems, the American public responded to inflammatory newspaper reports of British seizures of ships and sailors with heated calls for war. Madison hesitated, but finally yielded to popular clamor and sent a message to Congress in November 1811, listing the British attacks on U.S. shipping. He did not ask for a declaration of war, for which the nation was not prepared, but he suggested that Congress "will feel the duty of putting the United States into an armor and an attitude demanded by the crisis, and corresponding with the national spirit and expectations." Congress responded with appropriations for additional military and naval forces, and later granted Madison's request to recharter the national bank, to secure credit for those expenditures.

Bolstered by this support, Madison sent another message to Congress, on June 1, 1812, cataloging the "indignities and injuries" the British had inflicted on the United States, including the impressment of sailors, the naval blockade of American ports, and the instigation of Indian attacks on frontier settlements. Declaring that a "state of war" existed between the two nations, Madison presented the lawmakers with "a solemn question which the Constitution wisely confides to the legislative department of the Government." Three days later, the House of Representatives voted, by a margin of 79 to 49, for a declaration of war. The Senate first voted to limit the American response to reprisals against British ships, but it finally approved the declaration, on June 17, by a vote of 19 to 13, authorizing the president to use "the whole land and naval force of the United States" against the British.

What his critics derided as "Mr. Madison's war" was actually one he had tried hard to avoid. Once the fighting began, however, the public rallied around the president and, in the 1812 election, rewarded his seeming resolve with a second term. Madison, in fact, never expected to win the war on the military front, but he hoped the

British—then embroiled in yet another war with France—would accept a settlement that would protect American shipping and commerce. The British, however, responded to the war declaration with confidence. Both on land and on sea, British forces vastly outnumbered the American militiamen and seamen who fought the war. Indeed, the U.S. Navy had only twelve warships to oppose a British fleet of six hundred vessels. One military disaster followed another, as American militia surrendered Detroit to a small British detachment and the Royal Navy bottled up the tiny U.S. fleet in port. The most stunning blow came in 1814, when the Royal Marines took Washington and burned the White House and the Capitol. But American naval victories on the Great Lakes and the rout of British forces in Canada evened the score, and the British leaders decided that North America had become a "quagmire" (to borrow a term later applied to U.S. intervention in Vietnam). Peace talks between the two warring nations, held in neutral Belgium, finally produced a peace treaty in December 1814. Neither side "won" the War of 1812, but the illusion of victory gave President Madison a political boost that propelled his handpicked successor, James Monroe—who had served as both secretary of state and secretary of war—into the White House in 1817.

Most Americans know little or nothing about the War of 1812; few even connect it with the "Star-Spangled Banner." But it has lasting significance as the first war declared by Congress (the first of only five in the nation's history, in fact). More important, President Madison left the "solemn question" of declaring war to the body invested with that power by the Constitution. Faced with similar provocations by hostile nations—or, in many cases, lesser challenges—later presidents have responded with unilateral force, disregarding the mandate that Madison, as the Constitution's leading Framer, well knew.

The War of 1812 did produce a significant, but largely forgotten, Supreme Court decision. Although the case of *Martin v. Mott* began in September 1814—just three months before the war ended—the Court did not issue its ruling until 1827, with no explanation of why the case languished on the Court's docket for thirteen years. The case involved a New York militiaman, Jacob Mott, who was called for service by the state's governor, acting on the orders of President Madison. Mott refused to report for duty, for reasons he kept to himself, although "Mr. Madison's war" was highly unpopular in New York and other northern states. In fact, delegates from several northeastern states had met in Connecticut to consider seceding from the Union, more a show of rhetoric than resolve. At any rate, Mott was convicted by a court-martial and fined $96, which he refused to pay. He was later sued by the deputy federal marshal, named Martin, who had tried but failed to collect the fine.

Mott was prosecuted under a 1795 federal law providing that "whenever the United States shall be invaded, or be in imminent danger of invasion from any foreign nation or Indian tribe, it shall be lawful for the President of the United States to call forth such number of the militia of the State or States most convenient to the place of danger, or place of action, as he may judge necessary to repel such invasion," and to issue orders for militia service. In passing this law, Congress had delegated to the president its constitutional power "to provide for calling forth the militia, to execute the laws of the Union, suppress insurrections, and repel invasions." Mott argued at his court-martial that, in September 1814, New York faced no "imminent danger" of British invasion. Purely on the facts, Mott had a good case, as British troops had been routed in Canada and posed no threat to New York when he was called to duty. But as a matter of law, his legal defense, however ingenious, was doomed to failure. Justice Joseph Story wrote for a unanimous Supreme Court in affirming Mott's conviction. He found "no ground for a doubt" that presidents could summon the militia to meet any danger of invasion, whether "imminent" or not. "One of the best means to repel invasion," Story noted, "is to provide the requisite force for action before the invader has reached the soil" of the endangered state.

The Court's ruling in *Martin v. Mott* rested on the president's power as commander in chief of both federal troops and the state militias. The congressional delegation to the president of authority to call forth the militia was, Story wrote, a "limited power, confined to cases of actual invasion, or of imminent danger of invasion." But a decision about the exercise of this power "belongs exclusively to the President" and was not subject to challenge. Story raised the rhetorical question of whether calls to service were "open to be contested by every militia-man who refuses to obey the orders of the President." The answer was obvious. "Such a course would be subversive of all discipline," Story observed, "and expose the best disposed officers to the chances of ruinous litigation."

What most concerned the Court in *Martin v. Mott* was the prospect that future presidents might be dragged into court and forced "to establish the facts by competent proofs" that grounds existed for calling troops to service. Story worried that "the disclosure of the evidence might reveal important secrets of state, which the public interest, and even safety, might imperiously demand to be kept in concealment." Later presidents were, in fact, dragged into court by recalcitrant soldiers, and even by members of Congress, challenging the chief executive's dispatch of troops to fight in such undeclared wars as Vietnam and Iraq. As we will see, federal judges summarily dismissed these cases, on grounds that echoed Story's holding in Mott's case. And subsequent presidents would claim that "secrets of state" were protected from disclosure to the courts and the public. Jacob Mott's refusal to fight in a declared war—his challenge of President Madison's clear power to compel his service— unwittingly paved the way for judicial expansion of the commander in chief clause and judicial contraction of congressional power to limit executive authority to commit troops to combat.

Ironically, the climactic battle of the War of 1812 was fought two weeks after American and British diplomats had ended the war, with the Treaty of Ghent, on December 24, 1814. It was equally ironic that the Battle of New Orleans took place in the Louisiana Territory, whose purchase from the French in 1803 had marked the first great expansion of the nascent American empire. That battle was actually a series of engagements that raged, on both the waters and the land surrounding New Orleans, for more than two weeks. In the first major combat, on December 23, the outnumbered U.S. troops of General Andrew Jackson fought the superior British force to a stalemate. But on New Year's Day 1815, Jackson's troops inflicted severe casualties on the British. One week later, on January 8, celebrated now as victory day in the Battle of New Orleans, two British generals died in combat and their forces suffered over two thousand casualties, with only seventy-one American deaths. The remaining British troops fled by sea, and Jackson became an instant hero, paving his road to the White House fifteen years later.

President Thomas Jefferson's purchase of Louisiana reflected the rapid growth of the American economy in the early years of the nineteenth century. This vast tract of land, which spanned more than 800,000 square miles, from the Gulf of Mexico to the Canadian border, more than doubled the area of the United States. The French, who first claimed Louisiana in the seventeenth century, had ceded the territory to Spain in 1762, but regained the area in 1800 with the secret Treaty of San Ildefonso. Envisioning a great French empire in the New World, Napoleon Bonaparte had hoped to use the Mississippi Valley as a source of food and trade to supply the French island of Hispaniola, in the Caribbean. But the revolt of Haitian slaves in 1801, and the decimation by yellow fever of thousands of French troops who had been sent to crush the rebellion, convinced Napoleon that Hispaniola must be abandoned. Without that island, the French had little use for Louisiana. Engaged in war with England, and strapped for funds to support his troops in Europe, Napoleon offered the territory to the United States for $15 million. President Jefferson, who had earlier sent emissaries to Paris to negotiate a purchase of land on the lower Mississippi and to guarantee free navigation on the river, was delighted to acquire the whole territory on such bargain terms.

Jefferson's unilateral act in making the Louisiana Purchase raised a constitutional question, one the Framers had not anticipated in 1787. The Constitution empowers the president "to make treaties" with foreign nations but only with the "advice and consent" of the Senate, and with the concurrence of "two thirds of the Senators present" for the ratification vote. Acting quickly to accept the French offer to sell Louisiana, Jefferson had sealed the deal without the formality of a treaty. But the Senate, whose members knew what a bargain the president had struck, raised no objections, and ratified an after-the-fact treaty with France in October 1803. Jefferson's political foes could have challenged the Louisiana Purchase in court, arguing that the Constitution did not grant him the power to acquire new territory, or allow Congress to approve such purchases by treaty. The Constitution's Framers had, in fact, included no provision that dealt with the addition of territory to the original thirteen states. And in 1803, the Supreme Court was firmly controlled by Chief Justice John Marshall, placed in that post by John Adams, the man Jefferson had defeated in 1800. But Marshall, who believed firmly in executive power, spoke warmly, in several of his judicial opinions, of the "American empire," which he envisioned in expansive terms. So the Louisiana Purchase became a fait accompli, setting an unwritten precedent for later expansion of U.S. territory.

In a case that came to the Court a quarter of a century after the Louisiana Purchase, Chief Justice Marshall did, in fact, establish a judicial precedent for the acquisition of territories by treaty. Following Spain's cession of Florida to the United States in 1819, during the first term of President Monroe, the nation owned all the land south of Canada from the Atlantic to the Rocky Mountains. Under the treaty with "his Catholic majesty" of Spain, the inhabitants of Florida "shall be incorporated in the Union of the United States, as soon as may be consistent with the principles of the federal Constitution; and admitted to the enjoyment of the privileges, rights, and immunities of citizens of the United States." One right of American citizens is to bring lawsuits in state and federal courts, with jurisdiction in the Supreme Court to review "admiralty and maritime" cases. But did the residents of territories such as Florida have the same right, and did territorial courts have jurisdiction over such cases? Article IV of the Constitution gives Congress the power "to make all needful rules and regulations respecting the territory" of the United States. Under this provision, Congress had established a territorial government in Florida in 1822, and had created a system of territorial courts.

Out of the treaty with Spain, the constitutional provision in Article IV, and the federal law establishing the Florida territorial courts, a complex and confusing case reached the Supreme Court in 1828, under the intriguing title *American Insurance Company v. 356 Bales of Cotton.* The Court's opinion, written by Marshall, included such arcane legal terms as "libellant," "salvor," and "in personam." Boiled down, the case involved the competing claims of the insurance company and David Canter to the proceeds from the sale of 584 bales of cotton salvaged from the *Point à Petre,* a cargo ship that had been wrecked off the coast of Florida on a voyage from New Orleans to France. A territorial court in Florida had awarded Canter 76 percent of the proceeds, or 356 bales of cotton, worth some $1,800. The question before the Supreme Court, after the insurance company claimed that the Florida court had no jurisdiction over the case and that Canter had "fraudulently" sold the cotton, concerned the Court's power to review maritime cases from territorial courts.

On these facts the *American Insurance* case seemingly had no relevance to the broader question of whether Congress had the right to acquire territories by treaties with foreign nations. Indeed, Marshall—in the course of upholding Canter's salvage claim—simply assumed the existence of this power, despite the Constitution's silence on the issue. He also assumed that Congress, by establishing a territorial government in Florida, had authorized its legislature to create courts with jurisdiction over maritime cases, such as Canter's salvage claim. These were important holdings, resting on Marshall's expansive views of presidential and congressional responsibilities. But they were not nearly as significant as his statement in one crucial sentence of the opinion. "The Constitution confers absolutely on the government of the Union," Marshall wrote, "the powers of making war, and of making treaties; consequently, that government possesses the power of acquiring territory, either by conquest or by treaty."

Neither the *American Insurance* case itself, nor the acquisition of Florida by treaty, had anything to do with the war-powers clause in the Constitution. Congress had not declared war on Spain before the cession of Florida, nor had the Louisiana Purchase followed any declaration of war against France. Of course, nations such as England and France had expanded their empires through military conquest, but those countries were not governed by constitutions that limited the powers of their rulers and lawmakers. The Constitution spoke only of treaties as the means of resolving disputes between the United States and other nations, even those against whom Congress had declared war. The term "conquest" was entirely foreign to both the wording and the principles of the Constitution. The European imperial powers had often followed their conquest of weaker nations with treaties that were little more than forced surrender. The United States had, in fact, imposed such unfair treaties on many Indian tribes, and taken their lands through military conquest. But Chief Justice Marshall had offered the Court's sanction, in the seemingly insignificant *American Insurance* case, for a much greater exercise of American conquest, to feed the nation's growing appetite for land and wealth.

The United States took its first major step toward territorial expansion by conquest through war against Mexico in 1846, a conflict provoked by President James K. Polk. The Mexican War stemmed from, and followed, the annexation of Texas, and its admission to statehood, in 1845. Nine years earlier, the Anglo settlers of Texas had won their independence from Mexico, after a long and bloody struggle with Mexican forces that most Americans remember for the Battle of the Alamo, in San Antonio in March 1836: The outnumbered Texans who defended the fortress all died at the hands of the Mexican forces. But that defeat was followed a month later, on April 21, by the victory of Texan troops, commanded by Sam Houston, over the Mexicans at the Battle of San Jacinto. Shouts of "Remember the Alamo" spurred Houston's troops in that climactic engagement. Following the retreat of the surviving Mexicans, the Republic of Texas was born, with Houston as its first president. Although the Mexican government recognized the independence of Texas as a fact, it refused to abandon its claims to the lost territory.

Both houses of Congress hailed the Texas Republic with resolutions stating that its independence "ought to be acknowledged by the United States" as soon as the new republic "had in successful operation a civil government capable of performing the duties and fulfilling the obligations of an independent power." Despite this expression of congressional sentiment, President Andrew Jackson was reluctant to recognize Texas as a sovereign nation; taking this step, he thought, might provoke war with Mexico. According to Jackson, moreover, recognition of Texas by executive action would invade the powers of Congress. "It will always be considered consistent with the spirit of the Constitution," the president told Congress in response to its resolutions, that the power of recognition "should be exercised, when probably leading to war, with a previous understanding with that body by whom war alone can be declared, and by whom all the provisions for sustaining its perils must be furnished."

Notwithstanding their determination to free Texas from Mexican rule, Sam Houston and other leaders of the Texas Republic viewed themselves as Americans and worked to achieve statehood. After just nine years of independence, Texas was annexed to the United States by an act of Congress. In his first message to Congress, President Polk lauded the addition of Texas to the Union. "This accession to our territory has been a bloodless achievement," he said. "No arm of force has been raised to produce the result. The sword has no part in the victory." These were disingenuous words, as Polk looked toward the sword in his campaign to capture more Mexican territory and to expand the American empire to the Pacific. He had his eye on lands that extended to the southern boundary of what is now Oregon.

Polk used disputed claims with Mexico over the southern boundaries with Texas, and demands for Mexican compensation for "injuries" to American citizens during the war for independence, as the pretext for negotiations with the Mexican government in 1845, shortly after Texas joined the Union. In October 1845 the president named John Slidell, a Louisiana Democrat in the House of Representatives, as his envoy, but the Mexican government refused to receive him. Rejecting Polk's demands for settlement of claims for injuries to

Texans, the Mexicans made clear they would discuss only the boundary issues with Slidell. Nonetheless, Slidell traveled to Mexico City and stayed until March 1846, when the government there "insultingly refused," as Polk told Congress, to accept his credentials or conduct any negotiations with him. Very likely, Polk knew the outcome of this diplomatic charade, given Mexico's firm refusal to consider any payments for injuries for which it denied responsibility.

Slidell's failed mission had a broader goal. Polk had instructed the envoy to offer the Mexicans a "pecuniary consideration" for the American purchase of a vast tract of territory, including New Mexico and Upper California. Polk confided in his diary that he wanted Slidell to make this overture because he feared that England "had her eye" on California and was determined "to possess it if she could." In reality, this ostensible concern was just a fig leaf to cover Polk's territorial ambitions. The president also knew, from discussions with Spanish diplomats, that the Mexican government was virtually bankrupt and faced domestic opposition to any sale of its territory. To avoid "another revolution by which they would be overthrown," Polk recorded his Spanish visitors telling him that the Mexicans "must appear to be forced to agree to such a proposition."

There is little doubt that Polk, in pursuit of his territorial ambitions, intended all along to provoke a war with Mexico. Nor is there much doubt that he intended to begin this war on his own initiative, with military action against the weak and divided Mexican government. And surely Polk had planned this aggression, which he knew would involve "acts of war" against Mexico, without prior declaration of war by Congress. On January 16, 1846, the president ordered General Zachary Taylor to position troops on the border separating Texas from Mexico, on the Rio Grande and within sight of the Mexican military post at Matamoros. Fearing an attack on his forces, the Mexican commander at Matamoros demanded that Taylor withdraw the U.S. troops. Instead of complying, Taylor sent troops across the Rio Grande to reconnoiter the area and probe the Mexican defenses. These provocative moves finally goaded the Mexicans into crossing the river on April 24, 1846, engaging in combat that killed or injured sixteen American soldiers. In later battles with Mexican forces on U.S. territory, in early May, Taylor's forces were victorious.

Even before news of the battles reached Washington, Polk had informed his cabinet that he would ask Congress "to confer authority on the Executive to take redress into our own hands by aggressive measures" if Mexican forces crossed the Rio Grande. And immediately after he learned of the April 24 battle, Polk sent a message to Congress, on May 11, informing its members that "Mexico has passed the boundary of the United States, has invaded our territory and shed American blood on American soil." Declaring that "war exists" between the two countries, Polk asked Congress for a formal declaration of war.

The president's request was not granted without objections from members of Congress who felt that they were being stampeded by the popular clamor for war. Senator John Calhoun of South Carolina denounced Polk for having declared war on his own. "The president has announced that there is war," Calhoun said, but "there is no war according to the sense of our Constitution." Drawing a distinction between "hostilities and war," he warned against confounding the two states of armed conflict. "There may be invasion without war," Calhoun stated, "and the president is authorized to repel invasion without war." But it was the "sacred duty" of Congress "to determine whether war shall be declared or not. If we have declared war, a state of war exists, and not until then." Senator John Clayton of Delaware "condemned" Polk for having provoked Mexico into combat with American troops. "I do not see on what principle it can be shown that the President, without consulting Congress and obtaining its sanction for the procedure," Clayton complained, "has a right to send an army to take up a position, where, it must be foreseen, the inevitable consequence would be war." But their colleagues rejected the counsel of Calhoun and Clayton. After the House voted on May 11 to declare war, by the overwhelming margin of 174 to 14, the Senate followed suit two days later with even less dissent, by a vote of 40 to 2.

Unlike "Mr. Madison's war" with England in 1812, President Polk's Mexican War was both popular and successful, fought not to a stalemate but to a decisive American victory. After the forces of General Taylor took the city of Veracruz, and those commanded by General Stephen Kearny routed Mexican troops in California, General Winfield Scott led the soldiers who captured Mexico City in August 1847. Defeated on the battlefield, Mexico's leaders fled their capital and found refuge in the city of Guadalupe Hidalgo. On February 2, 1848, they signed a peace treaty with the United States, ceding more than half their nation's territory, in return for the face-saving payment of $15 million as compensation for war-related damages to Mexican property. In return for this sum, equal to the amount President Jefferson had paid to France in 1803 for the Louisiana Purchase, the United States acquired just as large an addition to its continental territory.

By any measure, the Mexican War represented the expansion, through conquest, of the American empire, notwithstanding the one-sided treaty with Mexico that ratified the acquisition of land. The Mexican War also marked the first major exercise of presidential war making, with Congress adding its approval only after Polk had approved military actions along the Rio Grande, with the "inevitable consequence," as Senator Clayton argued to no avail, of provoking the war that Congress later declared. The disputed border between Texas and Mexico had little to do with Polk's territorial ambitions, however. In fact, on May 13, 1846, the same day that Congress voted for war, Secretary of State James Buchanan—himself a later president—showed Polk a dispatch that he proposed sending to U.S. envoys in England, France, and other countries. Buchanan wanted the diplomats to assure those nations that "our object was not to dismember Mexico or to make conquests" and that the United States had no desire "to acquire either California or New Mexico or any other portion of the Mexican territory." But these were exactly Polk's designs, and he told Buchanan it was "unnecessary and improper" to send the dispatch. In his diary Polk wrote that "it was clear that in making peace we would if practicable obtain California and such other portion of the Mexican territory as would be sufficient to indemnify our claimants on Mexico, and to defray the expenses of the war which that power by her long continued wrongs and injuries had forced us to wage."

Although the California gold rush had not begun when Polk wrote these words, the Mexican lands he coveted for the American empire were surely worth more than $15 million, the amount he offered Mexico for more than half its territory. Polk himself paid a much greater price for victory in a war that began and ended with widespread popular support. Like several of his successors, Polk discovered that the voters care more about domestic blunders than foreign battles. Elected as a proslavery Democrat, Polk supported the admission of Texas to the Union as a slave state. The expansion of slavery into the territories became the dominant issue in the 1846 congressional elections, and the opposition Whigs (soon to become the Republicans) won control of the House. The slavery question affected political debate over the Mexican War, with the status of slavery in California at stake. Even before the war officially ended, with the signing of the Treaty of Guadalupe Hidalgo, the Whig majority in the House used a resolution lauding Zachary Taylor as a way to rebuke Polk, offering an amendment deploring "a war unnecessarily and unconstitutionally begun by the President of the United States." After the amendment carried by the narrow margin of 85 to 81, the resolution's sponsors dropped their move to confer a gold medal on Taylor. Having won their point, the Whigs later voted for the original resolution, and Taylor finally received his medal. In fact, when Polk honored his pledge to serve just one term as president, Taylor rode his wartime acclaim into the White House as the Whig candidate. Another Whig, a first-term House member from Illinois, later explained his vote for the amendment condemning Polk's actions. "Allow the President to invade a neighboring nation, whenever he shall deem it necessary to repel an invasion," Abraham Lincoln wrote to a friend, "and you allow him to make war at pleasure." The authors of the Constitution, Lincoln added, had placed the war power in the hands of Congress because they "resolved to so frame the Constitution that *no one man* should hold the power" of taking the nation into war.

The congressional Whigs delivered a direct rebuke to Polk for his war of conquest against Mexico. The Supreme Court delivered an indirect rebuke in 1850, in a seemingly insignificant case, involving the collection of import duties on a cargo of hides and other goods. The money at issue, a bit more than $1,500, was close to the disputed amount in the *American Insurance* case of 1828, in which Chief Justice Marshall had ruled that the government "possesses the power of acquiring territory, either by conquest or by treaty." The case of *Fleming v. Page* stemmed from the American occupation of the Mexican port of Tampico in 1847. The previous year, Congress had passed a law that reduced import duties on goods imported from ports that were under American "dominion" and control. Congress had clearly intended to make it less costly for U.S. firms to import goods from conquered Mexican territories. But when the *Catharine*, chartered by the trading company of Fleming & Marshall, arrived from Tampico in Philadelphia, James Page, the port's customs collector, demanded payment of the higher duties required of imports from foreign ports. Fleming & Marshall paid the duties under protest, and then sued Page to recover the contested funds, claiming that Tampico had been part of the United States when the cargo was shipped and was not a foreign port.

When the case reached the Supreme Court, the Mexican War had ended and Tampico had returned to Mexican sovereignty. Chief Justice Roger Taney, who had succeeded Marshall after his death in 1835, wrote for the Court in the *Fleming* case. There was no doubt, Taney said, that Tampico had been "subject to the sovereignty and dominion of the United States" when the *Catharine* left the port with its cargo. "The Mexican authorities had been driven out" by American forces, "and the country was in the exclusive and firm possession of the United States." Under the "law of nations," Taney noted, other countries were obliged to regard Mexico "as the territory of the United States, and to respect it as such." The status of Mexico, however, did not depend on the law of nations "but upon our own Constitution and acts of Congress." Taney then cast a skeptical judicial eye on the 1846 customs law that Congress had passed. That statute had not authorized American military officials to establish a customs house in Tampico, or to issue a "coasting manifest" to the *Catharine* for shipping cargo "from one port of the United States to another." Rather, those measures had been taken by officials acting under orders from the president "in his character of commander-in-chief" of the military forces. But that executive power, Taney wrote, does not "imply an authority to the President to enlarge the limits of the United States by subjugating the enemy's country." Only Congress, by ratifying a treaty that followed victory in a declared war, held that power. Consequently, before Congress ratified the Treaty of Guadalupe Hidalgo in 1848, Tampico was not "a part of the United States," and duties imposed on cargoes shipped from that port were subject to the higher rates collected on goods from foreign ports.

The bottom line of Taney's opinion was that Fleming & Marshall must pay the disputed customs duties. But the Court's ruling had a broader reach, in holding that the president's powers as commander in chief "are purely military" and do not extend to "the treaty-making power or the legislative authority" that only Congress can exercise under the Constitution. In treating Tampico as "a part of the United States," and by authorizing military officials to issue a coasting manifest to the *Catharine* for shipping cargo "from one port of the United States to another," President Polk had assumed powers given only to Congress.

It may be tempting, in hindsight, to dismiss cases like *American Insurance* and *Fleming* as historical artifacts. After all, they did not directly challenge the powers of presidents to meet the threat of military aggression by other nations. But in its rulings in both cases, the Court upheld the right of the United States to expand its territory by "conquest or treaty," in the identical words of two chief justices. Significantly, however, both John Marshall and Roger Taney—who, between them, headed the Court for sixty-three years—recognized that only Congress, and not the president, could take the nation into war and ratify a treaty that enlarged its boundaries.

In 1846, James Polk made no secret of his expansionist aims in provoking the Mexican War. Using the Texas boundary dispute with Mexico to pursue his goal of securing "California and the fine bay of San Francisco" from the weaker nation, he instigated the first military aggression on behalf of the American empire, which now spanned the continent. And for the American troops, the war was a relatively easy experience, with modest casualties and few scenes of battlefield carnage. Nonetheless, the Mexican War was hardly a popular conflict. Mexico may have been a weak nation, but Polk was also a weak president, hobbled by his one-term campaign promise and by the strong and often strident opposition from the Whigs in Congress. As we have seen, the House of Representatives had censured Polk for his actions, which were "unnecessarily and unconstitutionally begun" and the Supreme Court, in the *Fleming* case, implicitly rebuked the president for having, in effect, usurped congressional power to make laws regarding trade and commerce.

Polk left office in 1849, and died a few months later. His successor, Zachary Taylor, who gained renown as a hero of the Mexican War, died within a year of his election. None of the three men who served as president during the next decade—Millard Fillmore, Franklin Pierce, and James Buchanan—shared Polk's imperial ambitions, and none engaged in military adventures. In fact, both Pierce and Buchanan acted with restraint in the one episode in which American forces took hostile action against a foreign country. In 1854, when Pierce was president and Buchanan served as ambassador to England, the American warship *Cyane* was ordered to the Nicaraguan port of Greytown, from which bananas and hardwoods were shipped to the United States. Tensions between Nicaraguans and Americans in Greytown had been growing, largely over business disputes, and an American diplomat had complained about supposed insults by local officials. When the *Cyane* arrived in port, its commander went ashore and demanded an apology to the diplomat. The Nicaraguans refused, and the ship's commander issued a proclamation that he would bombard the town if amends were not promptly made. The proclamation also warned residents to leave Greytown for their own safety. When the time for the apology expired with no satisfaction, the commander carried out his threat and the *Cyane* shelled the town for several hours, inflicting no injuries but destroying a good deal of property, some owned by Americans.

President Pierce reported this obvious act of war to Congress, stressing that residents of the "offending town" had been duly warned of the impending bombardment and even provided with launches from the *Cyane* to remove and safeguard their property. Pierce referred to the "mischievous" Nicaraguans as mostly "blacks and persons of mixed blood" who had been stealing from warehouses owned by Americans. The Greytown episode had a comic-opera air, and both President Pierce and Ambassador Buchanan seemed embarrassed by the event. The British had expressed concern to Buchanan that its diplomats and citizens in Nicaragua might become endangered by the Greytown conflict. The ambassador to London told British officials that the ship's commander had acted without authority, although Pierce's secretary of state later instructed Buchanan to defend the bombardment as necessary to protect American lives and property, an unconvincing claim that caused him further embarrassment.

However much a historical footnote, the Greytown episode did produce a judicial opinion that later presidents—as recently as Bill Clinton and George W. Bush—have cited to justify their military incursions in Somalia and Iraq. In 1860, ruling on a suit by an American resident of Greytown against the U.S. government for property damage, a federal circuit court in New York rejected his claim. Upholding the *Cyane* commander's actions, the court, in *Durand v. Hollins*, made a sweeping assertion of presidential war-making power. The duty of protecting "the lives or property" of American citizens abroad, the court said, "must, of necessity, rest in the discretion of the president. Acts of lawless violence, or of threatened violence to the citizen or his property, cannot be anticipated . . . and may, not infrequently, require the most prompt and decided action." The *Durand* ruling was not, of course, a binding decision of the Supreme Court. Nevertheless, it is easy to see why subsequent presidents eagerly pointed to its affirmation of what became known as "inherent" presidential power to initiate military action to protect American citizens and property in foreign countries.

But the Greytown bombardment was not launched—with or without executive sanction—to protect U.S. lives or property. It began with a supposed insult to an American diplomat, and the Nicaraguans had not threatened anyone's life or moved to seize American property. In fact, after Buchanan became president, in 1857, he expressly disclaimed any power to initiate military action without prior congressional approval. Speaking as a former diplomat, he told Congress in 1858 that presidential authority in foreign affairs "is limited to the employment of diplomacy alone. When this fails, it can proceed no further." The president, he added, "cannot legitimately resort to force without the direct authority of Congress, except in resisting and repelling hostile attacks." The next year, in 1859, Buchanan restated his position: "Without the authority of Congress the Executive cannot lawfully direct any force, however near it may be to the scene of difficulty, to enter the territory of Mexico, Nicaragua, or New Grenada for the purpose of defending the persons and property of American citizens." (New Grenada was the name of what is now Colombia.) In this sentence, Buchanan issued a veiled but obvious rebuke to his White House predecessors Polk and Pierce.

By the mid-nineteenth century, the United States had grown rapidly in both population and territory, becoming a nation that rivaled—and often contended with—the European imperial powers that had long dominated international trade and markets. The American people had become embroiled in two declared wars, against England and Mexico, and presidents had sent ships and troops into several countries without formal declarations of war by Congress. During this period, the Supreme Court and the lower federal courts decided some half-dozen cases that raised issues of presidential war-making powers, handing down rulings that have since been cited on both sides of judicial conflicts over those powers. Most important, the first half of the nineteenth century marked the emergence of the expansionist—and often overtly imperialist—forces that have entangled the nation in even greater wars, both declared and undeclared. But another conflict, fought not to expand its territory but to prevent the country from being torn asunder, halted the expansionist drive until the close of the century. The Civil War, nonetheless, provoked some of the most significant legal challenges to presidential wartime powers, in cases that deserve the attention they receive in the next chapter.

4

"THE GREAT EXIGENCIES
OF GOVERNMENT":

The Civil War

None of the presidents who occupied the White House during the 1850s faced as many problems in foreign affairs as they did with the issue that dominated American politics and divided the country on sectional lines. That issue, of course, was slavery. Domestic conflicts over slavery may seem tangential or even irrelevant to issues of war powers, but the fierce battles over slavery—military, political, and legal—resulted in a struggle that raised serious questions of congressional and presidential powers, particularly because of Lincoln's wartime suspension of the writ of habeas corpus and the trials of suspected Confederate sympathizers before military tribunals while the federal courts remained open. Several Supreme Court rulings in 2004, in cases stemming from the detention of alleged "enemy combatants" during and after the war in Afghanistan, suggest how relevant the judicial decisions during the Civil War remain. The similarity between conflicts over slavery and the war on terror provides an instructive link between the past and the present in American life.

Well before the Constitution was drafted and adopted, conflicts over slavery had stirred passions on both sides of the issue and placed the effort to forge the "United States" in peril. The "Great Compromise" over slavery at the Constitutional Convention, which papered over the chasm between opponents and defenders of slavery, had proved to be neither great nor lasting. Their hand forced by southern delegates who threatened to bolt the convention and destroy James Madison's plan for a strong federal government, northern delegates capitulated and agreed to legitimize the institution of slavery, in three clauses that protected the human "property" of southern slave owners. Within three decades of the Constitution's ratification, in 1788, the growing abolitionist movement had created fear among southerners that Congress might restrict the expansion of slavery into the territories west of the Mississippi, which lured many slave owners who sought cheap land. With the Missouri Compromise of 1820, Congress did, in fact, limit the reach of slavery, admitting Missouri to the Union as a slave state but banning the practice in territories north of that state's southern border.

As an effort to defuse the explosive national conflict, the Missouri Compromise had the opposite effect. Over the next thirty years, each chamber of Congress resounded with heated rhetoric on both sides, and passions outside the Capitol burst into flames. In 1854, the abolitionist leader William Lloyd Garrison addressed an antislavery rally on the Boston Common to protest the return of an escaped slave to his owner. Holding up a copy of the Constitution, Garrison denounced it as "a covenant with death and an agreement with hell." With those words, he put a torch to the Constitution and burned it to ashes. "So perish all compromises with tyranny!" the abolitionist cried, echoed by the shouts of the assembled crowd. Farther west, the territory of Kansas became the first battleground in the Civil War, after Congress, in 1854, repealed the Missouri Compromise and adopted a law that put the slavery issue before territorial voters. After a proslavery posse sacked and burned the town of Lawrence in 1856, killing several "free-staters" during the attack, a fanatical abolitionist named John Brown gathered his followers and, in retaliation, murdered five proslavery settlers in Pottawatomie. The Pottawatomie Massacre foreshadowed Brown's doomed assault on the Harpers

Ferry arsenal in 1859, his tragic response to the Supreme Court's ruling two years earlier in the *Dred Scott* case, the most infamous decision in the Court's history.

In rejecting the claim of a slave named Dred Scott that his residence
in the free state of Illinois had emancipated him, Chief Justice Roger
Taney spoke in cold, hard words. Holding that slaves were simply
"property" and could be "bought and sold, and treated as an ordinary article of merchandise," Taney described blacks as "beings of
an inferior order, and altogether unfit to associate with the white
race, either in social or political relations; and so far inferior, that
they had no rights that the white man was bound to respect; and that
the negro might justly and lawfully be reduced to slavery for his own
benefit." But the chief justice went beyond this blatant expression of
racism to strike down the recently repealed Missouri Compromise as
an unconstitutional exercise of congressional power to regulate the
territories. This aspect of Taney's opinion, in effect "nationalizing"
slavery, tossed more fuel on the already blazing conflict over the
expansion of slavery into the territories.

The Court's ruling in the *Dred Scott* case became the central issue
in the 1858 senate campaign in Illinois, in which Abraham Lincoln,
running for the newly formed Republican Party, challenged Democratic senator Stephen Douglas. The two men debated up and down
the state, with Lincoln denouncing his opponent's "popular sovereignty" proposal to let territorial voters decide whether to enter the
Union as slave states or free states. "The *Dred Scott* decision was
erroneous," Lincoln said, and Douglas was complicit in a "conspiracy to perpetuate and nationalize slavery." Douglas, in turn, accused
Lincoln of conducting "warfare on the Supreme Court." The incum-
bent senator bested Lincoln in this election, but they faced each
other a second time, in the 1860 presidential campaign, with *Dred
Scott* again the central issue. In the rematch, Lincoln, aided by a split
within the Democratic ranks, won the election, but with less than 40
percent of the popular vote.

There may seem to be little, if any, connection between the
Supreme Court's decision in the *Dred Scott* case and later judicial

rulings on conflicts between presidential and congressional powers over wartime actions. But the link is actually close. Not only did *Dred Scott* further divide the nation on sectional lines; it created a fissure within the Democratic Party that allowed Lincoln to gain the White House for the Republicans. Lincoln's election, as we know, so inflamed the defenders of slavery that threats of secession from the Union moved quickly from political rhetoric to reality. On February 8, 1861, one month before Lincoln's inauguration, seven of the southern states announced the formation of the Confederate States of America. And on April 12, just five weeks after Lincoln took office, Confederate troops fired on Fort Sumter in South Carolina; its beleaguered Union defenders waved the white flag of surrender on April 14. On the same day, Lincoln called the Congress into special session, citing "the power vested in me by the Constitution" to call up the state militias and "to cause the laws to be duly executed." The Civil War had begun. Before it ended, in 1865, some 600,000 people—most of them young men in blue or gray uniforms—had lost their lives in the bloodiest war in American history.

The Civil War was fought not only on battlefields whose names evoke scenes of carnage—Antietam, Chancellorsville, Gettysburg, and many more—but also in courtrooms. Two important Supreme Court decisions stemmed from Lincoln's proclamations, issued while Congress was in recess, imposing a naval blockade on the Confederate states and suspending the writ of habeas corpus during the war. Lincoln's suspension of habeas corpus provoked another significant judicial decision, not from the Supreme Court but from Chief Justice Roger Taney while he was riding circuit in a lower federal court. Between them, these decisions illustrate the Court's difficult task of resolving disputes over presidential power during wartime—in this case, a war that began as a domestic insurrection but soon became a conflict between "belligerent" nations, each claiming sovereignty over its territory. Never before, or since, has the country faced a crisis of this magnitude or cost in lives.

Unlike several later presidents, including Harry Truman, Bill Clinton, and both of the Bushes, Lincoln disavowed any claims that he was acting with constitutional authority. Soon after Congress returned to session in 1861, he told its members that his actions, "whether strictly legal or not, were ventured upon under what appeared to be a popular demand and a public necessity, trusting then, as now, that Congress would readily ratify them." Lincoln was not the first president, and certainly not the last, to rely on after-the-fact congressional sanction for actions that stretched the boundaries of executive power. But the Confederate secession, and the quick spread of hostilities after the bombardment of Fort Sumter, forced Lincoln to move promptly and decisively; moreover, he acknowledged that Congress held the ultimate lawmaking power. Lincoln faced a dilemma in responding to the outbreak of hostilities. Although the Civil War began as a domestic insurrection, it was also a military attack on the United States by a belligerent nation within its own borders, a situation no president—before or after Lincoln— has confronted. Congress, recognizing the urgency of the situation that confronted the president, passed legislation "approving, legalizing, and making valid all the acts, proclamations, and orders of the President, etc., as if they had been issued and done under the previous express authority and direction of the Congress of the United States." Although similar expressions of after-the-fact congressional ratification of White House maneuvers would become commonplace, they could not change the extraconstitutional nature of the presidential initiatives.

In its first decision on Lincoln's wartime proclamations, the Supreme Court ruled on his power to impose a naval blockade on the Confederate states. On April 17, 1861, he clamped a blockade on the first seven states that had seceded from the Union; two weeks later, after Virginia and North Carolina joined the Confederacy, he included them in the blockade. Under his proclamations, neutral countries were put on notice that their ships were subject to seizure and to the sale of their cargo as prizes of war. Lincoln took these steps to cut off trade between the Confederate states and England, which had become the primary market for southern cotton, tobacco, and other goods. The blockade was also designed to prevent the shipment of arms and other military supplies from England and other nations to the Confederates. The British government was officially neutral in the Civil War, but the lure of wartime profits tempted many private merchants and traders to slip past the U.S. Navy into southern ports.

What became known as the *Prize Cases* began with the seizure of a British vessel, the *Hiawatha,* and a Mexican ship, the *Brilliante.* The *Hiawatha* was seized in the port of Hampton Roads, Virginia, bound for England with a cargo of tobacco. The *Brilliante,* carrying a cargo of flour, had been cleared by port officials in New Orleans for return to Mexico, but was seized when it anchored near Mobile, Alabama. Both vessels had been seized before Congress ratified Lincoln's blockade orders, on July 13, 1861, and their owners filed suit in federal court for the return of their property. The *Prize Cases* also involved two other ships, the *Crenshaw* and the *Amy Warwick,* which belonged to Virginia residents and had been seized as enemy property under the blockade proclamation, which covered "all persons in armed rebellion" against the Union. Like the *Hiawatha,* the *Crenshaw* was headed for England with a cargo of tobacco, and was seized at the mouth of the James River in Virginia. The *Amy Warwick,* loaded with coffee from Brazil, was seized in Hampton Roads. The British owners of the *Hiawatha* and those of the two Virginia vessels claimed they had been given no notice of the blockade, while the owners of the *Brilliante* argued that its clearance for the return voyage to Mexico had exempted the vessel from the blockade orders.

The justices who decided the *Prize Cases* in 1863, with the Civil War still raging, faced two major questions, stated at the outset of Justice Robert Grier's majority opinion. The first related to the British and Mexican vessels, owned by citizens of neutral countries: "Had the President a right to institute a blockade of ports in possession of persons in armed rebellion against the Government, on the principles of international law, as known and acknowledged among civilized States?" Grier's second question involved the vessels owned by residents of one of the "rebellious" states: "Was the property of persons domiciled or residing within those States a proper subject of capture on the sea as 'enemies' property'?" Behind these two legal issues stood a broader constitutional question, which the Supreme Court faced in the *Prize Cases* for the first time: Can a civil war, begun as a domestic insurrection by states in the Union, become an "actual" war that authorizes the president to exercise his powers as commander in chief of the armed forces, even though Congress had not formally declared war against the rebellious states?

A bare majority of five justices answered the last question in President Lincoln's favor. Writing for this majority, Grier noted that "Congress alone has the power to declare a national or foreign war. It cannot declare war against a State, or any number of States, by virtue of any clause in the Constitution." To get around this constitutional barrier, Grier took a circuitous route. Referring to the British and Mexican vessels, Grier stated that ships of "neutral" countries "have a right to enter ports of a friendly nation for the purposes of trade and commerce, but are bound to recognize the rights of a belligerent engaged in actual war" to impose a blockade "for the purpose of subduing the enemy." So were the Union and the Confederacy "belligerents" in an "actual" war? International law does not normally recognize the contesting parties in a civil war as independent nations, whose "belligerent" status would allow either one to impose a blockade that neutrals would be required to respect. Justice Grier, however, wrote that "it is not necessary to constitute war, that both parties should be acknowledged as independent nations. A war may exist where one of the belligerents claims sovereign rights against the other."

Grier turned this broad statement into an effective recognition of the Confederacy as an independent nation at war with the Union. "When the party in rebellion," he wrote, "have declared their independence; have cast off their allegiance; have organized armies; have commenced hostilities against their former sovereign, the world acknowledges them as belligerents, and the contest a war." The justice ignored the fact that both President Lincoln and Congress treated the Civil War as a domestic insurrection. But under Grier's definition, Lincoln did not possess the constitutional power to enforce a blockade of Confederate ports on neutral countries without a congressional declaration of war. Grier solved this problem by placing the war power in Lincoln's hands. Despite the president's refusal to acknowledge the Confederacy as an independent nation, his treatment of the rebellious states as belligerents "is a question to be decided *by him*," Grier wrote, "and this Court must be governed by the decisions and acts of the political department of the Government to which this power was entrusted." Lincoln's enforcement of the blockade on neutral vessels, however, was regarded by international law as an act of war, and only Congress was entrusted with that power.

Justice Grier turned to the second question raised in the *Prize Cases*, whether the *Amy Warwick* and the *Crenshaw*, the vessels owned by Virginians, could be seized as "enemies' property." The "belligerent" states of the Confederacy, he wrote, claimed "to be acknowledged by the world as a sovereign State. Their right to do so is now being decided by wager of battle." All the land and property in the Confederacy "is enemies' territory, because it is held in possession of an organized, hostile and belligerent power." Grier noted that President Lincoln recognized, in his blockade proclamation, that "great numbers" of those who resided in the Confederacy remained "loyal in their feelings" to the Union. Nonetheless, those "whose property may be used to increase the revenues of the hostile power are, in this contest, liable to be treated as enemies, though not foreigners. They have cast off their allegiance and made war on their Government, and are none the less enemies because they are traitors" to the Union. Profits from the sale of the tobacco on the *Crenshaw*, and the coffee on the *Amy Warwick*, Grier reasoned, would add "wealth and strength" to the Confederacy and were thus "regarded as legitimate prize, without regard to the domicile of the owner, and much more so if he reside and trade" within its territory.

Grier's majority opinion in the *Prize Cases* had far-reaching ramifications, going well beyond the unique situation of the Civil War. His approval of after-the-fact congressional ratification of Lincoln's blockade proclamation, which Grier admitted constituted an act of war, provided legal ammunition that later presidents have fired in judicial battles over their acts of war. The Court's majority also gave future presidents a potent legal weapon by deferring to Lincoln's decision to impose the naval blockade without congressional sanction. Grier's statement that this was "a question to be decided *by him,* and this Court must be governed by the decisions and acts of the political department of the Government" provides a concise definition of what later became known as the "political question" doctrine. The Court, in effect, had ducked its constitutional duty to police the acts of the other branches of government when they are challenged as exceeding their powers. This is perhaps the most troubling aspect of Grier's opinion. By shielding the president from judicial oversight, the Court abdicated its responsibility to "say what the law is," in the memorable phrase of Chief Justice John Marshall, writing in *Marbury v. Madison* in 1803. The Court's power of judicial review of the acts of both Congress and the president, Marshall stressed in this historic opinion, rested on the Constitution's command, in Article VI, that its provisions "shall be the supreme law of the land" and its grant to the Supreme Court, in Article III, of the power to decide "all cases, in law and equity, arising under this Constitution." But Justice Grier's invocation of the "political question" doctrine effectively exempted Lincoln from the Court's duty to hold his actions up to judicial scrutiny.

Justice Benjamin Nelson wrote for the four dissenters in the *Prize Cases,* who included Chief Justice Roger Taney, nearing the end of his twenty-eight-year tenure as the Court's leader. Increasingly feeble at eighty-six, and just one year from death, Taney roused himself from a sickbed to preside at the Court's session at which Nelson read his judicial rebuke of Lincoln. Nelson did not mince words. The Constitution, he noted, granted the power to declare war exclusively to Congress. "It cannot be delegated or surrendered to the Executive," Nelson said. The president "had no power to set on foot a blockade under the law of nations," he added. Lincoln's blockade proclamation, and the seizures of the four ships, Nelson concluded, were "without any Constitutional authority; and void; and, on principle, no subsequent ratification could make them valid." In the *Prize*

Cases, the dissenters obviously felt, the Court majority had neglected to "say what the law is." To them, the law at issue was not the act by which Congress subsequently ratified Lincoln's blockade proclamation but the Constitution itself, the "supreme law of the land."

In light of recent wars, from Vietnam through Iraq, in which Congress granted blank-check authorization for presidential actions, it is worth speculating whether the shift of one vote in the *Prize Cases* might have persuaded later justices that "no subsequent ratification could make them valid," as Nelson had argued. Most likely, in deciding challenges to congressional authorizations, without formal declarations of war, the Court either would have simply ignored the *Prize Cases* as precedent or would have distinguished the ruling against Lincoln on the ground that an "internal" naval blockade was factually different from "external" military action. Nonetheless, the sharp conflict between the Court's majority and its minority in the *Prize Cases* exposed a constitutional division over presidential war-making powers that subsequent judicial decisions on this crucial issue have failed to resolve.

Another of Lincoln's proclamations moved the Civil War into judicial chambers. On April 27, 1861, the president responded to a crisis that began eight days earlier. Thousands of Union troops had been called to duty in Northern states and were being rushed to the capital to defend it from Confederate attack, passing through Maryland by train. Maryland had not seceded from the Union, but it was a slave state and many of its residents sympathized with the Confederacy. On April 19, some twenty thousand Confederate supporters in Baltimore tried to prevent Union soldiers from transferring from one train to another. Although bayonet-wielding troops pushed the mob back, military officials got word of plots to blow up bridges along the train route through the state. They prevailed on Lincoln to issue a proclamation suspending the writ of habeas corpus in those parts of Maryland along the route between Philadelphia and Washington. Lincoln's order allowed Union officers to arrest and detain without trial anyone in the area suspected of threatening "public safety."

The "Great Writ" of habeas corpus had deep roots in English law. The Latin words mean "you should have the body," and the writ commands an official—usually a sheriff or a prison warden—to bring the "body" of a prisoner before a judge, to decide the legality of his or her detention. The writ is designed to protect individuals from arbitrary arrest and detention; it was first placed into English law by the Habeas Corpus Act of 1679. But this law was not enforced in the American colonies, and British officials arrested and imprisoned thousands of people, holding them without charges and without recourse to judicial review of their detention. After the Revolutionary War ended with American independence, still fresh resentment over the arbitrary behavior of British colonial officials prompted the Framers to provide, in Section 9 of Article I, that "the privilege of the writ of habeas corpus should not be suspended, unless when, in cases of rebellion or invasion, the public safety may require it." Significantly, this provision was placed in the article dealing with the powers of Congress, and not those of the president. Phrased as a negative limitation on congressional powers, the "suspension" clause did not authorize the president to suspend the writ of habeas corpus without prior and express direction from Congress. Lincoln clearly felt that the emergency confronting the Union with the outbreak of civil war, and the safe passage of Union troops and supplies to defend the capital, justified his proclamation, but, just as clearly, he acted without congressional authorization in suspending the writ.

The first judicial test of Lincoln's orders to Union military officials, granting them power to arrest and detain any person suspected of aiding the Confederate cause, began one month after his proclamation. On May 25, 1861, at two o'clock in the morning, Union soldiers burst into the home of John Merryman in Cockeysville, Maryland. After ordering him out of bed, they took him to nearby Fort McHenry, in Baltimore, dumping him in a cell. Merryman was hardly picked at random for arrest. A lawyer and state legislator, as well as a vocal supporter of the Confederacy, he was suspected of organizing a plot to blow up railroad bridges to block the passage of Union troops and supplies.

The day after his arrest, Merryman hastily drafted a petition for a writ of habeas corpus, and his lawyer rushed to Washington and presented it to Chief Justice Taney. As part of the Judiciary Act, Congress had passed a law at its first session, in 1789, authorizing any federal judge, including Supreme Court justices, to consider petitions for writs of habeas corpus. Each justice, then and now, is assigned to a federal judicial circuit—most often the one that includes his or her home state—and is responsible for handling emergency petitions from that circuit. The chief justice was a Maryland native, and Fort McHenry was in his circuit. Taney decided to hear arguments on Merryman's petition at the federal courthouse in Baltimore, rather than in Washington, to avoid pulling General George Cadwalader, who commanded Fort McHenry and to whom the petition was directed, away from his military post.

At the hearing before Taney, Merryman's lawyer demanded that military officials produce a copy of the warrant under which his client was arrested, but the army officer who appeared for General Cadwalader refused the demand. He presented Taney, instead, with a "return" to the petition, which simply claimed that Merryman had been arrested on charges of treason and rebellion. Taney then granted Merryman's petition, quickly drafted a writ of habeas corpus, and instructed the officer to return to Fort McHenry and serve the writ on Cadwalader. Later that day, the officer returned to the courthouse and reported to Taney that Cadwalader had refused to accept service of the writ. This act of defiance confronted Taney with a dilemma, and only two options. He could send a federal marshal to Fort McHenry, with orders to arrest Cadwalader for contempt of court and bring him before Taney. Or he could avoid such a direct challenge to military authority by letting Merryman remain in military custody.

Acting with restraint and prudence, Taney chose the latter option. But he did not simply bow to superior force and recalcitrance. He took up his pen and wrote a five-thousand-word opinion, castigating

President Lincoln. Ironically, just the month before, Taney had administered the presidential oath of office, in which Lincoln swore to "faithfully execute" his duties and to "defend the Constitution of the United States." Writing as a circuit judge in *Ex parte Merryman,* the chief justice first noted that General Cadwalader's "return" to the habeas corpus writ did not allege "any offense against the laws of the United States" by Merryman but, rather, "general charges of treason and rebellion, without proof, and without giving the names of witnesses" to Merryman's supposed crimes. "Having the prisoner thus in custody upon these vague and unsupported accusations," Taney said, Cadwalader "refuses to obey the writ of habeas corpus, upon the ground that he is duly authorized by the president to suspend it."

The chief justice then recounted the arguments of the military officer who spoke for Cadwalader at the hearing in Baltimore. Raising his bushy eyebrows with rhetorical flair, Taney continued. "I certainly listened to it with some surprise," he wrote, "for I had supposed it to be one of those points of constitutional law upon which there was no difference of opinion, and that it was admitted on all hands, that the privilege of the writ could not be suspended, except by act of Congress." Taney would not have granted the habeas corpus writ for Merryman if Congress had given President Lincoln the authority to suspend it. "Congress is, of necessity, the judge of whether the public safety does or does not require it, and their judgment is conclusive." But the Constitution, in specifying presidential powers, did not authorize Lincoln to suspend the writ on his own prerogative. "There is not a word in it that can furnish the slightest ground to justify the exercise of the power" that Lincoln had asserted in his proclamation, Taney wrote.

The chief justice devoted most of his opinion to reviewing the history of the Great Writ, from its origins in the Magna Carta, through enactment of the Habeas Corpus Act by Parliament, and its place in the U.S. Constitution. His point was that the writ "firmly secured the liberty of the subject against the usurpation and oppression of the executive branch of the government," whether headed by a king or a president. Returning to Merryman's case, Taney expressed his resentment at military "usurpation" of the judicial branch of government. He charged the military officials who acted on Lincoln's orders of having, "by force of arms, thrust aside the judicial authorities and officers to whom the Constitution has confided the power and duty of interpreting and administering the laws, and substituted a military government in its place, to be administered and executed by military officers." If General Cadwalader had sufficient evidence to charge Merryman with crimes under federal law, Taney pointed out, he should have brought that evidence before a federal attorney, who could then decide whether to issue a warrant for Merryman's arrest. If he had been arrested, a federal judge would have heard the evidence and decided whether to commit Merryman to jail pending trial, release him on bail, or discharge him from custody. But Cadwalader had decided, Taney wrote, to commit Merryman "without a hearing, even before himself, to close custody, in a strongly garrisoned fort, to be there held, it would seem, during the pleasure of those who committed him." Because of this unchecked and arbitrary power, Taney warned, "the people of the United States are no longer living under a government of laws, but every citizen holds life, liberty, and property at the will and pleasure of the army officer in whose military district he may happen to be found."

After these strong words, Taney threw up his hands in surrender. "I have exercised all the power which the Constitution and laws confer upon me," he wrote, "but that power has been resisted by a force too strong for me to overcome." He ended his opinion with a challenge to the president, directing the court's clerk to transmit a copy to Lincoln. "It will then remain for that high officer," Taney concluded, "in fulfillment of his constitutional obligation to 'take care that the laws be faithfully executed,' to determine what measures he will take to cause the civil process of the United States to be respected and enforced."

Lincoln did not appreciate this judicial lecture, from a political foe with a personal animus against him. Taney was certainly not a Confederate sympathizer, eager to release John Merryman to continue plotting to blow up bridges. But Taney had written the infamous *Dred Scott* opinion, stripping all blacks of their citizenship and "nationalizing" slavery in the territories—a decision that Lincoln had denounced in his campaigns for the Senate and the presidency. In replying to Taney, in a Fourth of July speech to a joint session of Congress, the president defended his suspension of habeas corpus in pointed words. Speaking of the laws Congress had passed to ratify his wartime actions, Lincoln asked rhetorically whether those statutes must "be allowed to finally fail of execution even had it been perfectly clear that by the use of the means necessary to their execution some single law, made in such extreme tenderness of the citizen's liberty that practically it relieves more of the guilty than of the innocent, should to a very limited extent be violated. To state the question more directly, are all the laws but one to go unexecuted, and the government itself go to pieces less that one be violated?"

Lincoln's dismissal of habeas corpus as a "single law" that protected more guilty than innocent citizens speaks volumes about his attitude toward the Great Writ, of both English and American law. Confronted with organized campaigns by Confederate sympathizers to disrupt Union military efforts, Lincoln felt justified in suspending the writ. Congress did, in fact, later ratify the president's suspension proclamations, with a law passed in March 1863—after Lincoln had imposed a nationwide suspension of habeas corpus, on August 8, 1862, in response to opposition to the military draft that had begun the previous month, sparking riots in New York and several other cities. Before the Civil War ended, more than 10,000 people had been arrested and jailed without recourse to habeas corpus. Lincoln's suspension of the "single law" protecting every American from arbitrary arrest and detention became the greatest violation of constitutional rights until the mass incarceration of some 120,000 Americans of Japanese ancestry during World War II.

Lincoln's suspension of habeas corpus produced yet another legal challenge to executive power, one that raised a different—but in many ways more significant—issue than the one brought up by Cadwalader's refusal to bring Merryman before Taney in 1861. The case of Lambdin P. Milligan also resulted from his arrest by military officers, acting without a judicial warrant. But in contrast to Merryman, who was soon released from confinement and never brought to trial, Milligan was tried before a military commission and sentenced to hang for "inciting insurrection" and "affording aid and comfort to rebels against the authority of the United States." Also in contrast to *Merryman*, the case of *Ex parte Milligan* reached the Supreme Court and resulted in a landmark decision with continuing significance.

The *Milligan* case stemmed from the very real dangers posed to Union forces by Confederate sympathizers in states along the Ohio River, particularly in Kentucky, Ohio, and Indiana. Members of secret societies with names such as the Knights of the Golden Circle, the Order of American Knights, and the Cirque de Belgique—groups that later banded together as the Sons of Liberty—were better known as Copperheads, after the poisonous snake whose brown-and-copper skin provided camouflage among fallen leaves. Many Copperheads led the lives of respectable citizens by day and plotted against the Union at night. Lambdin Milligan was a lawyer in southern Indiana, a Copperhead stronghold, and was suspected by Union military officials of belonging to the Sons of Liberty. During the fall of 1864, rumors of a plot to release Confederate prisoners of war from prison camps in Ohio reached Union military agents. The plotters, supposedly led by Milligan, planned to break into Union depots, steal arms, and launch an attack on the camps. Acting on these reports, General Alvin P. Hovey, who commanded the military district of Indiana, ordered Milligan's arrest on October 5, 1864, along with that of three other suspected plotters who belonged to the Sons of Liberty. Milligan and his fellow prisoners were taken to Indianapolis, where they were charged with "inciting insurrection" and providing "aid and comfort" to the Confederate cause.

The most significant aspect of the trial of Milligan and the other suspected plotters was that it took place before a military commission and not a civilian court. Lincoln had issued proclamations giving commanders broad powers to establish tribunals that could try civilians for offenses such as those brought against Milligan. On December 18, 1864, the military tribunal found all four defendants guilty and sentenced them to death by hanging. Milligan and his fellow defendants were lucky, however. According to the rules of the military tribunal that convicted them, its findings and sentences had to be reviewed by higher officers and, if approved, death warrants must be signed by the president. By the time the papers reached Washington, a Union victory over the Confederacy had become all but certain, and Lincoln did not sign the warrants. But they remained in his office, and Milligan remained in military custody, still under a death sentence.

Lincoln himself died from an assassin's bullet on April 15, 1865, just six days after General Robert E. Lee surrendered his Confederate troops—and his failed cause—to General Ulysses S. Grant at Appomattox Court House, in Virginia. The Civil War had ended, and it seemed likely that Lambdin Milligan had survived the bloody conflict. But his fate rested in the hands of Lincoln's successor in the White House, Andrew Johnson, who assumed office after serving just one month as vice president. Milligan's luck turned bad when Johnson signed his death warrant and set his execution for May 19.

By this time, Milligan had recruited a battery of lawyers—including a future president, James Garfield, then a member of the House of Representatives from Ohio—to press his case. Ten days before his scheduled execution, Milligan's attorneys filed a petition in the federal circuit court for Indiana, seeking his "discharge from unlawful imprisonment." They argued that the military tribunal had no jurisdiction over civilians, because Indiana had been under no danger of Confederate invasion when Milligan was arrested; that martial law had not been imposed; and that federal courts in the state were functioning at the time. In fact, they noted, a federal grand jury was in session when Milligan was tried by the military tribunal, and had adjourned without indicting him for any crime. It was then fairly common for circuit judges to "divide" over cases that raised significant constitutional issues, sending them to the Supreme Court for resolution, without the delay of writing opinions. The "divided" case of *Ex parte Milligan* thus reached the Court in the fall of 1865 but was not argued until March 5, 1866. Milligan, however, no longer faced the hangman's noose. After his lawyers filed their appeal, President Johnson commuted his death sentence, and he remained in military custody to await the Court's final decision.

The Court that decided the *Milligan* case was no longer headed by Roger Taney, whose opinion in *Merryman* had castigated Lincoln for suspending the writ of habeas corpus. Taney died in 1864, and Lincoln named Salmon P. Chase of Ohio to replace him. A former senator, governor, and Treasury secretary in Lincoln's wartime cabinet, Chase had gained notoriety before the Civil War for his legal defense of fugitive slaves. He had sought the Republican presidential nomination in 1860, and had considered another contest against Lincoln in 1864, although he finally withdrew from contention. Placing him on the Supreme Court as chief justice removed an obstacle to Lincoln's second term, but also cemented Republican control of the Court. Five of the justices who decided the *Milligan* case owed their seats on the bench to Lincoln.

Whether the justices would have decided the case as they did if Lincoln had remained in office, we cannot know. But his death removed any sense of personal loyalty or deference to the former president. Ruling on April 3, 1866, the Court unanimously ordered that Lambdin Milligan be released from military custody. Although Justice David Davis had been placed on the Court in 1862 by Lincoln and was a home-state friend and political ally, his *Milligan* opinion exceeded that of Taney, in *Merryman,* in denouncing Lincoln's exercise of wartime powers. Davis began his opinion by noting that Milligan was "not a resident of one of the rebellious states, or a prisoner of war," but a civilian who was arrested, tried, convicted, and sentenced to death by a military commission. He stated the central question before the Court in these words: "Had this tribunal the legal power and authority to try and punish this man?"

Davis underscored the gravity of this case, and of the issues it raised. "No graver question was ever considered by this court," he wrote, "nor one which more nearly concerns the rights of the whole people, for it is the birthright of every American citizen when charged with crime, to be tried and punished according to law." The Constitution itself, in three of the first ten amendments, lays out the protections of citizens accused of crimes. The Fourth Amendment, which guards against "unreasonable search and seizure," requires proof of "probable cause" for the issuance of a judicial arrest warrant. The Fifth, besides mandating a grand jury indictment before formal charges and trial, says that no person shall "be deprived of life, liberty, or property without due process of law." And the Sixth, of particular importance in the *Milligan* case, guarantees the accused person "the right to a speedy and public trial by an impartial jury of the state and district wherein the crime shall have been committed." Milligan received none of these basic constitutional protections, from the time of his arrest through his sentencing to death, Davis stated.

But he did not deny the president any power to declare martial law in areas of actual combat, or even in those that were threatened by hostile invasion. "This is not a question of the power to proclaim martial law," Davis wrote, "when war exists in a community and the courts and civil authorities are overthrown." Nor did he question "what rule a military commander, at the head of his army, can impose on states in rebellion to cripple their resources and quell the insurrection." Davis left undecided the authority to establish military tribunals in localities subject to martial law. But Indiana was not such a territory. "On her soil there was no hostile foot" at the time of Milligan's arrest, and no real prospect of imminent Confederate invasion. Those facts ended "all pretext for martial law" in the state, Davis declared firmly. The only proper course under which Milligan could have been charged and tried for "conspiracy" to aid the Confederacy, Davis wrote, was to secure his indictment by a grand jury and bring him before a civilian court. "If this had been done," Davis added, "the Constitution would have been vindicated" and "the securities for personal liberty preserved and defended." The federal court with jurisdiction over Milligan was open, "peacefully transacted its business," and adjourned with no indictment against him. "It needed no bayonets to protect it," Davis said, "and required no military aid to execute its judgments."

Justice Davis put his strong feelings about the broader issues in the *Milligan* case in words that have great relevance today, and which deserve full quotation: "The Constitution of the United States is a law for rulers and people, equally in war and in peace, and covers with the shield of its protection all classes of men, at all times, and under all circumstances. No doctrine, involving more pernicious consequences, was ever invented by the wit of man than that any of its provisions can be suspended during any of the great exigencies of government. Such a doctrine leads directly to anarchism or despotism, but the theory of necessity on which it is based is false; for the Government, within the Constitution, has all the powers granted to it, which are necessary to preserve its existence, as has been happily proved by the result of the great effort to throw off its just authority."

With these words, Justice Davis placed the protections of the Bill of Rights beyond the reach of government officials, civilian or military, elected or appointed. But succeeding generations of officials, including most of the presidents who followed Lincoln, have ignored this stern judicial lecture. The Union survived the Civil War, at great cost in lives on both sides of the bloody conflict. And the Constitution survived as well, but at great cost to the principles of civil liberty and the rule of law. The *Milligan* decision, with its warning against presidential claims of "unlimited power" during times of national crisis, should have foreclosed any further assaults on the Constitution. But as Justice Davis warned, officials who are "ambitious of power" and who display their "contempt of law" have repeatedly placed the Constitution in grave peril.

We will see in a later chapter that the Supreme Court, despite its reluctance to rule on after-the-fact congressional authorizations of presidential war-making powers, recently struck down the indefinite detention of American citizens suspected of being "enemy combatants" in the war on terror. Ruling in June 2004, the Court granted the habeas corpus petition of Yaser Esam Hamdi, an American-born citizen who had been seized in Afghanistan in 2001 and held in military prisons for more than two years, without charges being filed against him and without access to counsel. In a companion case, the Court extended habeas corpus protection to more than six hundred suspected "enemy combatants" held at the Guantánamo naval base in Cuba; none of them were U.S. citizens but all were detained on American territory.

Drawing a link between past and present, the parallels between the cases of John Merryman and Yaser Hamdi are striking, despite their different circumstances. Holding that the Constitution does not provide the president with a "blank check" during wartime, Justice Sandra Day O'Connor—who wrote for the Court in Hamdi's challenge to his detention—used words and reasoning that echoed those of Chief Justice Taney in Merryman's case. The cases of Lambdin Milligan and the Guantánamo detainees, even more different in circumstances, also have illuminating parallels. Most important, in all these cases, separated by more than a century, presidential subversion of the Constitution was emphatically rejected by justices who recognized that both Confederate sympathizers and suspected "enemy combatants" are protected, by the Great Writ, from indefinite detention at the will of any president.

5

"REMEMBER THE *MAINE*":

The Birth of Imperial America

Although the Confederate surrender in April 1865 ended the human carnage of the Civil War, the reunited nation has struggled, ever since, to heal the still-festering wounds of that bloody conflict. Despite the enormous casualties and costs of the war, however, the country's economy rebounded with robust health and vigor. Factories that had churned out huge quantities of munitions and other military supplies, mostly in the Union states, quickly shifted to producing consumer goods like stoves and shovels. The completion of the transcontinental railroad in 1869 symbolized the web of commerce that stretched from the Atlantic to the Pacific coasts. Entrepreneurs like Andrew Carnegie and John D. Rockefeller built financial empires based on steel and oil, while Thomas Edison and other inventors spurred advances in communication by telephone and telegraph. Even in the defeated Confederacy, the cotton industry slowly recovered, and the South developed its own iron and steel mills.

Most important, during the last three decades of the nineteenth century, the nation's population more than doubled, from 31 million in 1870 to 76 million by 1900. Millions of these new Americans

were immigrants who poured into the United States through the narrow funnel of Ellis Island, completing steamship voyages that began
in Poland, Russia, Italy, Greece, and other countries of eastern and
southern Europe. The vast majority of these immigrants were poor,
spoke little or no English, and had only a strong back or nimble fin-
gers to offer employers. But the voracious appetite of the American
economy crammed the newcomers into factories, mills, and sweat-
shops, to labor at low wages for long hours. For most immigrants, of
course, even a demeaning job and a crowded tenement were better
than the grinding poverty and dirt-floor homes they had left behind.
In the thirty years that followed the Civil War, these new Americans
joined native-born citizens in fueling the greatest economic boom
the world had ever seen, with an output of manufactured goods and
agricultural products worth some $10 billion in 1898.

The spurt in population and in the products of farms and factories
had a significant impact on the nation's role in the world economy.
By 1893, the United States was second only to England in foreign
trade, with cotton and oil as the leading American exports. Although
90 percent of American goods were consumed by the domestic market, the 10 percent sold overseas accounted for more than a billion
dollars in highly profitable trade. A major by-product of such rapid
growth was the ideology of expansion. Among the upper echelons of
politicians and businessmen, the lure of foreign markets led many to
advocate territorial as well as financial gain. Senator Albert Beveridge
of Indiana declared in 1897, "American factories are making more
than the American people can use; American soil is producing more
than they can consume. Fate has written our policy for us; the trade
of the world must and shall be ours." In a magazine article, another
senator, Henry Cabot Lodge of Massachusetts, outlined his program, whose centerpiece was to be the long-sought canal that would
connect the Atlantic and the Pacific and thus cut the time and cost of
foreign trade. The most likely site for the canal, at that time, was not
through Panama: "In the interests of our commerce," Lodge wrote,
"we should build the Nicaragua canal, and for the protection of that
canal and for the sake of our commercial supremacy in the Pacific we

should control the Hawaiian islands." On the other side of the canal, "the island of Cuba . . . will become a necessity." Lodge viewed territorial expansion as an imperative. "The great nations are rapidly absorbing for their future expansion and their present defense all the waste places of the earth," he said. "It is a movement which makes for civilization and the advancement of the race. As one of the great nations of the world the United States must not fall out of the line of march."

Along with talk of territorial expansion came militaristic bluster. The loudest voice belonged to Theodore Roosevelt, who glorified both war and white supremacy; indeed, he denounced the 1893 decision not to annex Hawaii as "a crime against white civilization," viewing the Pacific islands as a barrier against the "yellow peril" of Asian migration. Later, Roosevelt spoke at the Naval War College: "All the great masterful races have been fighting races," he declared. "No triumph of peace is quite so great as the supreme triumph of war." One likely site for military confrontation caught his eye. Roosevelt and other hawks urged political leaders to intervene in the Cuban rebellion against Spanish rule. During the 1890s, American investments in Cuba had grown to some $50 million, and annual trade between Cuba and the United States exceeded $100 million. Because the Cuban revolt threatened American investments and trade, both Presidents Grover Cleveland and William McKinley faced pressure to intervene, and to support the rebel demand for Cuban independence. In 1896, Congress adopted a resolution extending the "friendly offices" of the United States to Spain in recognizing an independent Cuba. But the Spanish government rejected the offer.

That same year, congressional leaders sent a delegation to the White House, telling President Cleveland that sentiment on Capitol Hill had turned against further diplomacy. "We have about decided to declare war against Spain over the Cuban question," they told Cleveland. "Conditions are intolerable." The chief executive refused, however, to yield to the hawks. "There will be no war with Spain over Cuba while I am President." The exchange following those blunt words has probably never been repeated since that Oval Office meeting. One member of the congressional delegation reminded Cleveland that the Constitution gave Congress the power to declare war. That was true, the president responded, but the Constitution also made him commander in chief of the armed forces. "I will not mobilize the army," he said firmly. Presidents have repeatedly, of course, mobilized the army and deployed the navy without congressional declarations of war, and without any effective legislative or judicial sanctions. Cleveland's reply turned the coin over. What action could Congress take if it declared war and the president refused to send troops into combat? Under the Constitution, the only remedy would be impeachment, a prospect that did not faze Cleveland.

William McKinley, the probusiness Republican who replaced the probusiness Democrat Cleveland, took office in March 1897 with a professed desire to avoid war in Cuba. Presumably having American interests in mind, McKinley instructed his minister to Spain to redouble his efforts to settle the conflict, because "it injuriously affects the normal function of business, and tends to delay the condition of prosperity." But the situation changed abruptly on February 15, 1898, when a massive explosion ripped through the American battleship *Maine,* sitting at anchor in Havana's harbor as a visible symbol of U.S. might. When the *Maine* sank, with the loss of 266 crew members, the American public reacted with shock and outrage, suspecting the Spanish of blowing up the ship. Considering that such an obvious act of war would certainly provoke a full-scale conflict, Spain had nothing to gain from blowing up the *Maine.* McKinley ordered an inquiry into the cause of the blast; he reported to Congress on April 11 that the *Maine* had been destroyed "by an exterior explosion—that of a submarine mine." Later and more thorough studies concluded that the explosion, from whatever source, took place inside the ship. But those reports were not released until after the war ended. In the eyes of the American public, Spain was guilty of killing nearly three hundred sailors, and pressure mounted for a declaration of war.

Reluctantly, McKinley bowed to the war hawks in Congress. On April 20, 1898, both houses adopted a resolution offered by Senator

Henry M. Teller, a Colorado Republican. The Teller Amendment, which was attached to a proposed declaration of war, stated congressional resolve that "the people of the Island of Cuba are, and of right ought to be, free and independent." Congress demanded that Spain "at once relinquish its authority and government in the Island of Cuba and withdraw its land and naval forces from Cuba and Cuban waters." Furthermore, it authorized President McKinley to "use the entire land and naval forces of the United States" to enforce the demand for Spanish withdrawal from Cuba. Even so, the Teller Amendment, in disclaiming any intention "to exercise sovereignty, jurisdiction, or control" over Cuba, once its residents gained independence, and in expressing U.S. determination "to leave the government and control of the Island to its people," rebuffed the advocates of outright American annexation of Cuba.

The congressional war hawks finally prevailed, and Congress formally declared war on Spain on April 25, by the overwhelming margin of 311 to 6 in the House, but with a much closer Senate vote, 42 to 35. One prominent Republican senator, John C. Spooner of Wisconsin, lamented that "possibly the President could have worked out the business without war, but the current was too strong, the demagogues too numerous, and the fall elections too near." Politics had trumped diplomacy, and the prospect of a quick and easy victory over Spain quieted the critics of this military adventure.

The victory in the Spanish-American War was relatively quick, but not as easy as most of its advocates had expected. American troops, unaccustomed to combat in tropical climates, sweltered in the summer heat and pouring rain, and were bogged down in the dense underbrush and steep hills around the city of Santiago de Cuba, where the fiercest fighting took place, at the island's eastern end. Malaria and dysentery felled more U.S. soldiers than Spanish guns, but the Americans had a huge advantage in firepower, from naval cannons and army artillery. All that most people recall about the shortest of America's five declared wars—the fighting lasted less than four months—is the famous charge of Teddy Roosevelt's Rough Riders up San Juan Hill, overlooking the Santiago harbor. As assistant secretary of the navy in the McKinley administration, Roosevelt had argued vociferously for war with Spain. When it came, he resigned his post to organize a volunteer cavalry brigade, and his exploits in Cuba not only brought him fame but soon propelled him to public office, first as New York's governor in 1898 and then as McKinley's vice president in 1900. Two days after Roosevelt's troops dislodged the Spanish from San Juan Hill, on July 1, 1898, the Spanish fleet fled the harbor, effectively surrendering control of Cuba. The Spanish accepted an armistice on August 12, and the Senate ratified a peace treaty on February 6, 1899.

If the only goal in declaring war on Spain was to secure Cuban independence, there would have been no obvious violations of their constitutional roles by either Congress or President McKinley. But that was not the fundamental motivation. The real aim of war hawks like Teddy Roosevelt, and of many business leaders who produced goods for export, was territorial expansion. Before the Spanish-American War, the United States possessed no formal colonies and was not, strictly speaking, an imperial power. After the war, however, the country joined the ranks of imperial nations; in fact, it now headed the "line of march" around the globe, as Henry Cabot Lodge had urged.

Although Cuba itself was not turned into an outright American colony, it became one in all but name, with its nominal independence a facade for U.S. control. In a preview of later military occupations, from Germany and Japan after World War II through Iraq after Saddam Hussein was deposed in 2003, American troops remained in Cuba for several years. And, like those countries, Cuba was forced to adopt a constitution to suit the United States. In July 1900 the Cubans began a constitutional convention, whose delegates were abruptly informed that the U.S. Congress intended to attach a measure that, in effect, would turn Cuba into an American protectorate. McKinley's secretary of war, Elihu Root, drafted a set of stipulations for the Cuban constitution that became known as the Platt Amendment, after Orville Platt, the Connecticut senator who attached them to an army appropriations bill in February 1901. The central provision of the Platt Amendment stated that "the government of Cuba consents that the United States may intervene for the preservation of Cuban independence," even without a request for assistance by the island nation. What was crucial to its continued independence, of course, was not American protection against invasion by other countries but Cuban protection of American property and investments against expropriation or trade barriers. To maintain such protection, the Platt Amendment required the Cubans to "sell or lease to the United States lands necessary for coaling or naval stations," a provision under which the United States later secured a perpetual lease on the Guantánamo Bay naval station in eastern Cuba.

Confronted with demands that, according to a report to the Cuban constitutional convention, would result in "feeble and miserable governments," the delegates, at first, firmly rejected the Platt Amendment. But finally, yielding to intense American pressure, the delegates capitulated and added the demeaning provisions to the new constitution. General Leonard Wood, who headed the American military occupation of Cuba, wrote to Vice President Roosevelt: "There is, of course, little or no independence left Cuba under the Platt Amendment." The occupation troops left Cuba in 1904, but, under the "intervention" clause, the United States sent more troops in 1906, 1912, 1917, and 1920, not to protect Cuban independence but to quash popular uprisings against American domination of the island's economy. However, rising Cuban nationalism and domestic criticism of the Platt Amendment led to its repeal in 1934 as part of President Franklin Roosevelt's Good Neighbor policy toward Latin America, although the United States hung on to its lease on Guantánamo Bay, where an American naval base controlled the Caribbean.

In many ways, the Spanish-American War had less to do with Cuba than with American interests in the Pacific. In fact, the day before Congress declared war on Spain in April 1898, President McKinley sent a cable to Admiral George Dewey, who commanded the Pacific fleet: "Proceed at once to Philippine Islands. Commence operations at once, particularly against the Spanish fleet. You must capture vessels or destroy." Dewey did just that. At dawn on May 1, his squadron of seven vessels, including cruisers and destroyers, entered Manila Bay and returned fire from the Spanish shore batteries. By noon, all ten ships of the Spanish fleet had been sunk by the devastating barrage from Dewey's guns, with not a single American casualty. The Spanish had ruled the Philippines for centuries and had battled native insurgencies for years before their defeats in Cuba and Manila Bay. Without much regret, Spain ceded the Philippines to the United States in the peace treaty of 1899, along with the Caribbean island of Puerto Rico and the Pacific island of Guam, in exchange for a total payment of $20 million.

With its effective control of Cuba, and its acquisition through force of the Philippines—with Puerto Rico and Guam thrown in for good measure—the United States entered the twentieth century as a full-fledged imperial nation. The constitutional formalities had been observed in declaring war on Spain, although it seems clear that economic and political control of Cuba, rather than a Spanish military attack on American soil or against U. S. citizens in Cuba, had motivated Congress. The sinking of the *Maine*, however much the public believed Spain was responsible, provided a convenient pretext for a war that, in reality, the advocates of expansion were simply waiting to launch. And despite the close Senate vote on declaring war, it was a popular war, quick and relatively bloodless, turning Teddy Roosevelt and his Rough Riders into instant heroes.

There were no such heroes in the long and bloody war to subdue the Philippines, which rebelled against U.S. rule in 1899. Led by Emilio Aguinaldo, who had fought the Spanish for years, the Filipino rebels waged a three-year struggle against seventy thousand American troops. It was a brutal confrontation, marked by numerous American atrocities. One American officer, Major Littleton Waller, was court-martialed for shooting eleven unarmed Filipinos. In his defense, Waller claimed that his commanding general, Jacob Smith, "instructed him to kill and burn, and said that the more he killed and burned the better pleased he would be." Waller asked General Smith "to define the age limit for killing, and he replied 'Everything over ten.'" When the Senate held hearings, in 1902, on charges of American atrocities, military commanders freely admitted giving orders to burn Filipino homes. One senator, noting that "women and little children" bore the brunt of this punishment, asked an army general whether this conduct fell within the rules of civilized warfare. "These people are not civilized," the general replied.

By themselves, the Philippines represented a rich source of mahogany, rice, coal, and other goods for the American market. But the islands were also stepping stones to the mainland of Asia, a vastly greater market. Senator Albert Beveridge, an unabashed apostle of empire, laid out his goals in January 1900. "The Philippines are ours forever," he told his Senate colleagues. "And just beyond the Philippines are China's illimitable markets. We will not retreat from either. The Pacific is our ocean. Where shall we turn for consumers of our surplus? Geography answers the question. China is our natural customer. The Philippines give us a base at the door of all the East."

Shortly after Beveridge made this speech, the door to China began to close. A group of Chinese revolutionaries, members of a secret society called the Righteous and Harmonious Fists and known in the West as the Boxers, demanded the expulsion of all foreigners from the country. The Boxers surrounded foreign legations in Peking (now Beijing) and threatened the lives of Americans and other outsiders. In response to the Boxer Rebellion, nations with economic interests in China—including England, France, Russia, Germany, and Japan—formed an international expeditionary force, to which McKinley added five thousand American troops. Within two months, the international troops crushed the rebellion and imposed on the weakened Chinese government, headed by the Dowager Empress, the Boxer Protocol of 1901. Under its terms, European powers had the right to maintain military forces in the capital, effectively placing the government under house arrest; the protocol also demanded a huge indemnity to the occupying nations for losses they claimed from the rebellion.

McKinley had dispatched the troops while Congress was in

recess, and he later explained that his actions "involved no war against the Chinese nation" but, rather, a limited incursion to protect U.S. lives and property, the favorite excuse of presidents who send troops abroad without prior congressional sanction. As we have seen, the Constitution's Framers contemplated emergency situations, such as reprisal against sudden attack on Americans and their property, or their seizure and detention. And each emergency situation has unique facts and circumstances, making any "bright line" rule to govern presidential actions difficult to fashion and apply. Were the lives of the Americans in Peking, during the Boxer Rebellion, truly in danger? Could diplomacy have secured their protection and, if necessary, safe passage from the troubled area in China? Should U.S. troops have limited their actions to protecting Americans, or should they have joined the international forces in crushing the rebellion?

These are questions, of course, for which the Constitution's text provides no simple answers. But however close to an elusive and shifting boundary President McKinley stepped, his successor boldly stomped across it, swinging his "big stick" of military force with a Rough Rider's swagger. Theodore Roosevelt paid no attention to Congress in his interventionist forays into the nations south of the United States. All of Central and Latin America had long been considered part of the American "sphere of influence" from which European powers were admitted only for trade and commerce. The famous Monroe Doctrine (1823) had warned outsiders that the United States "should consider any attempt on their part to extend their system to any portion of this hemisphere as dangerous to our peace and safety." President James Monroe, however, did not assert that he could enforce the doctrine with unilateral presidential action; should enforcement require a military response, only Congress could authorize it.

The Rough Rider had no such compunctions about sending American troops into foreign countries. In his annual message to Congress in 1904, TR announced what became known as the Roosevelt Corollary to the Monroe Doctrine. No southern nations whose government acted with "reasonable efficiency and decency in social and political matters" and that "keeps order and pays its obligations" had reason to fear American intervention. What Roosevelt had in mind, primarily, was the payment of debts owed to the United States and protection of U.S. property against expropriation. He sounded like the headmaster of a strict boarding school. "Chronic wrongdoing, or an impotence which results in a general loosening of the ties of civilized society," he warned, might result in American intervention, but "only in the last resort."

In fact, Roosevelt had used the "big stick" of military force even before this message. In 1903, the government of Colombia refused to ratify a one-sided treaty that would allow the United States to build a canal across the isthmus of Panama, which was then a province of Colombia. Roosevelt then encouraged a revolt by Panamanians and sent warships to prevent Colombia from sending troops to Panama. Once the revolutionaries took control, protected by American forces, Roosevelt recognized Panama as an independent nation. The maneuver was, pure and simple, war against Colombia, which posed no military threat to the United States. Congress did nothing to block this exercise of presidential war making, and grabbing Panama from Colombia met with popular acclaim. The Senate quickly ratified a treaty with the new Republic of Panama, giving the United States control of the Canal Zone, which not only became a boon to shipping but provided an American military base at the crucial juncture of Central and South America, from which troops could be dispatched to "wrongdoing" countries in the area. Later, TR boasted, "I took the canal zone and let Congress debate, and while the debate goes on the canal does also."

Carrying out his threat to punish nations that failed to pay their debts, Roosevelt sent troops to the Dominican Republic in 1905. The Dominicans, who had run up some $32 million in foreign debt, sought to negotiate agreements with creditor nations, including the United States. Roosevelt wanted to work out a payment schedule through a presidential agreement, but Senate leaders insisted that only a treaty would have binding force. Treaties require a two-thirds majority in the Senate, and Democrats had enough votes to block a treaty with the Dominicans. During this political impasse, the Italian government sent a warship to Santo Domingo to enforce demands for debt repayment. Roosevelt responded to this incursion by warning the Italians away from "American" waters, and by sending troops to occupy the Dominican capital. In 1907 the Senate finally ratified a treaty that settled the American claims, and Roosevelt's military intervention was effectively ratified by congressional silence.

TR's muscular, pugnacious approach to foreign policy set the tone for later presidents, even those who acknowledged that their actions depended on congressional approval. William Howard Taft, who succeeded Roosevelt in 1909, was an experienced lawyer who later served as chief justice of the Supreme Court, the only former president to join the bench. Taft understood the Constitution far better than Roosevelt, but he followed the Rough Rider in sending troops into several countries, including Nicaragua, Honduras, Mexico, and Cuba. Each incursion resulted from pressure to protect U.S. business interests, not from any military attack by those nations. Taft did, however, tell Congress in 1911 of his "serious doubt" that he possessed the power "under any circumstances" to send troops into foreign countries—in this case, Mexico—even to protect American lives and property. Taft did not view his role as commander in chief as giving him the power to order military intervention abroad, and in any event, he "would not exercise it without express congressional approval," he assured the lawmakers.

It would be difficult to imagine a greater contrast in presidents than between Woodrow Wilson and Teddy Roosevelt. The two were separated by the four years of Taft's administration, but Roosevelt still exemplified for many Americans the active chief executive, taking charge of foreign policy with hardly a nod to Congress. What scholars later called the "imperial presidency" began with Roosevelt, with his vision of a globe-circling American empire of territory and trade, supported by the ever-present threat of military intervention against "wrongdoing" countries. Wilson, who took office in 1913 as the first Democrat since Grover Cleveland, looked and sounded nothing like Roosevelt. A noted scholar and former president of Princeton University, Wilson had written an influential book, *Congressional Government,* which began as his doctoral dissertation in political science at Johns Hopkins University. Few people are aware that Wilson also received a law degree from the University of Virginia, although he practiced for less than a year before moving to academic life. As the only president with an earned doctorate, Wilson had a professorial look about him. But he was also a skilled politician. He won the election of 1912 with just 42 percent of the popular vote, but with a plurality over both Taft and Roosevelt. Running as the Progressive Party candidate, Roosevelt actually bested Taft, who ran a poor third as the Republican candidate. Taft might have defeated Wilson in a two-man contest, but Roosevelt's insurgent candidacy split the GOP vote between the Bull Moose reformers and the bull elephants in the party's conservative wing.

Despite his cerebral looks and image, Wilson was hardly a namby-pamby in foreign affairs. In 1914 he sent naval forces to the Mexican port of Veracruz, ostensibly to avenge an "insult" to some American sailors who had been arrested for rowdy shore-time behavior. Mexican authorities had quickly released the sailors, with apologies from President Victoriano Huerta. But this gesture failed to satisfy Wilson, who demanded a formal salute of twenty-one guns from the Mexicans to the U.S. vessels. Huerta's refusal to offer this symbol of obeisance provoked Wilson to ask Congress for approval of military action. "No doubt I could do what is necessary in the circumstances to enforce respect for our government without recourse to the congress," Wilson said, "and yet not exceed my constitutional powers as President; but I do not wish to act in a manner possibly of so grave consequence" without prior congressional authorization. The House of Representatives immediately granted Wilson the power he sought, but the Senate, refusing to be stampeded, began debating the issue. Wilson had no patience for delay, and promptly ordered troops to occupy Veracruz. The Senate later approved the joint resolution, which disclaimed "any purpose to make war upon Mexico."

American forces did, in fact, commit acts of aggression against
Mexico, bombarding Veracruz at the cost of one hundred lives,
occupying the city for seven months, and forcing the downfall of the
Huerta government—all because of the supposedly humiliating
demand for a twenty-one-gun salute to U.S. warships.

The next year, in 1915, Wilson sent troops to Haiti to support an
insurrection against a government the United States considered hostile
to its business interests. He took this action without prior congressional authorization. "I fear we have not the legal authority to do
what we apparently ought to do," Wilson admitted to his secretary
of state, William Jennings Bryan. American troops occupied Haiti
until 1934, effectively ruling the country as a colony. On the other
side of the island of Hispaniola, Wilson sent troops into the
Dominican Republic in 1916; they occupied the country for eight
years. And every president from Taft through Herbert Hoover sent
troops or warships to Nicaragua, with the purpose of affecting the
outcome of that country's presidential elections. Between 1909 and
1933, there was hardly a year during which U.S. troops did not
patrol the streets of Managua, the capital. During these years the
Roosevelt Corollary to the Monroe Doctrine turned the Caribbean
and Central America into a gigantic American colony, in fact if not
in name.

It is important to note, before we move to American involvement
in World War I, that none of the expansionist and territory-grabbing
events recounted in this chapter provoked any constitutional challenges to presidential actions. Opponents of the Spanish-American
War, the subjugation and annexation of the Philippines, and American
military intervention in Latin America voiced their objections in
Congress and in the press but did not ask the federal courts to block
any of these imperialistic adventures. Given the conservative, probusiness makeup of the federal judiciary at the time, the absence of
challenges in court was not surprising. But there was no serious
repression of the anti-imperialists by the federal government through
restrictions on speech and the press. As we will see, opponents of

World War I would face lengthy prison terms for "subversive" speech and writings against what its denouncers called the "imperialist" war. Such acts of repression by the government placed the war powers of Congress and President Wilson in direct conflict with the First Amendment, with the Supreme Court as the arbiter of how much criticism the Constitution must tolerate during wartime.

6

"WE MUST HAVE NO CRITICISM NOW":

The War to End All Wars

The United States entered World War I almost three years after hostilities broke out in Europe, and only after President Woodrow Wilson, abandoning the neutrality policy that most Americans had supported, virtually demanded that Congress declare war on Germany. Wilson was responding not to a sudden, unprovoked German attack on American soil but to the shelling and torpedoing of ships that carried war supplies and munitions to England and its allies. However much those submarine attacks outraged the American public, it was, in fact, the supposedly neutral Americans, and not the Germans, who violated the rules of war and of international law in sending ships across the Atlantic. But "war fever" is highly contagious, and the Wilson administration—aided by a compliant press and the government's own propaganda machine—created an epidemic that infected both the public and the Congress. On the final vote, just six members of the Senate and fifty in the House opposed the war declaration. From a constitutional perspective, of course, it would not have mattered if Congress had declared war by a single-vote majority in each chamber. Nor did it matter that Germany had not launched an all-out invasion of the United States. Under the Constitution, war can be declared with only a simple majority in the Senate and in the House, and the document lays down no conditions for the legislative call to arms.

Wilson did not hesitate to commit "acts of war" against the weaker nations within the American sphere of influence, without prior congressional approval. But he exercised much greater caution in the European war that had begun in 1914 and that soon turned the Continent into a slaughterhouse. Before the Great War ended, in 1918, ten million soldiers died on the battlefield, and twenty million civilians perished from hunger and disease. During the first three years of the war, the United States proclaimed its neutrality between the belligerents. Wilson used words that Teddy Roosevelt would never have uttered: "There is such a thing as a nation being too proud to fight." American neutrality, however, reflected more than Wilson's moralistic worldview. In 1914 the economy had sunk into recession. "The war opened during a period of hard times," said the financier J. P. Morgan, Jr., son of the nation's most powerful banker. "Business throughout the country was depressed, farm prices were deflated, unemployment was serious, the heavy industries were working far below capacity and bank clearings were off." Morgan himself had no fear of losing his job, although millions of workers lost theirs. But as the iconoclastic writer Randolph Bourne said, "War is the health of the state." And the European war restored the American economy to a healthy state; by 1917, England and its allies had purchased more than $2 billion in supplies. Neutrality was good for business.

Most of that business involved shipping goods across the Atlantic, and neutrality became difficult after German submarines began sinking American merchant ships. The Germans had announced that any vessel, including passenger ships, was fair game for attack if it carried war supplies or munitions. In 1915 the British liner *Lusitania* was torpedoed and sunk by a German submarine, with a loss of 1,198 lives, including 124 Americans. Wilson denounced the attack on "innocent" civilians, but in fact the *Lusitania* carried a cargo of five million machine-gun cartridges and 1,248 cases of artillery shells, hidden behind a false manifest. Secretary of State William Jennings Bryan advised Wilson that Germany had the right, under the rules of war, to prevent contraband from reaching the Allies: "A ship carrying contraband should not rely upon passengers to protect her from attack—it would be like putting women and children in front of an army."

Bryan urged Wilson to press the Germans to refrain from submarine attacks on neutral ships, but the president considered such an appeal "both weak and futile." After he asked Congress, in December 1915, for funds to expand the army and build more warships, Bryan resigned his post. Wilson won a second term, in 1916, with the slogan "He Kept Us out of War," but he kept moving the nation toward war. Even before his second inauguration, in March 1917, Wilson broke diplomatic relations with Germany, citing its refusal to end attacks on ships that carried munitions. He also asked Congress for authority to arm merchant ships for protection against German submarines. "No doubt I already possess that authority without special warrant of law, by the plain implication of my constitutional duties and powers," Wilson said on February 26, but he wanted "to feel that the authority and the power of the Congress are behind me in whatever it may become necessary for me to do."

Three days later, on March 1, the House, by the lopsided vote of 403 to 13, gave Wilson the green light he had requested. But a small group of antiwar senators blocked the measure from coming to a vote, invoking the filibuster rule that allowed unlimited debate on the Senate floor. Led by Senator Robert LaFollette of Wisconsin, a maverick Republican known to admiring constituents as Fighting Bob, those senators held up the "arm the ships" bill until Congress ended its session, on March 4, the day before Wilson's inauguration. The president was so incensed that he leveled this blast at his critics: "The Senate of the United States is the only legislative body in the world which cannot act when its majority is ready for action. A little group of willful men, representing no opinion but their own, have rendered the great government of the United States helpless and contemptible."

The Senate filibuster sank the bill to authorize Wilson to arm merchant vessels, but this legislative blockade did not prevent him from getting what he really wanted, a congressional declaration of war on Germany. The president called Congress into special session on April 2, 1917; four days later, both chambers approved the declaration, by votes of 373 to 50 in the House, and 82 to 6 in the Senate. The fourth declaration of war by Congress became the first to embroil the United States in a global conflict, in which the rival imperial powers Great Britain and Germany were fighting for control of territories, markets, and raw materials around the world. The American government disclaimed any desire to expand its own empire during or after the war, but the lure of postwar foreign markets became a motivating factor in the plans of political and business leaders to exploit the power vacuums that followed the war's end.

As was true in both the wars against Mexico and Spain, the United States declared war on Germany without the provocation of a military attack on American soil. Despite his protestation in October 1916, as voters prepared to cast their presidential ballots, that "I am not expecting this country to get into war," Wilson had already begun placing the nation on a war footing, and his administration was cranking up a formidable propaganda machine to create excitement for a military undertaking that many Americans viewed with little or no enthusiasm. Once again, as with the Mexican and Spanish wars, Congress had followed the constitutional formality of granting the president's request for a declaration of war, however lame the pretext, for what—in those earlier wars—had been the lure of territorial expansion. In the case of World War I, Wilson engaged in what the historian Richard Hofstadter later called "rationalization of the flimsiest sort" in justifying the war declaration. After all, the British and Germans had both interfered with American shipping, and neither had violated the established rules of warfare, but Wilson had not suggested declaring war on England. He was forced, as

Hofstadter wrote, "to find legal reasons for policies that were based not upon law but upon the balance of power and economic necessities."

In retrospect, the United States had no compelling reason to enter the European war. Many Americans, of course, had ties of ancestry with England, and others with no ancestral link sympathized with the "plucky" British in their struggle with the "brutal" Germans, accused of raping Belgian nuns and similar atrocities. But some five million Americans had German relatives and forebears, many of them parents or grandparents. Blood ties were thus not the major factor in going to war, nor were the lurid—and largely fictitious—reports of German crimes against civilians. The one factor that most clearly prompted Wilson to shift from neutrality between England and Germany was his fear that a drawn-out war, with neither side able to force the other to surrender, would gravely damage or even destroy the international economic system on which U.S. trade and prosperity depended. That system, of course, depended on the raw materials and other goods that were shipped from the colonies that both England and Germany controlled, in Africa and Asia, and on the return flow of manufactured products from industrial nations into the global markets. Before the war, the United States had trailed only England in foreign trade, and business and political leaders joined Wilson in his concern about the possible collapse of the world's trading system. If American troops could bring a quicker end to the war, the easier it would be to revive a moribund world economy. For obvious reasons, few business leaders—and no politicians—expressed their support for American involvement in the war in such nakedly self-interested terms. "Making the world safe for democracy" had more appeal than "making the world safe for trade." But the United States was not fighting for democracy in the African and Asian colonies that belonged to England and Germany, nor, indeed, for democracy in those imperial powers. Despite his professed support for "self-determination" by all peoples, Wilson himself harbored the racist attitudes of most whites in his native state of Virginia, and had never promoted voting rights for black Americans, let alone for the "colored" people of Africa and Asia. He did, however, fervently back what he called in 1914 "the righteous conquest of foreign markets."

The conquest of foreign markets required a stable world order, one in which struggles between rival imperial nations would not break out into warfare. Despite the horrific loss of lives on both sides, World War I did not destroy the world economy. But it seriously damaged the confidence of investors and traders that the flow of capital and commerce would remain open, particularly because the colonial subjects of the chief combatants—Britain, France, and Germany—seized on the conflict to press their claims for self-determination and national sovereignty. Although Wilson had encouraged anticolonial sentiment with his rhetoric, he had no desire to foster the breakup of the colonial system. His vision for the postwar world rested on a new institution, the League of Nations, an international parliament whose members pledged to bring before the world body any disputes that might lead to military action. Every member nation would have an equal vote in the League's assembly, but major decisions would be made by a council with five permanent members—the United States, Britain, France, Italy, and Japan—and four members elected by the assembly to short terms. Should disputes between member nations threaten armed conflict, the League could impose economic sanctions and, as a last resort, employ military force against recalcitrant countries.

Wilson pressed for American participation in the League of Nations with evangelical zeal. Not only was such an international body a "practical necessity," he told the Senate in 1919, but it represented "the hope of the world" for a lasting peace. He challenged the senators who would vote on the proposal to join the League: "Shall we or any other free people hesitate to accept this great duty? Dare we reject it and break the heart of the world?" But the president faced a skeptical audience in his emotional appeal. Senator Henry Cabot Lodge, the Massachusetts Republican who headed the skeptics, conditioned his support for joining the League on adoption of fourteen "reservations" to Wilson's proposal for a "covenant" to the Treaty of Versailles, which would formally end the state of war between Germany and the victorious allies. The second of Lodge's reservations went to the heart of the constitutional balance between Congress and the president: "The United States assumes no obligation to preserve the territorial integrity or political independence of any other country or to interfere in controversies between nations," it read, "or to employ the military or naval forces of the United States under any article of the treaty for any purpose, unless in any particular case the Congress, which, under the Constitution, has the sole power to declare war or authorize the employment of the military or naval forces of the United States, shall by act or joint resolution so provide." Lodge was less concerned with formal declarations of war by Congress than with unilateral presidential directives to "employ" military forces without prior congressional approval.

Senator Lodge's reservation would have done nothing more, in fact, than to preserve the powers of Congress under the Constitution. Wilson, however, responded that Lodge proposed to "cut out the heart of this Covenant" and to produce the "nullification" of the treaty for the League of Nations. More than a decade earlier, Wilson had made clear his disdain for congressional limitations of presidential power over foreign relations. In his book *Constitutional Government in the United States,* published in 1908, Wilson had claimed for the president an "absolute" control over the nation's foreign policy. "The initiative in foreign affairs," he wrote, "which the president possesses without any restriction whatever, is virtually the power to control them absolutely." While conceding that presidents could not conclude a treaty without the Senate's consent, he asserted that "every step of diplomacy" remained under presidential control. "He need disclose no step of negotiation until it is complete, and when in any critical matter it is completed the government is virtually committed. Whatever its disinclination the Senate may feel itself committed also."

Wilson's dismissive view of senatorial powers over the treaty-making process did not sit well with Lodge and other critics of the League of Nations. During all of 1919, the two strong-willed men conducted a fierce public battle over the covenant that Wilson had proposed as part of the Treaty of Versailles, which had been hammered out by the Big Four—the United States, Britain, France, and Italy—at the Paris peace conference in January and February. On his return to the United States, Wilson presented the draft covenant for the League at a dinner meeting with congressional foreign policy leaders. Breaking bread at the White House did not break the deadlock over participation in the League; Wilson later compared the disputatious dinner to having "tea with the Mad Hatter." Two days after this meeting, Lodge took the Senate floor to proclaim his opposition to Wilson's draft of the covenant, and thirty-eight of his colleagues quickly signed a letter urging the separation of the League from the Versailles treaty. Wilson promptly declared that the League and the treaty were "inseparable" and that he would not back down on this issue. He then returned to Paris for final negotiations with the other Big Four leaders, which concluded with a glittering ceremony in the Hall of Mirrors in the Versailles Palace on June 28, 1919, at which the president signed the treaty ending the "war to end all wars." Ten days later, Germany ratified the treaty, grudgingly accepting the Allies' demands for billions of dollars in reparations, as well as stringent limitations on German armaments and military forces.

The day after Germany's ratification of the treaty, Wilson returned to the United States and presented it to the Senate with a dramatic flourish: "The stage is set, the destiny disclosed," he proclaimed on July 10. But the Senate was not willing to close the curtain on this play and take a bow with the president. Over a two-week period, between July 14 and 28, Lodge took the Senate floor and read aloud all 246 pages of the treaty, making clear his objections to every provision that he considered an intrusion on congressional powers over the direction of American foreign policy. Over the next two months, Lodge presided at hearings before the Senate Foreign Relations Committee, at which sixty witnesses testified, most of them critical of American participation in the League of Nations. While those hearings proceeded in Washington, Wilson took his campaign for the League on the road, beginning an eight-thousand-mile circuit of the country on September 4, with forty speeches in twenty-nine cities. At the same time, Senators William Borah of Nebraska and Hiram Johnson of California began their own cross-country tour, denouncing Wilson's proposal to join the League as a surrender of U.S. sovereignty to a world body that might drag the nation into another war, without the consent of Congress and—more important—of the American people.

Wilson and his Senate critics embarked on their grueling marathons by rail, the only means of crossing the country before airplanes, and before television made it possible to address the nation from the White House or a network studio in Washington. Unlike Teddy Roosevelt, who relished physical exertion and brimmed with stamina, Wilson hardly ever engaged in exercise more taxing than lifting a pen. His punishing trip to rally the country behind the League came to an abrupt end in Pueblo, Colorado, where the president collapsed on September 25, 1919. He returned to Washington and suffered a debilitating stroke on October 2, which his doctors concealed from the public behind the bland diagnosis of "exhaustion." Over the next seven months, Wilson remained in the White House, bedridden and barely able to move or speak. During this crucial period, his strong-willed wife, Edith, and his trusted adviser Colonel Edward House became virtual copresidents, making decisions in Wilson's name, while they assured the public—quite falsely—that he was fully in control of the government.

There is no way of knowing how Wilson's illness affected the outcome of his proposal for American participation in the League of Nations. Even at full strength, he would have faced great difficulty in persuading the Senate to ratify the covenant to the Versailles treaty. Before the advent of opinion polls, it was impossible to measure public sentiment on this question, but it seems likely that most Americans shared the skepticism of the Senate majority that voted to reject the treaty on November 19, 1919, by a margin of 53 to 38. Refusing to surrender in his battle for the League, however, Wilson prevailed on the Senate Democrats to back a watered-down version of Lodge's reservations to the treaty, but even this move failed to satisfy the "irreconcilables" who stood firm in opposing any provision that would allow the president to commit forces to combat without prior congressional approval. On March 19, 1920, after four months of futile negotiations and heated debate, the Senate once again rejected the treaty, this time by a vote of 49 to 35. Two months later, the two houses of Congress adopted a joint resolution to end the state of war with Germany. Bitter in defeat, Wilson vetoed the resolution, leaving the nation formally at war with a country that had ratified a peace treaty with its European foes almost a year before. Not until July 2, 1921, after Warren Harding had replaced Wilson as president, did Congress once again adopt a joint resolution that finally ended the war.

Viewed in the broad context of American history, the Senate's refusal to approve Wilson's proposal to join the League of Nations stands out as the most emphatic declaration of congressional supremacy in foreign relations. Lodge and the irreconcilables were not the kind of isolationists who rejected on principle, or for partisan reasons, participation in world bodies designed to prevent conflicts between other nations from erupting into warfare. Nor did Lodge and his colleagues have any quarrel with the goals of the League of Nations, which they fully endorsed. The point of Lodge's "reservations" to the treaty Wilson presented to the Senate, on a "take-it-or-leave-it" basis, was that no president had the authority to dispatch troops to the battlefield without prior congressional approval. The war-making power, Lodge insisted, the Constitution gives solely to the Congress, and it cannot be delegated to the president through any treaty, even one approved by the Senate. On this crucial issue, the Senate irreconcilables were reconciled with the Constitution but not with Wilson's view of absolute presidential power over the nation's foreign policies. Not until the administration of George W. Bush, as we shall see, did any of Wilson's successors make such broad claims of presidential supremacy in this field.

How did the president's handling of U.S. participation in World War I fare in the third branch of government? The declaration of war on Germany did not raise any constitutional issues, and the Supreme Court had no occasion to decide whether Wilson had exceeded his powers in taking actions that made war all but certain.

The Court did, however, decide several landmark cases that stemmed from the war's unpopularity and the government's intense campaign to crush dissent. Considering the heated—and often vitriolic—criticism of later wars, in Vietnam and more recently in Iraq, the Court's rulings in the World War I cases merit discussion, both for the precedent they established in First Amendment cases and for their relevance to subsequent efforts to limit critical speech during wartime. One fact about the Wilson administration's attitude toward dissent is clear: It viewed all opposition to its policies as "seditious," even treasonable. Early in 1917, one of Wilson's closest advisers, former secretary of war Elihu Root, laid down the law: "We must have no criticism now." A few months later, upset that his words had not been heeded, Root warned that "there are men walking around the streets . . . tonight who ought to be taken out at sunrise tomorrow and shot for treason."

Root did not name the men he wanted to shoot, but they certainly included the leaders of the Socialist Party, whose membership and voting support jumped rapidly after the United States entered the war. The day after Congress declared war, party leaders met in St. Louis and blasted the declaration as "a crime against the people of the United States." The party's charismatic leader, Eugene V. Debs, was a former railway union leader who had won close to a million votes in the 1912 presidential election, although a lesser-known Socialist candidate garnered just 600,000 votes in 1916. Opposition to the war, however, swelled the Socialist vote in 1917 municipal and state elections. The party's candidate for mayor of New York got 22 percent of the vote and ten Socialists were elected to (and later ejected from) the New York State Assembly, while the party's vote in Chicago's city elections jumped to 35 percent; it rose to 30 percent in Buffalo.

Emboldened by this rise in popular support, the Socialists mounted a campaign against the highly unpopular military draft, which Congress had approved in June 1917, subjecting all men between eighteen and thirty-five to conscription. Congress imposed the draft because voluntary enlistment had failed to meet the army's manpower needs; in the first six weeks after the United States entered the war, only 73,000 men volunteered, while the army needed a million recruits. But the draft met with resistance and evasion, as men called to duty claimed exemptions or simply ignored draft notices. In August 1917 the *New York Herald* reported that ninety of the first one hundred draftees in the city had claimed hardship and medical exemptions. Even in Georgia, Senator Thomas Hardwick decried "widespread opposition on the part of many thousands" of young men, with "largely attended mass meetings held in every part of the state" to protest the draft. Before the war ended, over 300,000 men were officially classified as draft evaders, more than 10 percent of those who reported for duty. The epidemic of draft resistance prompted Congress to pass the Espionage Act in June 1917, imposing maximum terms of twenty years in prison for anyone "who shall willfully cause or attempt to cause . . . refusal of duty in the military or naval forces of the United States, or obstruct the recruiting and enlistment services of the United States." Despite the law's title, the statute had less to do with espionage than with encouraging young men to resist the draft, and its targets were not German spies but Socialist organizers.

Unlike the more militant antidraft activists during the Vietnam War, the Socialists in World War I did not attempt to physically block the doors to military recruitment and induction centers. They relied instead on speeches and leaflets to spread their message that the United States had no business entering a war between rival imperialist nations, and that military conscription would turn American troops into cannon fodder to serve the interests of big business. It was a campaign of spoken and printed words, not of violent or obstructive acts. On its face, the Constitution protected the Socialist campaigners against the draft. After all, the First Amendment provides that "Congress shall make no law . . . abridging the freedom of speech or of the press; or the right of the people peaceably to assemble, and to petition the Government for a redress of grievances." But the Wilson administration had no tolerance for dissent, however peaceful its expression.

The initial case to test the First Amendment began in Philadelphia, not far from the Constitution's birthplace at Independence Hall. On August 13, 1917, members of the city's Socialist Party executive committee gathered for their monthly meeting, and directed their general secretary, Charles J. Schenck, to prepare a leaflet for mailing to men who were listed in the newspapers as having passed their army physical examinations. Schenck already had copies of a circular the party had been distributing in its antidraft campaign. It was headed "Long Live the Constitution of the United States," and it reprinted the words of the Thirteenth Amendment, which abolished slavery and "involuntary servitude." The leaflet employed what Justice Oliver Wendell Holmes later called "impassioned language" against the draft. "A conscript is little better than a convict," it read. "He is deprived of his liberty and of his right to think and act as a free man." The leaflet urged readers to join the party's effort to repeal the draft law. "Exercise your rights of free speech, peaceful assemblage, and petitioning the government for a redress of grievances," it stated. "Come to the headquarters of the Socialist Party, 1326 Arch Street, and sign a petition to Congress for repeal of the Conscription Act." The other side of the leaflet that Schenck prepared, and which he wrote, was headed "Assert Your Rights!" It denounced the war as an imperialist conflict, and informed readers of "your right to assert your opposition to the draft." Schenck's language did not ask draft-age men to take any action other than voicing their objections to the draft law.

The fifteen thousand copies of the leaflet that Schenck had arranged to have printed, for mailing to draftees, never made it to the mailboxes. Federal officials got wind of the leaflets, secured a search warrant for party headquarters, and arrested Schenck and four executive committee members, who were charged, under the Espionage Act, with conspiring to "obstruct the recruiting and enlistment services of the United States." After a four-day trial in December 1917, the federal judge who presided directed the jury to acquit three defendants for lack of evidence. Schenck and Dr.

Elizabeth Baer, the committee's secretary, were convicted; he received a six-month sentence, and the judge gave her a ninety-day term. Under rules allowing cases that challenged federal laws on constitutional grounds to bypass the circuit courts, their appeals went directly to the Supreme Court.

More than a year passed between the trial of Schenck and Baer and the Supreme Court's ruling in their cases, on March 3, 1919. By then, the Great War had ended, with the Armistice of November 1918. The draft had also ended, but not the government's campaign to punish its opponents. Justice Holmes wrote for a unanimous Court in *Schenck v. United States*, addressing, for the first time, the limits on free speech during wartime. He began writing his opinion with a bias against dissidents like Charles Schenck. Urging young men, however indirectly, to refuse military service struck a raw nerve in Holmes, who had volunteered for the Union army in the Civil War and had twice been gravely wounded. More than fifty years later, at the age of seventy-eight, the justice still believed that "man's destiny is to fight," as he wrote to a friend during World War I. He asked another, "Doesn't this squashy sentimentality of a big minority of our people about human life make you puke?"

Holmes told another friend that "we should deal with the act of speech as we deal with any other overt act that we don't like." And he did not like what Schenck had said about the draft law. In his *Schenck* opinion, Holmes looked at speech as an "act" that differed from such acts as firing a gun on a battlefield only in form. He made one concession to the First Amendment. "We admit that in many places and in ordinary times the defendants in saying all that was said in the circular would have been within their constitutional rights," Holmes began. He then robbed this concession of any relevance to the case, writing that "the character of every act depends upon the circumstances in which it is done." In these two sentences, Holmes set a trap for Schenck and Baer. He obviously felt that August 1917 was not an ordinary time and that the "circumstances" of their acts deprived them of constitutional protection. With an example of unprotected speech, Holmes sprang the trap: "The most stringent protection of free speech would not protect a man in falsely shouting fire in a theatre and causing a panic."

Perhaps no sentence in any Supreme Court opinion has been as widely—and as inaccurately—repeated. Those who cite the "shouting fire" phrase forget, most often, to include the "falsely" qualifier. Was Schenck falsely shouting fire in his leaflet? More important, what relevance did Holmes's example have to Schenck's appeal to "Assert Your Rights!"? A vivid example of unprotected speech, Holmes's words served only to inflame the reader to view Schenck as inciting panic. Holmes continued with another memorable sentence: "The question in every case is whether the words used are used in such circumstances and are of such a nature as to create a clear and present danger that they will bring about the substantive evils that Congress has a right to prevent." Although Holmes did not invent the "clear and present danger" test in First Amendment law, his *Schenck* opinion made it a catchword, repeated by judges in dozens of later cases. Like any legal phrase, its words require definition. How "clear" must the danger be, and who decides its clarity? How "present," and who decides its imminence? Holmes offered only this vague guidance to other judges: "It is a question of proximity and degree." In his view, Schenck had come too close to urging young men to resist the draft. Nor did Holmes agree, as the defense asserted, that the government was required to prove that Schenck's leaflet had induced any draftee to refuse induction. Simply showing "the tendency and the intent" of the leaflet to accomplish this aim was enough. Conceding that the leaflet, on its face, "confined itself to peaceful measures such as a petition for the repeal of the act," Holmes maintained that "it would not have been sent unless it had been intended to have some effect, and we do not see what effect it could be expected to have upon persons subject to the draft except to influence them to obstruct" military recruitment. By substituting "intent" for "effect" as the test for the impact of speech on those who hear or read its message, Holmes had excused the government from the burden of proving that any potential draftee in

Philadelphia had even thought about refusing induction, much less acted on the "intent" of Schenck's leaflets, which never reached the post office.

There is another troubling statement in the *Schenck* opinion: "When a nation is at war many things that might be said in time of peace are such a hindrance to its conduct that their utterance will not be endured so long as men fight and that no Court could regard them as protected by any constitutional right." But does the Constitution allow a distinction between peacetime and wartime speech? Holmes made no reference to the Court's 1866 opinion in the *Milligan* case. Holding that civilians could not be tried before military tribunals when federal courts were open and functioning, the *Ex parte Milligan* decision set a precedent that limited presidential power. "The Constitution of the United States is a law for rulers and people, equally in war and in peace, and covers with the shield of its protection all classes of men, at all times, and under all circumstances," the Court said in *Milligan*. None of its provisions, the justices added, "can be suspended during any of the great exigencies of government."

The *Schenck* decision had certainly suspended the First Amendment during the "great exigency" of World War I. And the "clear and present danger" test provided government prosecutors with a potent weapon against dissenters, even after the conflict ended. One of the ironies of the *Schenck* case is that Justice Holmes executed an abrupt about-face in a case decided just eight months later. Ruling on November 10, 1919, in *Abrams v. United States,* the Court upheld the convictions of five young Russian immigrants who lived in New York City and belonged to a small anarchist group. Jacob Abrams and his compatriots had printed leaflets that denounced American military intervention in the Russian civil war, between the "Reds" of the Bolshevik regime and the "White" forces fighting to restore the deposed government. President Wilson had sent eight thousand troops to Russia, through the back door of Siberia, to aid the Whites as part of an international military force headed by the British. Most Americans paid little heed to this intervention, but many Russian immigrants objected to Wilson's efforts to overthrow the Bolshevik government, which had signed a separate peace treaty with Germany in March 1918.

Jacob Abrams and his fellow anarchists used a primitive method of spreading their message. They printed leaflets in both English and Yiddish, urging workers to join a general strike against munitions production, and dropped them from tenement windows on the Lower East Side of Manhattan, miles from the nearest munitions factory. Several people brought copies they found on sidewalks to the police, who soon tracked down the hapless anarchists. They were charged under the Sedition Act, which Congress had enacted in 1918 as an amendment to the Espionage Act, for publishing "disloyal, scurrilous and abusive language" about the government, and with inciting "curtailment of production" of "ordnance and ammunition, necessary and essential to the prosecution of the war." A federal judge imposed ten-year sentences on Abrams and two other male defendants—one had died in jail under suspicious circumstances—with a five-year term for the only female, Mollie Steimer.

Seven members of the Supreme Court voted to uphold the convictions, citing the *Schenck* case for support. But Holmes had changed his mind about the "clear and present danger" test, after listening to friends who argued that *Schenck* went too far in punishing legitimate criticism of government policies. Along with Justice Louis Brandeis, Holmes wrote an eloquent dissent in the *Abrams* case, proposing a new judicial test in free-speech cases. To warrant punishment, he now asserted, speech must "so imminently threaten immediate interference" with the government's lawful programs "that an immediate check is required to save the country." None of the speech punished in any of the wartime Sedition Act cases could possibly have met this stringent standard. But Holmes was writing in dissent, and Abrams and his fellow anarchists went to federal penitentiaries.

It took another fifty years for Holmes to receive some posthumous vindication, during another war that became even more unpopular than World War I. The Supreme Court finally abandoned the "clear and present danger" test in 1969, during a period of intense criticism of the Vietnam War. Many of that war's opponents had echoed Charles Schenck in urging young men to refuse military induction, but the Court issued a landmark free-speech ruling in a case that had nothing to do with Vietnam. The case of *Brandenburg v. Ohio* involved a speech by a Ku Klux Klan leader, who had railed against blacks and Jews at a cross-burning rally in Ohio. Clarence Brandenburg had been convicted and sentenced to jail for violating the state's "criminal anarchy" law, which prohibited speech that advocated the use of force or violence to overthrow the government. Despite his offensive words, Brandenburg had not urged anyone to overthrow the Ohio government, or to commit acts of violence against blacks or Jews. Only speech "directed to inciting or producing imminent lawless action" could be punished under the First Amendment, the Court ruled. This new free-speech test went even beyond the standard Holmes had proposed in his *Abrams* dissent, making it virtually impossible to punish critics of the government's wartime policies, however vitriolic or inflammatory their rhetoric.

By itself, speech cannot stop a tank or a warship, nor can it stop a president from sending tanks and warships into combat. But speech—in the broad sense of verbal and written expression—can often change a climate of opinion, and persuade those who hold power, in Congress and the White House, to listen to the people's voices. Over the years since the *Brandenburg* ruling, in wars from Vietnam to Iraq, public support for those military adventures was eroded by critical speech that would earlier have been punished, as Charles Schenck was punished during World War I, by prosecution and prison terms. However much presidents after Wilson have subverted the Constitution by arrogating the war-making power to themselves, critical speech—even the inflammatory act of burning the American flag—has been protected from punishment by a Supreme Court that has studiously avoided the "political question" of presidential actions that are akin to burning the Constitution.

7

"THE SOLE ORGAN OF THE NATION":

The Birth of the Imperial Presidency

During the 1920s, and following the Senate's rejection of American participation in the League of Nations, foreign policy issues took a back seat to domestic concerns. Most Americans cared more about getting their share of consumer goods than pursuing the "conquest" of foreign markets for those products. The torrent of consumption that marked the Roaring Twenties—such emblems of middle-class status as automobiles, radios, vacuum cleaners, and refrigerators sold like the proverbial hotcakes—far outpaced consumer spending in any previous decade. The market for these goods, and the stock prices of the companies that produced them with assembly-line efficiency, grew so rapidly that Wall Street could hardly keep track of the profits amassed by shareholders in such firms as Ford, U.S. Steel, and Standard Oil, whose coffers were swelled by foreign sales. In retrospect, we now know that the "paper prosperity" of the 1920s enriched only a small fraction of the American public, while millions of factory workers struggled to pay their bills and family farmers were often forced to sell their crops and livestock at a loss.

In a very real sense, the 1920s became the incubator for the profound social and economic disruptions that spawned the Great Depression of the 1930s and the resurgence of international hostilities that culminated in World War II. Out of that global conflict, as we shall see, the Cold War between the United States and the Soviet Union created two rival empires, one ultimately "victorious" and the other crashing into economic and political defeat. But in the 1920s the American empire reached only from Puerto Rico to the Philippines, far smaller in territory and political control than the empires of Britain, France, and even the Netherlands, whose tentacles extended from the Middle East to Southeast Asia. U.S. business and political leaders focused their attention on what were dismissively called the banana republics of Central America, wracked by conflict between wealthy elites and radical peasants. The political instability of these countries provoked fears that Russian "Bolshevism" might gain a foothold in America's backyard and threaten the property and profits of companies like United Fruit and American Telephone and Telegraph.

One country bore the brunt of American intervention, leading to a confrontation between President Calvin Coolidge and Congress over the deployment of naval vessels and troops without congressional approval. The United States repeatedly engaged in military intervention in Nicaragua between 1909 and 1933, siding with the business-dominated oligarchy in an attempt to put down popular forces representing peasants and the middle class. In 1909, William Howard Taft dispatched the marines to back the Conservative Party, which, two years later, dislodged the Liberal Party in a military coup, provoking a rebellion by the Liberals. American troops crushed the rebels and remained in the capital of Managua as a "legation guard," but in reality to protect the Conservative government. The marines remained until 1925, when a string of coups ended with the naming of Adolfo Diaz to head a shaky government that confronted a popular insurgency. President Diaz appealed to the United States for aid, claiming that Mexico was behind the insurgents and was fomenting a "Bolshevist" uprising.

Responding to Diaz's appeal, Coolidge ordered naval vessels to

Nicaragua in 1926, but Congress balked at military intervention. Republican senator John Blaine of Wisconsin introduced an amendment to a naval appropriations bill, specifying that none of the funds "shall be used to pay any expenses incurred in connection with acts of hostility against a friendly foreign nation, or any belligerent intervention in the affairs of a foreign nation, or any intervention in the domestic affairs of any foreign nation, unless war has been declared by Congress or unless a state of war actually exists under recognized principles of international law." The Senate defeated Blaine's effort to wield the congressional power of the purse against the president's power of the sword, but opposition to intervention in Nicaragua persuaded Congress, in 1932, to assert, in another military-funding bill, that "no money appropriated in this Act shall be used to defray the expense of sending additional Marines to Nicaragua to supervise an election there." The ostensible purpose of using American troops to "supervise" Nicaraguan elections was merely a cover for supporting the conservative politicians who received healthy campaign contributions from United Fruit and other U.S. corporations. Not until Franklin D. Roosevelt succeeded Herbert Hoover as president in 1933 were the marines finally removed from Nicaragua.

Another episode, also during the years between the two world wars, turned the issue around and led to one of the Supreme Court's most expansive decisions in the field of foreign policy. The case of *United States v. Curtiss-Wright Corp.* was unusual: It arose from an instance in which Congress gave the president more power in foreign relations, rather than less. But the president was Franklin D. Roosevelt, and the Congress that passed the law at issue was dominated by New Dealers who, in effect, gave FDR a blank check to rescue the nation from the crippling impact of the Great Depression. The background of the *Curtiss-Wright* case began during the Hundred Days session of Congress, in 1933, when the overwhelming Democratic majority enacted a bushel of laws establishing such "alphabet agencies" as the National Industrial Recovery Act and the Agricultural Adjustment Act. Under the NIRA and the AAA, the president had the authority to approve regulations limiting production quotas and setting minimum prices and wages in more than a thousand industries; the government could also require manufacturers of food items to pay "processing taxes," which would be given directly to farmers who agreed to reduce their production in return for higher prices for their goods.

Both of the statutes were immediately challenged in federal courts as unlawful delegations of legislative power to the president. Judges had rarely invoked the "delegation doctrine" to strike down federal laws, but the conservative majority on the Supreme Court ruled, in two landmark cases decided in 1935, that Congress had yielded too much power to the president when it enacted the Recovery Act. In the first case, *Panama Refining Co. v. Ryan,* the Court held that Congress should not have delegated to the president the unchecked authority to approve production quotas in the oil industry, without setting any standard for doing so. The second decision, in *A. L. A. Schechter Poultry Co. v. United States,* had a far broader impact on the recovery effort. This case stemmed from the federal prosecution of the four Schechter brothers, who slaughtered and dressed poultry for the kosher market in New York City. The Schechters were convicted, under the Recovery Act, of multiple charges of violating the Live Poultry Code, by selling "unfit" chickens and paying their employees less than the minimum wage set by the code. The Court's unanimous decision in what the press called the "sick chicken" case held that Congress, in allowing the president to approve "codes of fair competition" for virtually every industry, had unlawfully delegated legislative power to the executive branch. Roosevelt, publicly chastising the Court for its "horse and buggy" view of the nation's ailing economy, privately instructed Justice Department lawyers to explore ways to curb the Court's ability to place judicial roadblocks on the path to recovery; he was setting the stage for the "Court-packing" plan that spurred a political backlash in 1937. Only the Court's 5-to-4 approval of a key New Deal measure, three months after FDR had proposed adding up to six new justices to join the "nine old men" blocking his recovery program, defused the explosive conflict between the president and the Court.

However much he chided the Court for its rulings in the *Panama Refining* and *Schechter* cases, FDR had no complaints about the *Curtiss-Wright* decision in December 1936. In contrast to its invocation of the "delegation doctrine" to strike down laws involving domestic policy, the Court unanimously upheld the power of Congress to grant authority to the president in making foreign policy. The *Curtiss-Wright* case had its origins in a remote area of South America, the Chaco region, between the continent's only two landlocked countries, Bolivia and Paraguay. The only navigable route to the Atlantic coast was the Paraguay River, which runs through the Chaco and which the Bolivians tried to seize in 1932. The three-year war that followed took the lives of more than 100,000 soldiers on both sides. Hoping to put a damper on this bloody conflict, Congress approved a resolution in May 1934 stating that "if the President finds that the prohibition of the sale of arms and munitions of war in the United States to those countries now engaged in armed conflict in the Chaco may contribute to the reestablishment of peace between those countries," he was authorized to issue a proclamation that made it unlawful to sell arms to either nation. Companies or individuals who violated such a proclamation faced both fines and prison terms. Roosevelt promptly issued a proclamation banning arms sales to the two nations and warned that "all violations of such provisions shall be rigorously prosecuted."

The Chaco conflict ended in 1935 with the defeat of Bolivia, and Roosevelt revoked the embargo on arms sales. In January 1936, however, federal prosecutors secured the indictment of the Curtiss-Wright company, charging it with having conspired with a shipping firm to sell and transport fifteen machine guns to Bolivia two years earlier. The firm's lawyers asked a federal district judge to dismiss the indictment, arguing that Congress had improperly delegated legislative power to the executive branch in the resolution allowing Roosevelt to impose the arms embargo. After the judge upheld this claim, government attorneys appealed his ruling to the Supreme Court. Speaking through Justice George Sutherland—a former Republican senator from Utah and a member of the Senate Foreign

Relations Committee—the Court distinguished the *Curtiss-Wright* case from its earlier delegation rulings. Sutherland posed this question: "Assuming (but not deciding) that the challenged delegation, if it were confined to internal affairs, would be invalid, may it nevertheless be sustained on the ground that its exclusive aim is to afford a remedy for a hurtful condition within foreign territory?" The answer depended on whether distinctions exist between the powers of the federal government over domestic policy and over foreign affairs. Sutherland saw "fundamental" differences between the two spheres. So fundamental, in fact, that he virtually dismissed the role of Congress—and the "delegation doctrine" as well—in the field of foreign policy.

Sutherland's opinion went far beyond anything the Court has ever said—before and after this ruling—about the scope of presidential authority in any field. The nation's sovereignty, and its very survival, he wrote, depended on "an effective control of international relations." Such control belonged only to the president, Sutherland argued: "In this vast external realm, with its important, complicated, delicate and manifold problems, the President alone has the power to speak or listen as a representative of the nation." Sutherland approvingly quoted John Marshall, who had served in Congress before John Adams named him chief justice in 1803. Speaking to the House in 1800, Marshall called the president "the sole organ of the nation in its external affairs, and its sole representative with foreign nations." To Sutherland, those words were so compelling that he turned them into a doctrine. In looking at the congressional resolution at issue in the *Curtiss-Wright* case, the Court was "dealing not alone with an authority vested in the President by an exertion of legislative power, but with such an authority plus the very delicate, plenary and exclusive power of the President as the sole organ of the federal government in the field of international relations—a power which does not require as a basis for its exercise an act of Congress," Sutherland wrote. The "sole organ" doctrine thus displaced Congress from any decision-making role in foreign policy. The justice explained why the president needed "freedom from statutory restriction":

"He, not Congress, has the better opportunity of knowing the conditions which prevail in foreign countries, and especially this is true in time of war. He has his confidential sources of information. He has his agents in the form of diplomatic, consular and other officials. Secrecy in respect to information gathered by them may be highly necessary, and the premature disclosure of it productive of harmful results."

Notably lacking from Sutherland's exposition of the "sole organ" doctrine was reference to any constitutional provision. The Constitution, of course, allows the president to "make treaties" with foreign nations, but only with the "advice and consent" of the Senate. It also makes the president the commander in chief of the armed forces, but also subject to congressional control of military appropriations. Roosevelt's proclamation of an arms embargo during the Chaco conflict involved neither a treaty nor the dispatch of American troops. Under Sutherland's reasoning, FDR could have issued the proclamation even without congressional action. In effect, the *Curtiss-Wright* opinion, without using the word, found an "inherent" presidential power over foreign affairs, whose source lay entirely outside the Constitution. It would be hard to imagine a single president, over the years since this decision, who would not eagerly embrace the "sole organ" doctrine. But its premises, as laid out by Justice Sutherland, are highly questionable. The president's "confidential sources of information" have often given him slanted, even untrue intelligence. And the "secrecy" that Sutherland found necessary in foreign affairs has frequently covered up evasions and even outright lies that presidents have made to both Congress and the public. The July 2004 report of the 9/11 commission offers the most detailed evidence and scathing criticism of the massive intelligence failures stemming from both the "secrecy" mania of the executive branch and congressional abdication of its oversight role in foreign policy.

The fighting in Chaco between Paraguay and Bolivia did not affect vital U.S. interests, and hardly anyone outside the State Department took much notice of this regional conflict. But when a war broke out in Europe the next year, many Americans cared passionately about that bloody and bitter conflict. It was not a rivalry between nations but a civil war that pitted the democratically elected government of Spain against rebels who launched an insurrection to overthrow the government. The Spanish civil war had much greater significance, and potential consequences, than similar confrontations in other parts of the world, such as South America. In fact, both sides in Spain had the backing of powerful states locked in ferocious ideological combat. The Republican government of Spain, based on a left-wing coalition that included Communists, Socialists, and anarchists, had the support of the Soviet Union and Socialist governments in Europe. On the other side, the right-wing rebels, headed by Francisco Franco, a defecting army officer, were aided by the Nazi regime in Germany and the Fascist government of Italy. The rise of Adolf Hitler and Benito Mussolini had created alarm, in many countries, that the shaky peace after World War I might soon fall apart. By 1936, Hitler and Mussolini were both rearming their nations and rattling sabers against Socialists and Communists. In return, the Soviet government beefed up the Red Army and warned darkly of German and Italian designs on their neighbors.

Against the backdrop of growing conflict between bitterly opposed ideologies on the left and the right, both sides in the Spanish civil war appealed for political support and material aid from their foreign backers. Despite an international arms embargo, large quantities of munitions—from rifles to planes—reached the Spanish combatants. In the United States, the beleaguered Spanish Republican forces received the fervent support of liberals and leftists, with the American Communist Party the most vocal and active in mobilizing its members and joining "Popular Front" groups. Many political conservatives had no sympathy for the Spanish Nationalists and recoiled from their support by Germany and Italy. But the American Catholic hierarchy, and many of the church's members, backed the Nationalists because they were allied with the Spanish church and because the Republicans were avowed secularists. Reports of churches being sacked and burned, and of priests and nuns being abused and even murdered, inflamed many American Catholics.

The Roosevelt administration took a hands-off position toward
the Spanish civil war, unwilling to antagonize two of the voting blocs
on which the Democratic coalition depended. On one side, many liberals and virtually all leftists supported the Spanish Republicans,
while Catholics in big cities like Boston, New York, and Chicago sympathized with the Nationalists. Congress had passed the Neutrality
Act of 1935, banning the export of munitions "upon the outbreak or
during the progress of war between, or among two or more foreign
states." But because the law did not apply to the contending sides in
a civil war, Congress enacted a separate measure, authorizing the
president to impose an arms embargo against Spain. When he issued
a proclamation to trigger the embargo, Roosevelt declared that "the
people of the United States and their representatives certainly were
not prepared in 1937 to risk the slightest chance of becoming
involved in a quarrel in Europe which had all the possibilities of
developing into a general European conflict." The embargo damaged
the Spanish Republicans more than the Franco-led rebels, who
obtained vast stores of munitions from Germany and Italy; in addition, the defeat of the Republican government and the rise of Franco
encouraged Hitler and Mussolini to prepare for the "general European
conflict" that Roosevelt had deplored.

That conflict began when Germany invaded Poland, on September
1, 1939. England and France immediately declared war on Germany
and its Axis partner Italy. Despite Roosevelt's repeated statements
that the United States would not be dragged into another European
war, it was clear that most Americans sympathized with the beleaguered Allies with whom U.S. troops had fought in the "war to end
all wars." Although the Roosevelt administration proclaimed neutrality, it also provided munitions to Britain and France. While praising the courage of the troops and peoples of the countries fighting
the Germans, FDR cautioned that his statements carried "no implication of military commitments. Only the Congress can make such
commitments."

After the French asked for American naval vessels—most of them
in mothballs since the end of World War I—to bolster its fleet,

Roosevelt said that any such transfer "would require Congressional action which might be difficult to get." In fact, Congress was reluctant to approve the French request; it passed a law in June 1940 providing that no ships could be transferred unless military officials "shall first certify that such material is not essential to the defense of the United States." British prime minister Winston Churchill also sought U.S. destroyers, and Roosevelt granted his request with an executive agreement in September 1940, giving the British fifty "over-age" destroyers in return for the use of British islands in the Atlantic and the Caribbean for military bases. FDR bypassed Congress in this deal, relying on an opinion by Attorney General Robert Jackson that the president's powers as commander in chief allowed him "to use all constitutional authority which he may possess to provide adequate bases and stations for the utilization of the naval and air weapons of the United States at their highest efficiency in our defense." Significantly, Jackson cited Justice Sutherland's 1936 opinion in the *Curtiss-Wright* case for support, but Jackson stretched that opinion, and the "sole organ" doctrine of presidential powers, far beyond even Sutherland's expansive statements. The arms embargo that FDR had imposed in the war between Paraguay and Bolivia was designed to deny munitions to those nations, while the "destroyers-for-bases" deal provided U.S. military goods to Britain. Roosevelt's executive agreement was, in fact, a treaty with England, but the Senate was not asked for its "advice and consent" on this unilateral exercise of presidential deal making.

Much like Woodrow Wilson before him, Franklin Roosevelt pledged that "we will not participate in foreign wars and we will not send our army, naval or air forces to fight in foreign lands outside the Americas except in case of attack." Speaking to a partisan audience in Boston on October 30, 1940, FDR promised that "your boys are not going to be sent into any foreign wars." But he continued to supply the British and their allies with equipment, finally persuading Congress to pass the Lend-Lease Act in March 1941, authorizing him to "sell, transfer title to, exchange, lease, lend, or otherwise dispose of" military supplies to countries he considered essential to the

nation's defense. Six months later, he initiated an act of war by issuing a "shoot-on-sight" order to the naval and air forces, instructing
them to attack any German or Italian vessels that entered waters off
the American coast, even beyond the territorial limits claimed by the
United States. American "boys" were being sent into combat by the
president, acting under his claims of inherent power as commander
in chief, but without congressional sanction or a formal declaration
of war. With hostile vessels prowling the Atlantic coast, and with the
"plucky" British in dire peril, Congress may well have approved the
president's actions. But the American people had been assured that
only "in case of attack" would troops be dispatched to fight. And
that attack took place, of course, on December 7, 1941, when Japanese planes bombed the naval base at Pearl Harbor, in Hawaii, sending more than two thousand American sailors to watery graves.
However much Roosevelt might have stretched his constitutional
powers before that date, the "day of infamy" silenced his critics. It
was no longer just the Constitution that was under attack but the
survival of the nation itself. Faced with this unprecedented crisis, the
American people placed their trust in a president who had vastly
expanded his domestic powers and those of the federal bureaucracy,
and who adroitly used his popular support to broaden his authority
in wartime.

In a real sense, the imperial presidency, which took full shape
during the Depression, created, in turn, the imperial America that
emerged from World War II as the most powerful nation on earth.
This link between domestic politics and foreign policy continues to
influence both aspects of American society. As we shall see, particularly during the presidencies of Richard Nixon, Lyndon Johnson,
and George W. Bush, a president's decline in domestic political support most often leads to increasing doubts about the wisdom of
his foreign policies. But Franklin Roosevelt suffered no such fate
as those successors, and thumbed his nose at the Constitution,
with few if any political repercussions. The vast expansion of
presidential powers during the Depression stemmed, in large part,

from Roosevelt's unmatched political skills, but it also reflected the growth of the United States as the world's dominant economic and military force, at a time when rival empires—both allies and adversaries—lost their abilities to block the expansion of the American empire.

8

"THE VERY BRINK OF
CONSTITUTIONAL POWER":

Japanese Americans and German Saboteurs

On December 8, 1941, the day after the Japanese attack on Pearl Harbor, President Franklin D. Roosevelt asked Congress to declare war on the first nation to launch a surprise attack on American territory. The Senate approved the resolution by a vote of 82 to 0, and the House followed suit by a vote of 388 to 1; the sole dissenter was Representative Jeanette Rankin of Montana, a staunch pacifist who had also voted in 1917 against declaring war on Germany. On December 11, both Germany and Italy declared war on the United States, and Congress reciprocated by recognizing a state of war with those Axis nations.

The Japanese attack on Pearl Harbor more than justified the congressional declaration of war against that nation, and Congress merely acknowledged the subsequent declarations of war against the United States by Germany and Italy. Those belligerent acts raised no constitutional issues, nor did Roosevelt's direction of military operations as commander in chief of the armed forces. The most serious constitutional questions during the war resulted from presidential orders that affected more than 100,000 American citizens and legal residents of this country. They were not engaged in an armed rebellion against the government, as the Confederate states had been during the Civil War. And they had not harshly criticized American participation in war, as had Eugene Debs, for example, during World War I. Even during those wars, the government did not round up and imprison an entire group of Americans, only because they "looked like the enemy" and were suspected of disloyalty solely on the basis of race and ancestry. But the treatment of Japanese Americans during World War II created a constitutional "disaster" for which all three branches of government shared culpability. This shameful episode in American history sheds light on the depth and persistence of anti-Asian racism, the capitulation of military officials and political leaders to such bigotry, and the Court's reliance on racial stereotypes to justify the suspension of constitutional protections.

Surprisingly, the initial reaction to the attack on Pearl Harbor, on the part of some West Coast newspapers and politicians, was one of appeals for tolerance and understanding toward Japanese Americans. Most of the "thousands of Japanese here and in other coast cities," the *Los Angeles Times* editorialized on December 8, 1941, were "good Americans, born and educated as such." Published in the city with the largest number of Japanese Americans, this influential paper urged that "there be no precipitation, no riots, no mob law." The *Times* was right in its positive characterization of this racial minority. The vast majority were "good Americans," in many ways more patriotic and law-abiding than their Caucasian neighbors. They were also unlike the more numerous Chinese, who first arrived during the 1850s to lay railroad track and pick vegetables and fruit and largely remained in low-skill, low-pay jobs. Japanese immigrants numbered only two thousand in 1890, many of them highly educated, and they prospered as farmers and shopkeepers. But they suffered from the same xenophobia and racism that led Congress to pass the Chinese Exclusion Act in 1882, although the flow of Japanese immigrants continued until 1924, when Congress closed the nation's door on all Asian countries. By 1940, more than 100,000 Japanese lived on the West Coast, some two-thirds of them native-born American citizens and the remainder legal residents who in 1924 Congress had specifically barred from U.S. citizenship.

The early appeals for tolerance and forbearance soon disappeared, however, as fears of a mainland Pearl Harbor spread among a jittery public. On January 16, 1942, Leland Ford, a member of Congress from Los Angeles, urged that "all Japanese, whether citizens or not, be placed in inland concentration camps." Two weeks later, the *Times* argued that "the rigors of war demand proper detention of Japanese and their immediate removal from the most acute danger spots" along the coast. Walter Lippmann, the nation's most respected columnist, deplored "the unwillingness of Washington to adopt a policy of mass evacuation and mass internment" of Japanese Americans. "Nobody's constitutional rights include the right to reside and do business on a battlefield," he wrote.

Faced with a rising tide of calls for the removal of all Japanese Americans from the West Coast, the Roosevelt administration asked military officials to recommend a course of action. They responded with unvarnished racism. In early February 1942, General John DeWitt, the West Coast army commander, submitted his "Final Recommendation" to Secretary of War Henry Stimson. "The Japanese race is an enemy race," DeWitt stated, "and while many second and third generation Japanese born on American soil, possessed of United States citizenship, have become 'Americanized,' the racial strains are undiluted." DeWitt used blunter language before a congressional panel: "A Jap's a Jap," he said; "it makes no difference whether he is an American citizen or not. I have no confidence in their loyalty whatsoever."

Although the "Final Recommendation" urged the mass evacuation and internment of Japanese Americans as a precaution against "sabotage and espionage" to aid the Japanese war effort, the report cited no evidence that any Japanese American had committed such crimes or had planned them. Using a kind of twisted logic, DeWitt blamed the lack of evidence on the sneaky nature of Japanese Americans: "The very fact that no sabotage has taken place to date is a disturbing and confirming indication that such action will be taken," he claimed. Conceding his inability to justify "the sheer military necessity" for mass evacuation and internment, DeWitt nonetheless pressed Stimson for authority to remove all Japanese Americans from the West Coast. The secretary of war initially hesitated, writing in his diary that mass internment "will make a tremendous hole in our constitutional system." But he finally agreed to present DeWitt's proposal to Roosevelt, who signed Executive Order 9066 on February 19, 1942, authorizing Stimson to designate military zones "from which any or all persons may be excluded."

Based on the presidential directive, General DeWitt first imposed a nighttime curfew on "all persons of Japanese ancestry" who lived on the West Coast, both native-born Americans and those designated as "enemy aliens," a category that included persons born in Japan, the first-generation immigrants whom Congress had made "ineligible" for citizenship. The curfew also applied to "enemy aliens" who held German or Italian citizenship, although it exempted American citizens whose families had come from either country. After a few weeks, DeWitt lifted the curfew on all Germans and Italians but left it in place for Japanese Americans until he issued "exclusion orders" that were backed by Congress with criminal penalties. Under the military orders, all Japanese Americans on the West Coast were given one week to dispose of all their possessions—except for what they could pack into one suitcase—and report to "assembly centers" located at fairgrounds and horse-racing tracks such as Santa Anita. While the "evacuees" lived in tents and horse stalls, Army engineers hastily built pine-board and tar-paper barracks in ten "relocation centers," mostly in deserts and mountains on Indian reservations in California, Arizona, Utah, Idaho, and Wyoming, with two in the Mississippi delta region of Arkansas. Each camp, surrounded by barbed-wire fences and guard towers manned by army troops with rifles and machine guns, housed about 10,000 Japanese Americans; each family was given a space that was separated from neighbors by sheets. Under these spartan conditions, more than 110,000 American citizens and legal residents who were never charged with crimes or given a hearing to challenge their detention were imprisoned for an indefinite period. The protections of the Bill of Rights did not exist within the barbed-wire enclosures that made up America's "concentration camps," a term that, for many people, evokes the horrors of the Nazi Holocaust but that Roosevelt used in describing the wartime internment camps.

What may seem surprising about the internment of Japanese Americans is that so few of its victims challenged their detention in court. But they faced the Hobson's choice of reporting to the camps or facing prison terms for refusing to obey the "exclusion orders" issued by military officials. At least in the camps, the evacuees could remain with their families and retain some semblance of communal life. So it is not surprising, in retrospect, that only three young men made the difficult choice to challenge the internment and face the virtual certainty of prosecution, conviction, and imprisonment. The stories of Gordon Hirabayashi, Minoru Yasui, and Fred Korematsu stand as testaments to personal courage and the determination to demand their rights as loyal U.S. citizens.

Gordon Hirabayashi was born in 1918 in Auburn, a rural town near Seattle, where his father—a Japanese immigrant and thus an "enemy alien" in the eyes of the law—ran a roadside fruit market. In high school Gordon became an Eagle Scout and served as president of the Auburn Christian Fellowship. When he entered the University of Washington in 1937, the young man joined the University Quaker Meeting and registered with his draft board as a conscientious objector. When General DeWitt imposed a nighttime curfew on all Japanese Americans, Gordon was living in the campus YMCA dormitory. He obeyed the curfew for more than a month, often running back to his dorm to beat the clock. He later recalled thinking, "Why the hell am I running back? Am I an American or not? Why am I running back and nobody else is?" When the exclusion orders reached Seattle, Gordon became a conscientious objector to internment. He went to the downtown FBI office and told Special Agent Francis Manion that he would not report to the assembly center at the Puyallup Fairgrounds. Manion recorded Gordon's statement that "he could not reconcile the will of God, a part of which was expressed in the Bill of Rights and the American Constitution, with the order discriminating against Japanese aliens and American citizens of Japanese ancestry." Arresting Gordon for violating both the curfew and the exclusion orders, Agent Manion placed him in the county jail to await trial.

Minoru Yasui did not share Gordon's pacifism. Born in 1916 in Hood River, Oregon, he entered the University of Oregon in 1933 and volunteered for the army's Reserve Officers' Training Corps. After receiving a second lieutenant's commission in 1937, Min attended the university's law school, graduating in 1939. Unable to find legal work in Oregon, he landed a job with the Japanese consulate in Chicago, and duly registered with the State Department as a foreign agent. The day after Pearl Harbor, Min resigned his consular post and returned to Oregon, where he received an order to report for duty at Fort Vancouver in Washington State. But when he arrived in uniform, army officers told him he was unacceptable for service and ordered him off the base. This rebuff on racial grounds triggered a stubborn reaction; Min returned eight times to Fort Vancouver and was turned away each time. Even before the exclusion orders reached Portland, Min decided to challenge the curfew. The night of March 28, 1942, he marched into the police headquarters and approached a sergeant. "I pulled out this order that said all persons of Japanese ancestry must be in their place of abode, and I pulled out my birth certificate and said, 'Look, I'm a person of Japanese ancestry, arrest me.'" The sergeant complied, and Min spent nine months in solitary confinement before his trial.

Fred Korematsu was born in 1919 in Oakland, California, and worked as a shipyard welder before the Pearl Harbor attack. He volunteered for the navy in 1941 but was turned down because of gastric ulcers. Fred did not challenge the internment from religious conviction or legal training. In fact, he tried to evade the exclusion orders by changing his name, altering his draft card, and undergoing plastic surgery on his eyelids and nose. His primary motivation was to remain with his Caucasian girlfriend, but his clumsy efforts to escape detection failed. On the afternoon of May 30, 1942, police officers in San Leandro, California, got a tip and picked him up on a street corner. The San Francisco newspapers reported Fred's arrest, and he soon received a jailhouse visit from Ernest Besig, the local director of the American Civil Liberties Union, who had been searching for a test case against the internment. Eagerly accepting Besig's offer of legal help, Fred gave him a handwritten statement arguing that Japanese Americans "should have been given a fair trial in order that they may defend their loyalty at court in a democratic way, but they were placed in imprisonment without a fair trial!" Unlike Gordon and Min, Fred was sent to an assembly center, the Tanforan Racetrack near San Francisco, to await trial for disobeying the exclusion order.

Despite the differing motivations of the test case defendants, their criminal trials in federal district court were uniformly brief and perfunctory. Judge Lloyd Black, who presided in Seattle at Gordon Hirabayashi's trial, rejected his lawyers' claims that General DeWitt's curfew and exclusion orders violated the due process clause of the Fifth Amendment by singling out a racial group for "special restrictions" not imposed on others. Noting the proximity of aircraft plants and naval bases to Seattle, Black pointed to "the fact that the parachutists and saboteurs, as well as the soldiers, of Japan make diabolically clever use of infiltration tactics. They are shrewd masters of tricky concealment among any who resemble them. With the aid of any artifice or treachery they seek such human camouflage and with uncanny skill discover and take advantage of any disloyalty among their kind." Judge Black directed the jurors to find Gordon guilty, which they did after ten minutes of deliberation, and Black sentenced Gordon to concurrent ninety-day terms, on both the curfew and the exclusion order violations.

Min Yasui's trial, in Portland, took a bit longer, largely because Judge Alger Fee took over the questioning from the government's lawyer, who had argued in a pretrial brief that "Jap citizens are inevitably bound, by intangible ties, to the people of the Empire of Japan. They are alike, physically and psychologically." Judge Fee surprised Min, who had never been to Japan, with questions about

Japanese customs and beliefs. "What is Shinto?" he abruptly asked. Min was clearly puzzled by the question. "Shinto? As I understand, Shinto is the national religion of Japan," he answered. "Do you give adherence to its precepts?" Fee continued. "My mother and father were Methodists in Japan," Min replied, "and I myself have been a Methodist in this country and I don't know the precepts of the Shinto religion." Fee heard the case without a jury, and pronounced Min guilty for his admitted curfew violation. Before passing sentence, Fee ruled, in a written opinion, that despite Min's American birth and citizenship, he considered him "a citizen of Japan and subject to the Emperor of Japan," a finding the judge based on "the nativity of his parents and the subtle nuances of traditional mores engrained in his race by centuries of social discipline." After linking Min to "the treacherous attack by the armed forces of Japan" on Pearl Harbor, Fee imposed the maximum penalty of one year in prison and a $5,000 fine.

Fred Korematsu came to trial in San Francisco before Judge Adolphus St. Sure, who differed from his Seattle and Portland colleagues in treating the defendant with respect. After an FBI agent testified about Fred's draft-card forgery and plastic surgery, Fred took the stand to explain his actions. His description of the doctor's work drew smiles in the courtroom. "I don't think he made any change in my appearance," Fred said, "for when I went to the Tanforan Assembly Center everyone knew me and my folks didn't know the difference." Fred told the judge that he had volunteered for military service before Pearl Harbor, but had been rejected on medical grounds. "As a citizen of the United States I am ready, willing, and able to bear arms for this country," he affirmed. This forthrightness impressed St. Sure, but he nonetheless found Fred guilty and sentenced him to a five-year probationary term. When Fred's lawyer announced his intention to appeal the conviction, the judge obligingly set bail at $2,500, but military police officers grabbed Fred and took him back to Tanforan, where his parents were confined in horse stalls, awaiting transfer to an internment camp in the Utah desert.

After circuit court judges upheld their convictions, all three defendants appealed to the Supreme Court, but the justices sent Fred Korematsu's case back to the circuit court for a ruling on his sentence, because the criminal statute passed by Congress to enforce the internment orders did not provide for probation. Before his case returned to the Supreme Court, the justices heard arguments in the Hirabayashi and Yasui cases, in April 1943. Solicitor General Charles Fahy defended DeWitt's orders, urging the justices to defer to Roosevelt's judgment, as commander in chief, that "military necessity" required the removal of all Japanese Americans from the West Coast. Fahy also pressed the "racial characteristics" claim that had persuaded Secretary of War Stimson to swallow his constitutional doubts about mass internment. Asserting that Japanese Americans "had never become assimilated" into American society, Fahy called it "not unreasonable" to fear that members of this racial group "might assist the enemy." Harold Evans, who argued for Gordon Hirabayashi, relied on the Court's 1866 ruling, in *Ex parte Milligan,* that "legislative authority over civilians may not be delegated to the military when the area in question is not strictly a military area." The *Milligan* decision, holding that Confederate sympathizers could not be tried by military tribunals while the civilian courts remained open, did not impress Justice Felix Frankfurter, an army prosecutor during World War I. "There's a lot in Milligan," he told Evans, "that will not stand scrutiny in 1943, a lot of talk that is purely political." Frankfurter did not elaborate on his cryptic statement, leaving Evans without a question to answer. "That's for this Court to decide," he weakly replied. Unlike Lambdin Milligan during the Civil War, Gordon Hirabayashi did receive a trial in a civilian court. But Evans might have reminded Frankfurter of the Court's firm statements in *Milligan* that the Constitution "is a law for rulers and people, equally in war and peace," and that none of its provisions "can be suspended during any of the great exigencies of government." Nevertheless, Hirabayashi—and every Japanese American on the West Coast— had effectively been sentenced to indefinite detention in the internment camps without being charged with any crime and without any hearing to determine their loyalty to the United States. In this respect, Gordon's perfunctory trial before Judge Black merely served to ratify the suspension of the Bill of Rights that led to the curfew and exclusion orders the young man was charged with violating.

The Court issued its *Hirabayashi v. United States* decision on June 21, 1943, along with a short opinion in the *Yasui v. United States* case, reversing Judge Fee's unfounded ruling that Yasui was not an American citizen. Chief Justice Harlan Fiske Stone wrote for a unanimous Court in upholding Hirabayashi's conviction for curfew violation. He sidestepped the conviction for violating the exclusion order, on the ground that Judge Black had imposed concurrent sentences on the two counts and that Hirabayashi faced no additional penalty for the exclusion violation. Stone most likely dodged the more difficult exclusion issue in hopes that government officials might end the internment program before Fred Korematsu's case, which directly challenged the exclusion orders, returned from the circuit court. In that event, the *Korematsu* case would become moot and the Court would be off the hook.

Stone first addressed the argument that Roosevelt had exceeded his constitutional powers as commander in chief by issuing an executive order without prior authorization by Congress. The chief justice finessed this issue by pointing to the after-the-fact ratification of Roosevelt's action. The law that followed the president's act imposed criminal penalties for violating the military orders. "We have no occasion to consider whether the President, acting alone, could lawfully have made the curfew order in question," Stone wrote, "or have authorized others to make it. For the President's action has the support of the Act of Congress, and we are immediately concerned with the question whether it is within the constitutional power of the national government, through the joint action of Congress and the Executive, to impose this restriction as an emergency war measure." Under this view, of course, presidents could issue any kind of orders, whether or not related to national defense, so long as Congress later ratified them. But under the Constitution, the president is empowered only to "execute" the laws passed by Congress, not to make them by executive order.

Writing in 1943, Chief Justice Stone had no desire to limit the president's wartime powers in any way. He found support for an expansive view of presidential powers in a quote from his immediate predecessor, Chief Justice Charles Evans Hughes. "The war power of the national government is 'the power to wage war successfully,'" Stone proclaimed. "It extends to every matter and activity so related to war as substantially to affect its conduct and progress." According to Stone, the government's responsibility is not limited to the battlefield but "embraces every phase of the national defense, including the protection of war materials and members of the armed forces" from the dangers of espionage and sabotage. Claims that Japanese Americans posed such dangers prompted the military orders that Gordon Hirabayashi had violated. In providing that Congress and the president share the war power, Stone wrote, the Constitution "has necessarily given to them wide scope for the exercise of judgment and discretion in determining the nature and extent of the threatened injury or danger and in the selection of the means for resisting it."

Having granted the president, acting with the later approval of Congress, "wide scope" to deal with the supposed dangers that Japanese Americans posed to the nation, Stone moved to the curfew orders as a means of preventing such threats. The curfew order that Gordon Hirabayashi had challenged applied solely to "persons of Japanese ancestry." This clear act of racial discrimination created a problem for Stone, who abhorred racism. "Distinctions between citizens solely because of their ancestry," he wrote, "are by their very nature odious to a free people whose institutions are founded upon the doctrine of equality." But "the danger of espionage and sabotage" by Japanese Americans overrode the Constitution's promise of "the equal protection of the laws" to every American, regardless of race or ancestry. Stone asserted that "those facts and circumstances which are relevant to measures for our national defense" provided military officials with reason "to place citizens of one ancestry in a different category from others." And what were the facts and circumstances that justified DeWitt's military orders? On this crucial issue, Stone accepted

Solicitor General Fahy's "racial characteristics" argument, without questioning its veracity.

"At a time of threatened Japanese attack upon this country," Stone wrote, "the nature of our inhabitants' attachments to the Japanese enemy was consequently a matter of grave concern." Citing the references, in the government's brief, to laws directed against Japanese immigrants, Stone concluded that such discrimination had "intensified their solidarity" and "prevented their assimilation as an integral part of the white population." It was thus "reasonable" for military authorities to consider Japanese Americans "a menace to the national defense and safety" and to restrict their movements through curfew orders. All these factors gave President Roosevelt and War Department officials "a rational basis for the decision" to "set these citizens apart from others who have no particular association with Japan." Stone simply ignored the fact that Gordon Hirabayashi had never been to Japan and had no association whatever with that country, other than his ancestry. Under his logic, native-born Americans who had never left this nation's shores were equally suspect if their ancestors had come from a country that government officials considered hostile to the United States. However faulty this logic, it has been applied by later administrations to justify the "watch lists" and FBI surveillance of Americans with family roots in Cuba, Iran, Iraq, and many other nations.

The Court's decision to uphold Hirabayashi's conviction was unanimous, but one justice, Frank Murphy, had earlier circulated a blistering dissent, finding a "melancholy resemblance" between the restrictions on Japanese Americans and "the treatment accorded to members of the Jewish race" in Germany. The Court's only Jewish member, Felix Frankfurter, asked Murphy to consider whether his statement might be read as "playing into the hands of the enemy." This appeal to wartime unity convinced Murphy to change his dissent into a concurrence, but he retained the comparison of Japanese Americans to German Jews and his conclusion that the military orders approached "the very brink of constitutional powers."

Chief Justice Stone's wish that government officials would end the internment program and thereby moot the *Korematsu* case was not granted before it returned to the Court in October 1944, after the circuit court affirmed the probationary sentence. The justices also heard argument in *Ex parte Endo,* which involved a habeas corpus petition filed by Mitsuye Endo, a young Japanese American woman who had volunteered, from an internment camp, to test the government's power to detain citizens the army had conceded were loyal. Her case had languished in the lower courts for more than two years before the Supreme Court agreed to consider Endo's appeal from a district court ruling that dismissed her petition. Since the government made no effort to defend the continued detention of loyal Japanese Americans, the central issue before the justices was the question, raised in the *Korematsu* case, of whether it could order their internment in the first place. Solicitor General Fahy returned to the Court's podium, but his defense of the exclusion orders took an abrupt turn from his *Hirabayashi* argument that the "racial characteristics" of Japanese Americans justified their removal from the West Coast. No longer were General DeWitt's orders a "reasonable" response to the dangers posed by "disloyal" members of a racial group. Now, Fahy asserted, the orders had in fact been designed to "prevent incidents involving violence between Japanese migrants" and Caucasians who blamed them for Pearl Harbor. Fred Korematsu had not met "the burden which rested upon him," Fahy claimed, to disprove the evidence "of hostility to the evacuees, which lay at the basis of the decision to impose detention" on them. This about-face in the government's position—reflecting the fact that Japanese forces posed no threat to the West Coast after 1943—eroded allegations based on the danger of espionage and sabotage by Japanese Americans.

The obvious absurdity of forcing Korematsu to prove that whites were not hostile toward Japanese Americans did not faze Justice Hugo Black, who wrote for six justices in upholding Korematsu's conviction. Ignoring Fahy's "blame the victim" argument, Black returned to the *Hirabayashi* decision for support, quoting Chief

Justice Stone's claim that the danger posed by "disloyal" Japanese Americans justified the curfew imposed on them. Black brushed aside complaints that removing people from their homes and imprisoning them in concentration camps imposed greater hardships than curfews. "But hardships are part of war," he replied, "and war is an aggregation of hardships." And the justice denied that racial animus had anything to do with the case. "Korematsu was not excluded from the Military Area because of hostility to him or his race," Black asserted. "He was excluded because we are at war with the Japanese Empire" and because "the military urgency of the situation demanded that all citizens of Japanese ancestry be segregated from the West Coast" until the danger passed.

Although Justice Murphy had reluctantly stood with his colleagues at "the very brink of constitutional power" in the *Hirabayashi* case, he broke ranks in *Korematsu*. The exclusion of Japanese Americans from their homes, he wrote in dissent, went over that brink "and falls into the ugly abyss of racism." Murphy had withdrawn his *Hirabayashi* dissent because he did not want to stand alone on the constitutional battlefield. But two colleagues stood with him in *Korematsu*. In his majority opinion, Justice Black had claimed that Fred Korematsu could have escaped the internment by leaving California before the exclusion orders became effective. Justice Owen Roberts replied, in his dissent, that an earlier order forbade Korematsu from leaving the state. He called the two orders "a cleverly devised trap to accomplish the real purpose of the military authorities, which was to lock him up in a concentration camp." In a separate dissent, Justice Robert Jackson accused the majority of validating "the principle of racial discrimination" under the guise of military necessity. "The principle then lies about like a loaded weapon, ready for the hand of any authority that can bring forward a plausible claim of an urgent need," he warned.

The Court issued its *Korematsu* decision on December 18, 1944, along with a unanimous ruling that reversed the dismissal of Mitsuye Endo's habeas corpus petition. Justice William O. Douglas wrote the *Endo* opinion for the Court, declining to reach "the underlying constitutional issues which have been argued." Endo's lawyers had asserted that because her loyalty had never been questioned, the government lacked any basis for her detention. Douglas simply held that military officials had "no authority to subject citizens who are concededly loyal" to continued detention, thereby avoiding a head-on collision with Justice Black's claim, in *Korematsu,* that Roosevelt had the power to order the evacuation of all Japanese Americans. Read together, the *Korematsu* and *Endo* opinions cannot be reconciled. But since the War Department had announced, the day before the Court issued its rulings, that the internment camps would be closed and that Japanese Americans would be "permitted the same freedom of movement throughout the United States as other loyal citizens and law-abiding aliens," the conflict between the two decisions troubled only a handful of constitutional scholars. After spending more than two years behind barbed-wire fences, the War Department's announcement left a bitter taste in the mouths of more than one hundred thousand loyal Japanese Americans, who swallowed their resentment, worked hard, sent their children to college, and finally became "assimilated as an integral part of the white population."

Underneath their image as a "model minority," however, many Japanese Americans remained bitter about their wartime treatment. Some of the internment survivors, and many of their children, marched for civil rights and against the Vietnam War during the 1960s and 1970s. Beginning with a small group in Seattle, some Japanese Americans launched a grassroots lobbying campaign, asking Congress to make symbolic payments for their loss of constitutional rights. The first victory of the "redress" movement came in 1980, when Congress established the blue-ribbon Commission on Wartime Relocation and Internment of Civilians, charged with reviewing the mass internment and recommending methods of restitution. The commission held hearings around the country, at which more than 750 people testified, many speaking for the first time about their wartime hardships and lingering pain. In a 467-page report in 1983, the commissioners unanimously agreed that Japanese Americans had suffered a "grave injustice" that resulted from "race prejudice, war hysteria, and a failure of political leadership." Congress finally enacted a redress bill in 1988 and President Reagan signed the national apology that accompanied the checks of $20,000 to the sixty thousand survivors of the internment camps.

Another form of redress came in the federal courts. In 1983, Gordon Hirabayashi, Min Yasui, and Fred Korematsu filed *coram nobis* petitions—from the Latin term for "error before us"—in the district courts in which they had been tried and convicted. Legal scholars and commission staff members had uncovered Justice and War Department records of warnings, from government lawyers to Solicitor General Fahy, about the falsity of General DeWitt's claims, in his "Final Report" on the mass evacuation, that Japanese Americans had engaged in espionage and sabotage. "Since this is not so," one Justice Department lawyer told Fahy, "it is highly unfair to this racial minority that these lies, put out in an official publication, go uncorrected" before the Supreme Court. Ruling in 1983 and 1984, federal judges in all three cases vacated the wartime convictions on the basis of governmental misconduct. "The judicial process is seriously impaired when the government's law enforcement officers violate their ethical obligations to the court," wrote Judge Marilyn Hall Patel in a posthumous rebuke to Fahy, erasing Korematsu's criminal conviction. In her ruling on Gordon Hirabayashi's petition, Circuit Judge Mary Schroeder stated that "a United States citizen who is convicted of a crime on account of race is lastingly aggrieved." The final act in the redress movement took place in the East Room of the White House in January 1998, when Bill Clinton placed the Presidential Medal of Freedom, the nation's highest civilian honor, around Fred Korematsu's neck. "A man of quiet bravery," Clinton said, "Fred Korematsu deserves our respect and thanks for his patient pursuit to preserve the civil liberties we hold dear."

The wartime internment of Japanese Americans and their patient pursuit of redress for the "grave injustice" they endured are reflections of two conflicting strains in American society. According to the relocation commission, as we noted, the internment decision resulted from "race prejudice, war hysteria, and a failure of political leadership." President Roosevelt issued Executive Order 9066 with little deliberation and with no evidence that Japanese Americans posed any danger of espionage or sabotage. In fact, he relied on the recommendation of an army general who publicly stated his belief that the "racial characteristics" of this Asian group predisposed them to disloyalty. The Supreme Court, too, based its decisions in the *Hirabayashi* and *Korematsu* cases on unquestioning deference to presidential war-making powers, coupled with the racist supposition that Japanese Americans, two-thirds of them native-born citizens, valued "their attachments to Japan and its institutions" above loyalty to the country of their birth or chosen residence. But the postscript to this story, in the successful redress movement of the 1980s and the judicial vacation of the criminal convictions of three young men who challenged the internment program, reflects the "patient pursuit" of justice that has marked the slow, often painful struggles of black Americans, gays and lesbians, and other groups that have been the victims of public hostility and political repression. In this regard, the story of the Japanese American internment vividly illustrates the enduring conflicts over the Constitution in wartime. Judge Patel put it well in her opinion vacating Fred Korematsu's conviction; she stated that although the Supreme Court's decision in his case "remains on the pages of our legal and political history," it stands as a "constant caution that in times of war or declared military necessity our institutions must be vigilant in protecting constitutional guarantees."

If the Constitution did not require that loyal Japanese Americans be afforded a trial in a civilian court before their indefinite detention in internment camps, did it require such a trial for German saboteurs who landed on American soil with detailed plans and explosives? The Supreme Court decided a case in 1942 that raised this question, with far-reaching implications and great relevance to the current war on terror. The establishment by President George W. Bush of military tribunals to try "enemy combatants" prompted government lawyers to dust off the Court's ruling in *Ex parte Quirin* and to argue that it supports the president's action. Whether or not it does, the Court's decision in the *Quirin* case raises life-and-death issues about the rush to judgment.

The government presented no evidence that any Japanese American had committed, or planned to commit, an act of espionage or sabotage. But there was ample evidence that eight Germans had surreptitiously entered the United States with plans and means to blow up bridges, tunnels, and buildings in major cities, along with industrial plants that produced vital war goods like aluminum and magnesium. The story of this abortive plot illustrates the continuing vulnerability of cities to portable, concealed bombs in the hands of terrorists who have made the kind of careful preparations the German saboteurs did. During the early months of World War II, German intelligence officials decided that sabotage within the United States would serve two purposes: crippling vital war production and demoralizing the American public, making them too fearful, for example, to visit department stores or travel by train. Lieutenant Walter Kappe of the Abwehr, the German intelligence branch, was detailed to this effort; he had spent several years in the United States and had been active in the pro-Nazi German-American Bund. Early in 1942, Kappe contacted German men who had returned from the United States to their homeland because of sympathy with Nazi aims. Kappe recruited twelve men in their twenties and thirties who volunteered for a sabotage mission. In Berlin they were instructed in incendiaries, explosives, timing devices, secret writing, and concealment of identity by blending into an American background. The saboteurs were taken to aluminum and magnesium plants, railroad shops, canals, locks, and other facilities to familiarize them with the vulnerable points of the targets they would attack. Finally, they were shown detailed maps, drawings, and photographs of potential targets, which they committed to memory, and received $175,000 in U.S. currency.

The plan would be executed by two four-man teams, which set off in German submarines from a base in occupied France, one team leaving on May 26, 1942, and the other two days later. The first group, headed by George John Dasch, landed on a beach near Amagansett, Long Island, New York, on June 13. They were dressed in German military uniforms, to ensure they would be treated as prisoners of war if they were immediately captured. Under cover of darkness, they changed into civilian clothes, and buried their uniforms and the explosives they brought ashore for later retrieval. Then, out of nowhere, a member of the U.S. Coast Guard, John Cullen, appeared. The saboteurs all spoke good English, but the mistake one of them made of saying something in German made Cullen even more suspicious of the four strange men on a beach in the middle of the night. George Dasch pulled out a wad of money and offered Cullen $260 to forget he had seen the group. Cullen took the money and left, but immediately reported the incident to the Coast Guard, which then informed the FBI. However, a search of the area turned up nothing, as the saboteurs had taken the first train from Amagansett to New York City.

The second four-man team, led by Edward Kerling, landed on June 17 at Ponte Vedra Beach, in Florida, south of Jacksonville. They were dressed in bathing suits but wore German army caps. This group also changed into civilian clothes and buried their caps and explosives. No one spotted them, and they left for a planned rendezvous with Dasch's group in Cincinnati on July 4, splitting up into pairs for initial visits to New York and Chicago. But the carefully planned sabotage plot soon fell apart. Dasch, perhaps suspecting that Cullen had given his superiors good descriptions of his team and fearing eventual capture—or perhaps simply from cold feet—told another team member, Ernest Burger, that he was pulling out and would turn himself in to the FBI. Burger agreed to give himself up as well. Dasch called the FBI office in New York on June 14, giving the name "Pastorius" and saying that he would telephone FBI headquarters in Washington the following week. He did so on June 19, from a Washington hotel, and directed the agents to his room. When they arrived, Dasch opened a briefcase containing $82,000; the evidence helped convince the agents of the story he told them, which eventually filled a 254-page confession. Armed with this information, FBI agents arrested the remaining members of Dasch's team—Burger, Heinrich Heinck, and Richard Quirin—in New York on June 20. Kerling and Werner Theil of the Florida team were also picked up in New York on June 23, and the remaining two members of Kerling's group, Herman Neubauer and Herbert Haupt, were arrested in Chicago on June 27.

Once in FBI custody, the eight saboteurs were turned over to army officials in Washington, while government lawyers debated what to do with them. President Roosevelt apparently favored trying them before a military court-martial. However, this process would require proof "beyond a reasonable doubt" of the saboteurs' guilt and a unanimous verdict for conviction. The government's case rested almost entirely on Dasch's lengthy confession and the shorter confessions of the other seven, along with the German uniforms and explosives that had been buried and later retrieved by federal agents. It was a strong case, but the defendants had not attempted any sabotage, carried no written plans, and stated they had no intention of following the German army's orders. They were certainly guilty of entering the country unlawfully and conspiring to commit sabotage, but government officials wanted to let the Germans know that any future sabotage plots would be dealt with severely. The best way to send the message was to convict and execute the captured saboteurs promptly. And the best way to accomplish that goal was to try the men before a military commission, with lower standards of proof and with just a two-thirds vote required for conviction.

FDR finally agreed with the military commission proposal, and issued an executive order on July 2, 1942, appointing a body of seven army officers to try the saboteurs. The commission would conduct the trial behind closed doors, and all proceedings would remain secret. The same day, citing his powers as commander in chief, Roosevelt issued a proclamation stating that "all persons who are subjects, citizens or residents of any nation at war with the United States and who during time of war enter or attempt to enter the United States through coastal or boundary defenses, and are charged with committing or attempting or preparing to commit sabotage, espionage, hostile or warlike acts, or violations of the laws of war, shall be subject to the law of war and to the jurisdiction of military tribunals." On July 3, the army's judge advocate general, Myron Cramer, lodged four charges against the defendants with the commission: The first simply alleged "violation of the law of war," the second and third charged them with "corresponding with or giving intelligence to the enemy" and with spying, and the fourth charged them with conspiracy to commit the first three offenses. Significantly, the "law of war" is not a written body of statutes but is, rather, a part of the broader "law of nations," which itself has no written form. But under the law of war, as understood and applied by virtually every nation for centuries, spying on behalf of the enemy during wartime is an offense punishable by death. Whether the German saboteurs were spies in the classic sense of gathering and communicating intelligence to their government was problematic in the *Quirin* case, but they had the facilities and training for intelligence gathering as well as sabotage.

The saboteurs were tried by the military commission in the Justice Department building in Washington, in a proceeding that began on July 8, 1942. Attorney General Francis Biddle and Cramer headed the prosecution, with Colonel Kenneth Royall (later secretary of the army) leading the defense team of lawyers. By all accounts, Royall and his colleagues did an exemplary job and zealously defended their clients. The testimony concluded on July 27, and Royall immediately filed habeas corpus petitions for all defendants with the federal district court in Washington, claiming that Roosevelt lacked the power to establish the military commission and that the defendants were entitled to trial in the civil courts, with all constitutional protections available to them. The district judge refused to accept the petitions, effectively denying them, and Royall then asked the Supreme Court to review the cases. The justices were on their annual summer recess, but Chief Justice Stone hastily convened a special term on July 29 for oral argument in *Ex parte Quirin*, the title of the case that included all eight defendants. This expedited schedule set a record for the Supreme Court, which heard argument on July 29 and 30 and issued its ruling the following day.

In just three sentences, the justices agreed without dissent—

Justice Murphy did not participate—that the charges against the defendants "allege an offense or offenses which the President is authorized to order tried before a military commission," that the commission "was lawfully constituted," and that the defendants "have not shown cause for being discharged by writ of habeas corpus." That brief order sealed the fate of the German saboteurs. The military commission reconvened, found all the defendants guilty, and sentenced them to death. Attorney General Biddle appealed to Roosevelt to commute the sentences of Dasch and Burger for their cooperation in capturing the remaining saboteurs. Roosevelt agreed, and Dasch received a thirty-year sentence and Burger a life term in federal prison. On August 8, 1942, the six other saboteurs were electrocuted in the District of Columbia jail.

But the *Quirin* case was not over. On October 29, almost three months after the executions, the Court issued a lengthy opinion, explaining and justifying its earlier refusal to consider the habeas corpus petitions. Chief Justice Stone wrote for the Court—again without Murphy's participation—and first addressed the government's claims that "petitioners must be denied access to the courts" and that "no court may afford the petitioners a hearing" at which they could challenge their trial before the military commission. It was a crucial issue, and one the Court would visit again in 2004, in cases involving the detention of "enemy combatants" seized and detained by the Bush administration. Attorney General Biddle had argued that federal courts were barred from hearing challenges to the military commission, or reviewing its findings and sentences, simply because Roosevelt had inserted a "no access" rule into his proclamation of July 2. This was an astounding claim of absolute presidential lawmaking power, and Biddle most likely swallowed his personal objections to his official position. In his opinion, Chief Justice Stone said that Roosevelt's proclamation could not bar "consideration by the courts of petitioners' contentions that the Constitution and laws of the United States constitutionally enacted forbid their trial by military commission." But Stone left unclear whether Congress could strip the federal courts of jurisdiction in future cases; he also dodged the issue of what kind of judicial "consideration" might apply. Because the Court had earlier refused to consider the saboteurs' habeas corpus petitions and had ruled that the military commission was "lawfully constituted," it is difficult to discern from Stone's opinion what judicial relief a defendant held for trial before a military commission might obtain. The chief justice explained that the Court had denied the "applications for leave to file petitions for habeas corpus" by the saboteurs but had granted their petitions for certiorari to challenge the refusal of the district court even to allow their lawyers to file the habeas petitions. Perhaps the best explanation for this tangled and confusing procedural history came in Stone's statement that the "public importance of the questions raised by their petitions" had persuaded the Court to hear the case.

Once he reached the substantive issues in the *Quirin* case, Stone picked a careful path through thorny constitutional questions. He began with a broad acknowledgment of the president's "exercise of his powers as Commander in Chief of the Army in time of war," which authorized him to carry into effect "all laws defining and punishing offenses against the law of nations, including those which pertain to the conduct of war." Much earlier, Congress had passed the Articles of War, which applied to military personnel and provided for trial of most offenses by court-martial. The articles also recognized military commissions for the trial of "offenses against the law of war not ordinarily tried by court-martial," including spying. But did the articles permit trial by commissions of persons—such as the saboteurs—who were not American military personnel? Stone answered by noting that the articles did not "exclude from that class 'any other person who by the law of war is subject to trial by military tribunals' and who may be tried by court-martial or military commission." But that "class" included only military personnel and specified groups of persons "associated or serving with the army." The German saboteurs belonged to none of the classes subject to the Articles of War, except by the broadest expansion of which Stone was capable.

Having concluded that the saboteurs could be tried by a military commission under the Articles of War, despite their lack of connection with the U.S. military, Stone had little trouble disposing of their claim to the protections of the Fifth and Sixth Amendments, which require grand jury indictment for a capital crime and trial by jury in a civil court. He asserted that grand juries and jury trials were "procedures unknown to military tribunals" when the Constitution was adopted and were unsuited for tribunals "called upon to function under conditions precluding resort to such procedures." But the "conditions" under which the saboteurs were tried hardly precluded civil trials. This was not a battlefield trial, far removed from civil courts. In fact, it was conducted at the Justice Department headquarters, just a few blocks from the federal district court and halfway between the White House and the Supreme Court.

The logic behind Stone's opinion seemed to be that if military personnel could be tried by court-martial without benefit of the Fifth and Sixth Amendments, "enemy belligerents" like the saboteurs were even less deserving of those protections. Long-standing practice may have supported the Court's decision to posthumously affirm the death sentences of the six executed saboteurs, but Stone evaded the clear command of the Fifth Amendment that "no person shall be held to answer for a capital, or otherwise infamous crime, unless on a presentment or indictment of a Grand Jury, except in cases arising in the land or naval forces" during wartime. In several cases, the Court has held that aliens, even those illegally in the country, are "persons" within the meaning of the Fifth Amendment, and are entitled to its protection.

There are compelling arguments on both sides of the *Quirin* case, which raised—but did not persuasively decide—several difficult constitutional issues. It seems unfair to permit military personnel to be tried and even sentenced to death by court-martial, without the protections that civilians enjoy, while extending those protections to "enemy belligerents" who sneak into the country, bent on sabotage that could kill thousands of Americans or cripple war production. But to return once again to the Court's words in the *Milligan* case, the Constitution "covers with the shield of its protection all classes

of men, at all times and under all circumstance," and none of its provisions "can be suspended during any of the great exigencies of government." The internment of Japanese Americans, held without
charge or trial, and the trial of the German saboteurs, conducted
behind closed doors, both show the fragility of the Constitution at
war. And both episodes were echoed by the roundup and detention
of several thousand Muslims from Middle Eastern countries following the terrorist attacks on the World Trade Center and the Pentagon
on September 11, 2001, and by the imprisonment of several hundred
suspected terrorists captured during the U.S. invasion of Afghanistan
that followed those attacks. As we shall see, the Supreme Court's
rulings in 2004 on George W. Bush's claim of "inherent" power to
detain those prisoners, indefinitely and without charges, showed
that the *Hirabayashi* and *Quirin* cases have been undermined as
precedent by greater judicial skepticism of unbridled and unchecked
presidential powers during wartime.

9

"A WORLD-WIDE AMERICAN EMPIRE":

The Imperial Presidency in the Cold War

The outline and future shape of the postwar American empire could be seen even before the United States entered World War II. Framers of the policies and institutions through which imperial ambitions were later pursued, both within and outside the Roosevelt administration, often spoke frankly, but only within the closed circle of government and business leaders, of their long-term goal of creating such an empire. FDR himself assumed the mantle of Woodrow Wilson, who had assured the American people, both during and after the nation's participation in World War I, that the United States had no territorial ambitions and no desire to become the world's "police officer." Wilson, as we have seen, had failed to persuade the Senate to bring the United States into the League of Nations—a reflection of his weakness as a political leader. Roosevelt, in contrast, employed his mastery of politics and his command of the imperial presidency to lay the groundwork for U.S. participation in the United Nations. Membership in the international organization, in turn, gave FDR's successor, Harry Truman, the opportunity to circumvent the Congress in sending American troops into Korea in 1950. The Asian conflict was the first of a long series of undeclared wars that have subverted the Constitution's command that only Congress has the power to declare war and to authorize the president to send troops into combat.

Despite their sharp differences in personal and political skills, Wilson and Roosevelt both sought to promote the American economic empire that grew rapidly during the 1920s and continued to expand during the Great Depression. Exports of agricultural products and manufactured goods propped up an ailing domestic economy, and trade agreements with smaller, weaker countries gave the United States a commanding position in the world economy. And the two presidents, as noted, disclaimed any territorial ambitions in the aftermath of Allied victories in the two world wars. In August 1941, four months before the United States entered the war, FDR met with Winston Churchill, on naval vessels anchored off the coast of Newfoundland. The two leaders hammered out what they called the Atlantic Charter, which stated that both nations "seek no aggrandizement, territorial or other," and pledged to respect "the right of all peoples to choose the form of government under which they will live." Behind this noble vision of the postwar world, evoking a Norman Rockwell painting of New England town meetings, however, lay a hard-headed acceptance of the imperial status quo.

Two weeks before Roosevelt and Churchill issued the Atlantic Charter, for example, Undersecretary of State Sumner Welles had promised the French that the United States, "mindful of its traditional friendship for France, has deeply sympathized with the desire of the French people to maintain their territories and to preserve them intact." The most important region in the French empire was that of Indochina, which supplied vital sources of tin and rubber to the Allied war effort. Vietnam, the largest, most populous part of Indochina, was already seething with nationalist sentiment, and the leaders of the Vietnamese independence movement seized on the Atlantic Charter to press their demands for self-determination. Yet the Roosevelt administration turned a deaf ear to these appeals. In late 1942, FDR assured the French that "it is thoroughly understood that French sovereignty will be re-established as soon as possible throughout all the territory, metropolitan or colonial, over which flew the French flag in 1939."

The United States did not covet the French colony of Indochina, but it did want to retain access to its tin and rubber. Far more important in postwar planning, however, was control of the vast petroleum supplies in the Middle East. This region of the world, dominated by the British, became the focus of American foreign policy during the war. Domestic production and transportation depended heavily on petroleum, and the oil fields of Texas and Oklahoma could not meet the insatiable appetite of businesses and consumers. Oil reserves in the Middle East, particularly in Saudi Arabia, far outstripped those in the United States, and the British stood in the way of access to this vital commodity. The Roosevelt administration showed no compunction in shouldering aside its wartime ally in the drive for postwar control of Saudi oil. Using the lure of Lend-Lease aid to the Saudis, American officials prevailed on King Ibn Saud to grant special privileges to the Arabian-American Oil Company, known as ARAMCO. With this assurance in hand, the British government reluctantly conceded its exclusive control of Saudi oil and signed a pact in 1944 that recognized "the principle of equal opportunity" for the petroleum companies of both nations.

The U.S. empire that now circles the globe had its roots in the expansive visions of the nation's founders and early leaders, but the blueprint for the present-day realization of those visions was drafted by people who recognized that the United States would emerge from World War II as the largest and strongest economy. The alliance of nations who conquered the Axis powers gave way to an alliance between American corporations and government officials who, jointly, shaped the evolving order; the latter-day cooperative venture was motivated by profit and secured by American political and military dominance after 1945. Early in the war, Secretary of State Cordell Hull looked forward to this prospect: "Leadership toward a new system of international relationships in trade and other economic affairs will devolve very largely upon the United States because of our great economic strength. We should assume this leadership, and the responsibility that goes with it, primarily for reasons of pure national self-interest." That self-interest, of course, had little regard for the self-determination of people in countries such as Vietnam, who came to view the noble promises of the Atlantic Charter as the empty words of imperialist leaders.

Furthermore, leaders like Hull foresaw the United States as able to impose its will on the weakened or devastated nations on both sides of the bloody conflict. They envisioned a postwar environment in which the country could secure and extend its military presence through a peacekeeping organization capable of deterring future acts of aggression, like those of Germany and Japan, that might otherwise culminate in regional or global war. Those two nations, of course, along with Italy and the other Axis powers, were no longer a threat to international stability. But there were two potential sources of instability that concerned many postwar planners, both inside and outside the American government. One stemmed from the political ferment and nationalist movements in the colonial possessions of Britain and France, as well as Belgium, Portugal, and the Netherlands. Struggles for independence had already begun in Vietnam and several African colonies, many of them led by avowed Communists. Another source of political instability was centered in Moscow. Despite the Soviet Union's wartime alliance with the nations fighting Germany and Japan, and the horrific losses to its military forces and civilian population—some twenty million Soviet soldiers and citizens died in the war—many American leaders suspected that Joseph Stalin had designs on countries around his nation's borders. Moscow was also the headquarters of the Communist International, the world federation of communist parties, including those in Africa and Asia. During the war, the Soviet government kept its foreign Communist followers on a tight leash, most of them concealing their ties to Moscow. Having watched newsreels of the Red Army helping to liberate the Nazi-occupied countries of Eastern Europe and driving through Germany to meet the Allied forces at the Elbe River, much of the American public looked forward to warm and lasting relations with the Soviet Union; many government and business leaders shared this rosy view. In late 1943, for instance, the White House received a memo from the Foreign Economic Administration, predicting that an "enormous post-war trade" between the United States and the Soviet Union was possible, based on Soviet payment in gold and raw materials. "The Russians want, and will want," the memo said, "machine tools, and the United States industry now has gigantic capacity and wants markets. The Russians will want railroad, automotive and air transport equipment, oil and refinery equipment, electrical machinery, and equipment for chemical, textile and food processing plants." In March of the following year, Assistant Treasury Secretary Harry Dexter White prepared a report listing expected American raw material needs and citing Soviet sources of manganese, chromium, mercury, lead, and other vital minerals. White suggested a $5 billion, thirty-year credit, to be repaid in raw materials. During 1945, American business looked on expanded Soviet trade with anticipation. In January, *Fortune* magazine reported that some seven hundred American companies were paying $250,000 to advertise in the *Catalogue of American Engineering and Industry,* prepared especially for the Soviets. The organ of the U.S. Chamber of Commerce, *Nation's Business,* reported in March 1945 that Soviet orders with General Electric, International Telephone and Telegraph, and Newport News Shipbuilding indicated that the USSR "will be a greater market than ever before for American business."

Even before the United States joined the war, some business leaders described their ultimate goals in blunt terms. Speaking to the Investment Bankers Association of New York in December 1940, Virgil Jordan, president of the National Industrial Conference Board, used these words: "Whatever the outcome of the war, America has embarked on a career of imperialism, both in world affairs and every other aspect of her life." Carrying out "our imperial responsibilities" meant the creation of a "solid base of internal unity and domestic prosperity" following the war. Advocacy of an American empire, based on dominance of the global economy, continued after the war. In early 1946, for example, the conservative writer Eugene Lyons wrote in *Nation's Business* that the weakness of the British forced the United States to "fill the vacuum by building a world-wide American empire."

President Roosevelt and other high-level officials did not, of course, speak of America's postwar aims in terms of empire. But they certainly encouraged both administration aides and business leaders to promote the nation's economic interests abroad. Protecting those interests from political instability, whether in Europe, Africa, or Asia, depended primarily on U.S. military strength. Even with a demobilized army and navy, the United States would retain enough forces to establish a military presence around the globe, with thousands of occupation troops stationed in Germany and Japan. The postwar occupation bases, which the United States still mostly maintains, formed the pillars of the worldwide network of military installations, in more than eighty countries, that now protect the global interests of the American empire.

Military strength alone could not guarantee the international stability on which U.S. interests depended, however. The collaboration of the other major partners in the Allied coalition, as junior partners in the emerging international system, would be necessary to its success. Early in 1943, the outline of a world body to establish this order took shape, with a resolution in the Senate proposing the creation of the United Nations. Senator Joseph Ball, a Minnesota Republican, was joined as sponsor by another GOP senator, Harold Burton of Ohio, and two Democrats, Lister Hill of Alabama and Carl Hatch of New Mexico. Moderate and respected members of the Senate, they had already cultivated the support of their colleagues. It was significant that the impetus for American participation in the United Nations came from the Senate and not President Roosevelt, although he had been consulted and concurred with Ball's proposal. Surely FDR remembered what had happened in 1919 and 1920, when the Senate emphatically rejected President Woodrow Wilson's effort to ram the Versailles Treaty and the League of Nations through the Senate. Knowing how jealously the Senate guarded its prerogatives, Roosevelt had no desire to make a similar mistake.

Senator Ball stressed, in introducing his resolution, that the "whole world, and our allies, know that it is the United States Senate which will finally decide what will be the foreign policy of our country when the war ends." He pointedly omitted the president from this statement, and just as pointedly omitted the House of Representatives. Under the Constitution, the Senate does not share its role in ratifying treaties with the House, but to claim that the upper chamber would "finally decide" the nation's foreign policy ruffled more than a few feathers in the House.

The lower chamber responded to the Ball resolution with one sponsored by J. William Fulbright, an Arkansas Democrat who later served in the Senate and became an outspoken critic of the Vietnam War. Fulbright's resolution, introduced in September 1943, was brief: "Resolved by the House of Representatives (the Senate concurring), That the Congress hereby expresses itself as favoring the creation of appropriate international machinery with power adequate to establish and to maintain a just and lasting peace, among the nations of the world, and as favoring American participation therein." Hamilton Fish, Jr., a conservative New York Republican, proposed ending the resolution with the words "through its constitutional processes." Although, as Fish was well aware, the Senate could ratify a treaty to join the United Nations without House approval, he preferred legislation that would require the two chambers to agree on a UN charter, still to be drafted. Fish warned Fulbright that he and other members of the House "are afraid that some secret commitments will be entered into and that Congress will be by-passed, and that the Constitution will be ignored." The New York representative did not spell out the "secret commitments" he feared, but they most likely related to the dispatch of troops by presidential order, without prior approval by Congress. Since Fulbright raised no objection to the "constitutional processes" wording, the House added it to the resolution, which was overwhelmingly adopted by a 360 to 29 margin.

Not wanting to be seen as following the lead of the lower chamber in foreign policy, the Senate did not concur in the Fulbright resolution. By a vote of 85 to 5, it adopted a resolution introduced by Tom Connally, a Texas Democrat, which included the "constitutional processes" wording of the House version but also specified that any treaty to join the United Nations would require two-thirds approval by the Senate. Significantly, there was little discussion during the debate over the Connally resolution about the role of Congress in approving the commitment of American troops to UN "peacekeeping" operations. This issue was, of course, a crucial one. It was clearly understood in Congress that a major function of the United Nations would be to act as an international "police force," able to call on member nations for troops to separate the combatants, and to maintain the peace in small-scale conflicts. But the Senate was not prepared to lay down any conditions on the use of U.S. forces until a UN charter was drafted and submitted to Congress.

Before the drafting process began, two high-level conferences took place, in 1943 and 1944, the first in Moscow and the second in Washington, at the Dumbarton Oaks estate in Georgetown. The United States, Britain, the Soviet Union, and China took part; both meetings produced broadly worded declarations of the need for a "general international organization for the maintenance of international peace and security." Two weeks after the Dumbarton Oaks conference, President Roosevelt assured Congress that he recognized the need for prior congressional approval of troop commitments to UN peacekeeping operations, but he also stressed that the UN "must have the power to act quickly and decisively to keep the peace by force, if necessary." In an analogy, the president said that a police officer who saw someone break into a house could hardly be expected "to go to the town hall and call a town meeting to issue a warrant before the felon could be arrested." Although the words were hardly reassuring to skeptical members of Congress, the lawmakers waited for the outcome of the drafting process under way in San Francisco in late 1945. Representatives of fifty nations worked for nine weeks to produce a draft charter intended to ensure a lasting peace. Four of the eight American delegates were members of Congress, evenly split by party: Tom Connally and Arthur Vandenberg from the Senate, and Sol Bloom and Charles Eaton from the House. The bipartisan delegation helped greatly to ease the charter through Congress.

The structure of the new body included the General Assembly, in which the votes of each member nation would have equal weight; the eleven-member Security Council, with five permanent members—the United States, Britain, France, China, and the Soviet Union—and six members elected by the General Assembly for two-year terms, with a rotating chairmanship. Each of the five permanent members could exercise a veto over Security Council resolutions. The UN would also include the Secretariat, headed by a secretary general; the International Court of Justice; and specialized agencies for humanitarian, scientific, and economic work. The most important provisions of the UN Charter dealt with procedures for the use of military forces, to be mobilized at the direction of the Security Council "in accordance with a special agreement or agreements" between the council and member states, "subject to ratification by the signatory states in accordance with their respective constitutional processes." For the United States, this provision left undecided the crucial issue of whether the president, acting alone, could dispatch troops for UN peacekeeping missions, or whether prior approval by Congress would be required.

During hearings on the UN Charter before the Senate Foreign Relations Committee, John Foster Dulles, a prominent Wall Street lawyer who had served as adviser to the U.S. delegation at San Francisco and later as secretary of state, was asked by Eugene Milliken, a Colorado Republican, if he saw a difference between "policing powers" and "real war problems." Milliken suggested that the former might allow the president to act without congressional approval, while the latter would require it. Dulles agreed: "If we are talking about a little bit of force necessary to be used as a police demonstration, that is the sort of thing that the President of the United States has done without concurrence by Congress since this Nation was founded." Dulles was partly correct. In a number of cases, presidents had dispatched troops to seek reprisal for damages or to protect citizens and their property—although many of these incidents were actually pretexts for intervening in the affairs of other countries, such as Nicaragua. And several presidents, notably Woodrow Wilson, had sent troops to join multinational forces, most often to aid one side in a civil war, as Wilson had done in sending troops to Russia in 1918. Where Dulles erred, however, was in not addressing the underlying question of whether a president could employ even "a little bit of force" that was not defensive in nature, without trespassing on congressional turf.

Senate ratification of the treaty approving participation in the United Nations was a foregone conclusion, given its bipartisan backing and overwhelming public support, but there were doubters and dissenters. Senator Burton Wheeler, a maverick Montana Democrat, argued that Congress was abdicating its constitutional war powers. "If it is to be contended that if we enter into this treaty we take the power away from Congress, and the President can send troops all over the world to fight battles everywhere," he thundered, "I say that the American people will never support any Senator or Representative who advocates such a policy; and make no mistake about it." Shortly after Wheeler sat down, the Senate approved the UN Charter by a vote of 89 to 2.

Once the charter had been adopted, Congress took up the issue of "special agreements" to authorize the commitment of military forces to UN peacekeeping missions, at the request of the Security Council. The hearings and debates in Congress on the UN Participation Act of 1945 resulted in two important limitations on unilateral presidential power. The first stipulated that, once Congress approved a special agreement with the Security Council for the use of force, the president could implement the agreement without further congressional action. The second provision made clear that presidents could not make any other agreements that might commit troops to combat without prior congressional approval. Undersecretary of State Dean Acheson, who later headed that department, assured the House Foreign Affairs Committee that it would be "entirely within the wisdom of Congress to approve or disapprove whatever special agreement the President negotiates" with the United Nations. He added that "until the special agreement has been negotiated and approved by the Congress, it has no force and effect." In its report on the UN Participation Act, the Senate Foreign Relations Committee noted that all its members "were agreed on the basic proposition that the military agreements could not be entered into solely by executive action." The final bill that Congress enacted, and President Truman signed, indicated emphatically that the White House could not deploy troops for UN military action on its own initiative. Thus, in approving U.S. participation in the United Nations, Congress had jealously guarded its constitutional war powers.

Before considering the first test of the UN Participation Act—President Truman's unilateral decision to send troops into Korea in 1950—we need to set the framework for the conflicts that led to the Korean War. Two momentous events in the five years that followed the Allied victory in World War II fundamentally changed the course of world history and led to a long series of struggles—some military and others political and economic—between the United States and the Communist bloc. It was, of course, the era of the Cold War, which dominated both domestic politics and foreign policy during the remainder of the twentieth century. A full account of the beginnings and later development of the Cold War is beyond the scope of this book, but a recounting of significant events is necessary to an understanding of the constitutional issues that arose from this global conflict.

The rosy forecast of friendly postwar relations and profitable trade between the United States and the Soviet Union quickly vanished in the wake of Soviet occupation and domination of much of Eastern Europe. In truth, the imposition of Soviet control over these countries, and their sudden transformation into satellites of the Stalinist regime, came as no surprise. When he met with Stalin at the Potsdam Conference in Germany in 1945, President Truman had, in fact, agreed to the establishment of a Soviet "sphere of influence" in Eastern Europe. But the vociferous response of some individuals and organizations in the United States—particularly the outrage of Americans of Polish ancestry—to the "Iron Curtain" that Churchill would later describe as falling across Europe created a political backlash that cost the Democratic Party control of the House in 1946.

For more than a century, the United States had exercised control, as expressed in the Monroe Doctrine, of its sphere of influence in Latin America and the Caribbean. But after World War II, American policy makers operated according to a double standard. While they were willing to concede the legitimate Soviet security needs in Eastern Europe, they wished to retain an "open door" in that region and the rest of Europe for U.S. economic and political influence—yet they would deny the Soviets reciprocal access to the Americas. What the United States wanted, War Department official John J. McCloy said, was "that we ought to have our cake and eat it too; that we ought to be able to operate under this regional arrangement [in Latin America], and at the same time intervene promptly in Europe." It was this kind of thinking, rooted in the postwar strength of the United States, that led to Truman's determination to face the Soviet Union with an "iron fist," as he said to Secretary of State James Byrnes.

Truman first shook his iron fist at the Soviets in conflicts over political turmoil in Greece and Turkey. In Greece, pro-Soviet forces had led the struggle against Nazi wartime occupation, after waging a liberation movement against the prewar right-wing monarchy and dictatorship. A popular left-wing group, the National Liberation Front (the EAM), had been put down by the British immediately after the war and the right-wing dictatorship restored. When the EAM launched a guerrilla movement against the regime, enlisting some seventeen thousand fighters, the British sought aid from the United States in crushing the rebellion. A State Department official later said: "Great Britain had within the hour handed the job of world leadership . . . to the United States." Turkey, standing athwart the Dardanelles and controlling access, from both Europe and the Soviet Union, to the vast oil reserves of the Middle East, was also torn by conflict between left-wing and right-wing forces.

The White House responded in the spring of 1947 by asking Congress to provide $400 million in military and economic aid to Greece and Turkey; the United States, Truman believed, must help "free peoples who are resisting attempted subjugation by armed minorities or by outside pressures." The Soviet Union, in fact, had stayed aloof from the Greek civil war, having promised Churchill a free hand in Greece, in return for Britain's giving the Soviets a free hand in Romania, Poland, and Bulgaria. But the United States applied outside pressure of its own in Greece, by providing the right-wing government with 74,000 tons of military equipment, including artillery, planes, and a stock of napalm. In addition, some 250 army officers took the field as "advisers" to the Greek forces. In 1949, the direct military aid succeeded in defeating the EAM rebellion. With "stability" restored in Greece, American corporations, including Esso, Dow Chemical, and Chrysler, moved in with investments and plants. The Truman Doctrine, coupling economic penetration of this region with the iron fist of military support for right-wing dictatorships, won the backing of Congress and much of the American public. But one conservative Republican member of Congress who opposed the aid bill for Greece and Turkey spoke in blunt terms: "The course sought to be established by this bill is in every respect a course toward imperialism." Truman, mindful of his domestic critics, cast the blame for regional discord on the nation's Cold War adversary. "Unhappily," he said, "one imperialistic nation, Soviet Russia, sought to take advantage of this world situation. It was for this reason, only, that we had to make sure of our military strength." In reality, the postwar conflict between the United States and the Soviet Union reflected the competing interests of two rival empires, with the American empire holding an enormous advantage in military and economic strength.

The second event of particular significance happened in January 1949, with the Communist victory in the Chinese civil war. The Communist forces, who had resisted the Japanese occupation of much of China before and during World War II, ousted the corrupt government of Chiang Kai-shek, which had been supported by the United States. Chiang and his Nationalist government fled the Chinese mainland and took refuge on the island of Taiwan, where they imposed a harsh rule on the native people. The Chinese revolution, led by Mao

Tse-tung, reflected the great upheaval of a long-subjugated people, whose vast country had been carved into slices of an economic pie consumed by Western nations, with only the crumbs left for the Chinese themselves.

U.S. leaders, having backed Chiang with more than $2 billion in military and economic aid during World War II, did not welcome the advent of Communist rule in the world's most populous nation. But the new Chinese government did not pose a direct military threat to the United States, with the massive Red Army occupied largely in reconstructing a devastated, poverty-stricken country. However, events in a much smaller country, which bordered China to the south, did threaten the stability of that region. Korea, which Japan had occupied for thirty-five years by brutal force, was liberated after the war. But the Korean peninsula itself was divided in half, along the thirty-eighth parallel. The Soviet Union and the United States had agreed on this division as the best means of preserving each country's influence in the separate halves of Korea. North Korea became a Communist dictatorship, and South Korea a right-wing dictatorship. The two Korean governments, equally bitter over the forced division and each proclaiming to represent all the Korean people, denounced each other and began an escalating pattern of saber rattling. But they were both weakened by the long Japanese occupation, which had drained Korea of its resources, and there seemed little prospect of the North-South conflict going beyond bellicose rhetoric.

That situation changed dramatically on June 25, 1950, when North Korean troops crossed the thirty-eighth parallel and invaded South Korea. The first large-scale invasion of one country by another since World War II also became the first opportunity for the United Nations to employ its peacekeeping machinery. What followed, over the three years before a shaky, often-violated cease-fire ended the bloody conflict, was in three respects a disaster. The greatest catastrophe was that some two million Koreans died in the civil war. Second, the Korean War represented a nightmare for the United Nations; it could not restore the peace, and its multinational peacekeeping force became, in effect, a very short tail on the massive American bulldog. The United States contributed more than 90 percent of the troops who fought in the Korean War, and controlled all the command decisions. Finally, this so-called police action proved disastrous to the constitutional principle of congressional primacy in the nation's war powers.

The day after the North Korean army invaded South Korea, the UN Security Council met in emergency session and ordered the invading forces to withdraw to positions above the thirty-eighth parallel. President Truman announced that "in accordance with the resolution of the Security Council, the United States will vigorously support the effort of the Council to terminate this serious breach of the peace." Predictably, the North Koreans ignored the UN order. The next day, Truman informed the American people that "I have ordered United States air and sea forces to give the [South] Korean Government troops cover and support." The United States, he said, "will continue to uphold the rule of law." Although Truman was referring to the law of international relations, and not to the "supreme law of the land," as set forth in the Constitution, he clearly broke the latter law, in three areas. First, the president committed military forces to combat, in what constituted an act of war, without prior congressional approval or a formal declaration of war. Second, he violated the provisions of the UN Charter—and thus a U.S. treaty obligation—by taking a unilateral military action even before the Security Council had called on member nations for their assistance. And third, Truman violated the UN Participation Act by ignoring its requirement for prior congressional approval of any special agreement with the United Nations for the commitment of U.S. forces. In fact, there was no special agreement at the time he gave the order for troops to provide "cover and support" for the South Korean forces.

Thus Truman had no legal or constitutional authority for his actions at the outset of the Korean War. He ordered U.S. forces to undertake acts of war in Korea, despite his claim, at a June 29 press conference, that "we are not at war." As Secretary of State Dean Acheson later admitted to a Senate committee, "in the usual sense of the word there is a war." The Korean confrontation, which Truman preferred to call a "police action," met every test of being a "formal" war, yet there had been no declaration of its status. Only Congress could take that step, which, in regard to the Korean conflict, it did not do. Further, Acheson's claims that all of Truman's responses "have been under the aegis of the United Nations" were not true. The Security Council did not pass a resolution calling for military deployment—the Soviet member boycotted the session—until June 27. Truman had ordered the forces into combat the day before. Indeed, Acheson later admitted that "some American action, said to be in support of the resolution of June 27, was in fact ordered, and possibly taken, prior to the resolution."

In committing the United States to the Korean War, Truman had violated the commands of the Constitution, of a binding treaty, and of a congressional statute. He all but slapped Congress in the face by ignoring its constitutional role in the war-making process, particularly its sole power to declare war. And how did Congress respond to the presidential usurpation of its prerogatives and directives? With hardly a whimper of protest. Over the past century, as we know, once the nation has gone to war, most of the doubters and dissenters close ranks behind the president and the troops. But the Korean War was not a popular war; in fact, it was the most unpopular conflict to that point in U.S. history. The Democrats lost the White House in 1952, after twenty years of control, largely because most voters felt that Korea was not worth the growing toll of American soldiers who died in combat. Only a few members of Congress, however, criticized Truman during the early months of the war. On the left, Representative Vito Marcantonio, the American Labor Party member from New York City, made this complaint: "When we agreed to the United Nations Charter we never agreed to supplant our Constitution with the United Nations Charter. The power to declare war and make war is vested in the representatives of the people, in the Congress of the United States." On the right, Senator Robert Taft, a respected Ohio Republican with White House ambitions, cautioned that if the president could take the country to war in

Korea "without congressional approval, he can go to war in Malaya or Indonesia or Iran or South America." Taft might have added, "or Vietnam, or Panama, or Afghanistan, or Iraq." In fact, not a single president since Franklin Roosevelt has gone before Congress to seek a declaration of war, while the nation has been engaged in wars—big and small—in every decade since the end of World War II. And with rare exceptions, Congress has tagged along, offering blank-check authorizations or after-the-fact approvals of unilateral executive-branch war making.

Although Truman's decision to commit troops to the Korean War did not produce any judicial test, the Supreme Court did rule on one of his wartime acts. In late 1951, long-standing conflicts between the United Steelworkers Union and the nation's steel companies led to threats of a strike that would shut down production. On December 18, the union gave notice that its members would go on strike when the existing collective bargaining contract expired, on December 31. The Federal Mediation and Conciliation Service intervened in an attempt to bring the two sides to the bargaining table, but the effort failed to resolve their differences. On December 22, Truman referred the dispute to the Federal Wage Stabilization Board to investigate and recommend the terms of a fair settlement. After dragging on for more than three months, this initiative also ended in a stalemate. On April 4, 1952, the union gave notice of a nationwide strike to begin in five days. A few hours before the deadline, Truman issued an executive order, directing Secretary of Commerce Charles Sawyer to take possession of the steel mills and keep them running. Informing the owners of the steel mills that they were now acting as managers for the United States, the commerce chief, in effect, made them federal employees, along with the union members. Sawyer directed his new employees, both managers and workers, to continue production under his supervision.

On April 9, with the strike averted, Truman reported his action to Congress, explaining that he had ordered the seizure of the steel mills to prevent an interruption of production for vital war materials, including tanks and planes. Meanwhile, the steel companies—

led by the Youngstown Sheet and Tube Company, in Ohio—dispatched their lawyers to the federal district court in Washington, seeking both a judicial declaration that Truman's executive order, and Sawyer's directives, were invalid as exceeding the constitutional powers of the executive branch, and an injunction to restrain their enforcement. In response, government lawyers claimed that even a brief strike would "endanger the well-being and safety of the nation." They also asserted that Truman had inherent power, "supported by the Constitution, by historical precedent, and by court decisions," to seize the mills. Rejecting these claims, the district judge issued a preliminary injunction on April 30, restraining Sawyer from "continuing the seizure and possession of the plants" and "from acting under the purported authority" of Truman's executive order. Government attorneys ran to the nearby federal court of appeals, which ordered a stay of the injunction while the case proceeded directly to the Supreme Court. "Deeming it best that the issues raised be promptly decided by this Court," the justices stated, they set the case of *Youngstown Sheet & Tube Co. v. Sawyer* for argument on May 12, 1952.

In the *Youngstown* case, the notion of "inherent" presidential powers was not one of "first impression" before the court, but the scope and magnitude of Truman's action—his order directed the takeover of every major steel mill in the country—gave the case extraordinary significance, as did the wartime setting. Although steel production continued while the Court deliberated, the prospect of a lengthy, crippling strike, if the justices ruled against the president, loomed in the background. The Court's decision, handed down on June 2, ended the speculation with a resounding judicial blast at the assertion of "inherent" powers. Hugo Black, perhaps the most fervent constitutional literalist in the Court's history, scoffed at this notion in his "opinion of the Court," speaking for the six justices in the majority. First, Black brushed aside, in one paragraph, the government's claim that the district court should not have issued the injunction, because the steel companies would not suffer "irreparable" harm from the seizure and had the remedy of full compensation for any lost income or profits. Observing that such damages would be difficult to calculate, Black ruled that the district court had ample grounds for enjoining the seizure.

The justice spelled out those grounds in eight forceful paragraphs. "The President's power, if any, to issue the order must stem either from an act of Congress or from the Constitution itself," he began. Black found no support for Truman's order in either source. "There is no statute that explicitly authorizes the President to take possession of property as he did here," he stated. "Indeed, we do not understand the Government to rely on statutory authorization for this seizure." Not only had Congress not given the president the seizure powers he claimed, Black added, but it had "refused to adopt that method of settling labor disputes" when it passed the Taft-Hartley labor relations act in 1947.

Now Black turned to the Constitution, noting that the government's lawyers had not pointed the Court to any specific constitutional language to support Truman's action. "The contention is that presidential power should be implied from the aggregate of his powers under the Constitution," Black wrote. The Constitution did vest the "executive power" in the president, required him to "take care that the laws be faithfully executed," and made him "Commander in Chief of the Army and Navy." But even if these express powers were combined, they provided no implied authority to make laws, which is what Truman's order had attempted. Notwithstanding the president's "broad powers" as commander in chief, Black said, they did not extend to taking over private property to head off labor disputes. "This is a job for the Nation's lawmakers, not for its military authorities," Black stated firmly. Neither did the president's "executive power" allow him to seize the mills. Congress could have enabled Truman to take such action, but it had not done so. Black ended his brief opinion with a pointed judicial lecture. "The Founders of this Nation entrusted the lawmaking power to Congress alone in both good and bad times," he wrote. "It would do no good to recall the historical events, the fears of power and the hopes for freedom that lay behind their choice. Such a review would but confirm our holding that this seizure order cannot stand."

The Court's majority opinion settled the *Youngstown* case, and restored the nation's steel mills to their owners. It also restored the lawmaking power over labor relations to Congress. But the black-and-white nature of Hugo Black's opinion did not satisfy Justice Robert Jackson, a former attorney general under President Franklin Roosevelt. He expressed his views in a concurring opinion that cited his experience "as legal advisor to a President in time of transition and public anxiety" during the Great Depression. Jackson issued a polite but pointed rebuke to Black for "dealing with the largest questions in the most narrow way." He stressed that Congress and presidents shared responsibility for integrating their "dispersed powers into a workable government." Looking for a "practical" way for the legislative and executive branches to collaborate in meeting the "grave dangers" that faced the country during wartime, Jackson outlined three situations in which presidential powers "fluctuate, depending upon their conjunction or disjunction with those of Congress." In the first, "when the President acts pursuant to an express or implied authorization of Congress, his authority is at its maximum, for it includes all that he possesses in his own right plus all that Congress can delegate." If Truman had seized the steel mills pursuant to congressional statute, his act "would be supported by the strongest of presumptions and the widest latitude of judicial interpretation," Jackson wrote. In the second, when the president acts without "either a congressional grant or denial of authority, he can only rely upon his own independent powers, but there is a zone of twilight in which he or Congress may have concurrent authority, or in which its distribution is uncertain." Within this "twilight zone," Jackson said, "any actual test of power is likely to depend on the imperatives of events and contemporary imponderables rather than on abstract theories of law." Jackson stated the third situation in the terms of a math teacher: "When the President takes measures incompatible with the expressed or implied will of Congress, this power is at its lowest ebb, for then he can rely only upon his own constitutional powers minus any constitutional powers of Congress over the matter." In other words, any powers held by the president would be subtracted from those of the Congress, with a result that could reach zero.

Applying this constitutional calculus to the *Youngstown* case, Jackson "eliminated" both the first and second of these situations. Congress had not authorized the president to seize the mills, nor did he possess "independent powers" in this matter. In fact, Congress had expressly denied him that power. Justices Black and Jackson wound up with the same sum for Truman's action, which was zero. But Jackson's calculations were based on a more nuanced approach—in effect, a sliding scale that balanced congressional and presidential authority. Jackson also took into account the "vast accretions of federal power" since the New Deal, which "have magnified the scope of presidential power." His opinion recognized a fact that would have great impact on later situations in which presidents acted without prior congressional approval: "Subtle shifts take place in the centers of real power that do not show on the face of the Constitution." As we will see, the center of "real power" over efforts to maintain and expand the American empire has shifted dramatically from Congress to the presidency.

The *Youngstown* decision was not unanimous. Chief Justice Fred Vinson spoke for the three dissenters, arguing for "inherent" presidential power to meet the "emergency" of the threatened steel strike. When President Truman named Vinson to head the Court after the sudden death of Harlan Fiske Stone in 1946, he placed at its helm a former Kentucky congressman who had served briefly as secretary of the Treasury in Truman's cabinet. A loyal Democrat and a poker-playing crony of the president, Vinson proved to be the weakest chief justice of the twentieth century, amiable but completely unable to patch over the personal animosities and ideological squabbles that divided the Court during his eight years in office.

Vinson's dissent in *Youngstown* accused the majority of ignoring "the gravity of the emergency and the immediacy of the threatened disaster" of a nationwide steel strike during wartime. In his view, it was Congress and not the president that had failed to meet this emergency by passing laws to authorize Truman's actions. The president had "expressed his desire to cooperate with any legislative proposals approving, regulating or rejecting the seizure of the steel mills," Vinson wrote. "Consequently, there is no evidence whatever of any Presidential purpose to defy Congress or act in any way inconsistent with the legislative will." This argument, of course, put the cart before the horse. Presidents, as Justices Black and Jackson both made clear, have the power under the Constitution only to "faithfully execute" the laws made by Congress, not to make laws themselves. Truman had acted, Vinson wrote, "to prevent immediate paralysis of the mobilization program," which in Vinson's mind provided the necessary legislative program the president was implementing with his seizure order. Forcing Truman to wait until Congress expressly authorized him to occupy the mills could well have endangered the war effort and the safety of the troops. Although Vinson did not use the term, his dissent adopted the claims of "inherent" executive powers that most of Truman's successors have made in justifying their wartime acts—from sending troops into combat to holding American citizens in detention without charges or access to lawyers for alleged complicity with terrorist groups.

The Korean War seriously eroded Truman's shaky base of public support and contributed to the Republican capture of the White House in 1952. In the following decade, the Vietnam War substantially undermined Lyndon Johnson's much stronger base of public support and played a major role in the Republican capture of the White House in 1968. Both presidents made sweeping claims of "inherent" powers to meet supposed threats to the nation's security, and both paid a heavy political price for their unilateral acts. Nonetheless, the fact that Truman and Johnson committed troops without incurring congressional or judicial sanctions illustrates the strength of the imperial presidency and the inability of the supposedly equal branches of government to stand up to chief executives who feel emboldened to take any unilateral military actions they see fit. The wars in Korea and Vietnam differed in many ways, but they both demonstrate the consequences of imperial hubris, the intoxication of personal and national power that has caused the downfall of leaders and nations alike. Disregard of the Constitution, and even disdain for its commands, is often an early warning sign of excessive self-confidence, which can infect the humble as well as the arrogant. As we shall see, the tragedy of Vietnam offers an instructive lesson in the pitfalls of the imperial presidency.

10

"WHAT EVERY SCHOOLBOY KNOWS":

Vietnam and Congressional Abdication

Many Americans—especially those born after 1960—view the Vietnam War as ancient history. A majority, in fact, cannot even recall the dates of U.S. involvement in that war, or locate Vietnam on a map. Most, however, know that the United States "lost" the war, and some remain convinced that antiwar protesters contributed to that painful, humiliating defeat. The word "Vietnam" still evokes strong emotions on both sides of the continuing debate over America's role in the world. But few Americans view the Vietnam War as part of a broader effort to maintain an empire that requires all sorts of military operations—from covert action by the CIA to full-scale invasion of countries such as Panama and Iraq—that presidents order and from which Congress is shut out. The decades of the 1960s through the 1980s show the imperial presidency at its height, while they foreshadow the consequences of presidential overreaching, with the invasion of Iraq in 2003 marking the possible "decline and fall" of the American empire.

Even before the Korean War ended, with a cease-fire in 1953, the Vietnam War had begun. In fact, the conflict in Indochina—which also includes Cambodia and Laos—started in 1946, when a revolutionary movement in Vietnam, led by Ho Chi Minh, turned its armed struggle for independence from the Japanese, who had occupied the country during World War II, against the French, who reasserted control of their former colony in 1945. Ho Chi Minh was a Communist, but the vast majority of Vietnamese who joined the Vietminh movement he headed were simply nationalists. He issued a Declaration of Independence for Vietnam in late 1945, modeled on (and borrowing language from) the American declaration of 1776. Listing the grievances against the French, it concluded: "The whole Vietnamese people, animated by a common purpose, are determined to fight to the bitter end against any attempt by the French colonists to reconquer their country."

The Vietminh forces were strongest in the northern part of Vietnam, and the French bombarded the port city of Haiphong in October 1946 in an effort to dislodge them. Over the next eight years, the Vietminh battled the French, who gradually lost control of the rural areas in which most Vietnamese lived. The French military effort depended heavily on American aid; by 1954, when the French surrendered after the climactic battle of Dien Bien Phu, the United States had poured more than $1 billion of aid, including 300,000 small arms and machine guns, into the failed campaign against the Vietminh.

The American public paid little attention to the struggle for control of Vietnam, particularly while the Korean War dominated the headlines. But Washington kept a close eye on Vietnam, for two reasons. First, there were fears that if Vietnam came under Communist control, revolutionary movements in other Southeast Asian countries might emulate the Vietminh, and the right-wing governments in this region, including those in Malaya and Indonesia, might topple like dominoes. The postwar conflict in Vietnam, in fact, gave rise to the "domino theory," which dominated American political and military thinking over the next three decades. Second, the United States had an economic interest in the area. Thus, in the ten years or so after World War II, the United States maintained a "security chain" of military bases in Asia, including naval and air bases in the Philippines, Taiwan, Japan, and South Korea. The bases were essential to U.S. dominance of the entire Pacific region, into which American corporations hoped to expand the foothold they had established before World War II. A secret National Security Council memo in 1952 linked the two reasons for concern about Vietnam: "Communist control of all of Southeast Asia would render the U.S. position in the Pacific offshore island chain precarious and would seriously jeopardize fundamental U.S. security interests in the Far East. Southeast Asia, especially Malaya and Indonesia, is the principal world source of natural rubber and tin, and a producer of petroleum and other strategically important commodities."

A congressional mission to Vietnam in 1953 underscored Washington's apprehension in the face of the increasing likelihood of a Vietminh victory over France. In a report, the commission noted that "Indochina is immensely wealthy in rice, rubber, coal and iron ore. Its position makes it a strategic key to the rest of Southeast Asia." Continued access to those resources was by no means a certainty: "If the French decided to withdraw, the U.S. would have to consider most seriously whether to take over in this area." The first step in U.S. involvement in Vietnam was the partitioning of the country in 1954, as the outcome of an international conference in Geneva. Under the Geneva Accords, the French agreed to withdraw into the southern part of Vietnam for two years, ceding control of the north to the victorious Vietminh. National elections would take place in 1956, to form a government that would unify the divided country. The U.S. government, however, feared that the Vietnamese people, both north and south, would vote for parties dominated by nationalist forces and that Ho Chi Minh would emerge as Vietnam's leader. To counter this prospect, the United States installed a puppet regime in South Vietnam, led by Ngo Dinh Diem, who had recently returned to Vietnam from exile in New Jersey. Supported almost entirely by American arms and economic aid, Diem blocked the national elections, which never took place. As the Defense Department history of the Vietnam War, better known as the Pentagon Papers, later concluded, "South Vietnam was essentially the creation of the United States."

Diem proved to be a disaster, both for the South Vietnamese people and for the United States. His regime, which was repressive and corrupt, jailed scores of critics, few of them Communists. Diem's police and military forces, trained and armed by American "advisers," controlled the South Vietnamese capital of Saigon and other major cities, but the government's empty promises of land reform alienated the country's peasant majority. Armed rebellion against the Diem government began in 1958, supported by the Communist regime in North Vietnam. Two years later, a broad coalition of nationalist forces in the south formed the National Liberation Front, whose military arm was known as the Vietcong.

Between 1954 and 1960, the Republican administration of Dwight D. Eisenhower violated the terms of the Geneva Accords, which permitted the United States to station 685 military advisers in South Vietnam. Without informing Congress, much less getting its approval, Eisenhower sent several thousand troops to Vietnam, some of them stretching their advisory role by engaging in combat with Vietcong forces. Despite these breaches of the accords, however, Eisenhower had resisted earlier calls for more drastic military action, including the use of tactical nuclear weapons, to rescue the French from impending defeat. He also made clear his unwillingness to act without congressional approval. "There is going to be no involvement of America in a war unless it is the result of the constitutional process that is placed upon Congress to declare it," he told a press conference in 1954. In addition, Eisenhower scribbled a note to Secretary of State John Foster Dulles, saying that in "the absence of some kind of arrangement getting support of Congress," it "would be completely unconstitutional & indefensible" to assist the French.

But the American military role in Vietnam rapidly escalated under President John F. Kennedy, who succeeded Eisenhower in 1961. Before his assassination in November 1963, Kennedy had not only increased the number of American troops in Vietnam to sixteen thousand but had approved a secret plan for covert military actions in Vietnam and the neighboring country of Laos, which North Vietnamese and Vietcong forces used as a sanctuary. According to the Pentagon Papers, these operations included the "dispatch of agents to North Vietnam" to engage in "sabotage and light harassment." However, all the American military aid to the Diem regime failed to halt its growing loss of control of the countryside, where the Vietcong held sway over much of the population. A cabal of disgruntled South Vietnamese army generals, working closely with CIA officers, plotted a military coup to depose Diem. Although Kennedy received regular briefings on their activities, he made no effort to warn Diem of the dangers he faced from his own generals. On November 1, 1963, South Vietnamese troops attacked the presidential palace in Saigon. Diem phoned U.S. ambassador Henry Cabot Lodge, pleading for help. "Some units have made a rebellion and I want to know what is the attitude of the United States," Diem said. "I do not feel well enough informed to be able to tell you," Lodge blandly replied. "I have heard the shooting, but am not acquainted with all the facts." The fact was that Lodge knew full well about the plot. Within hours, Diem fled the palace but was quickly grabbed by the plotters and executed. The Vietcong played no role in Diem's demise, but they reaped a harvest in popular support for their campaign against the string of American puppets that followed Diem, none of them capable of quelling the insurgency.

Vietnam soon became a "quagmire," a seemingly endless confrontation that would swallow hundreds of thousands of American troops, who won every major battle with the Vietcong but decisively lost the more important battle for the "hearts and minds" of the Vietnamese people. Lyndon B. Johnson, who suddenly moved from the vice presidency into the White House after Kennedy's death, struggled, with little success, to turn the tide in Vietnam by sending more troops, planes, and ships. In a futile effort to demoralize its people and disrupt the flow of North Vietnamese troops and supplies along the Ho Chi Minh Trail to the south, Johnson also authorized a massive air assault on North Vietnam. American troops were now fighting North Vietnamese regular forces that had crossed the border to aid the Vietcong; clearly, the United States was at war with North Vietnam. But Johnson conducted the war, even visiting American troops in South Vietnam to pledge his support for their efforts, without asking Congress for a declaration of hostilities. On their part, members of Congress expressed little opposition to Johnson's massive escalation of the war, supporting military appropriations and expansion of the draft. Moreover, Johnson had the backing of a substantial majority of the public and of the media, which reported uncritically on the "victories" of U.S. troops over Vietcong forces. During the early years of the war, few journalists questioned the rosy briefings by the military command in Saigon. For instance, the daily "body count" of dead Vietcong, which most of the press obligingly reported, was later shown to be vastly inflated and to include many civilians. The Johnson administration's official position, stated by Secretary of Defense Robert McNamara in 1964, was that the United States planned "to move our forces as rapidly out of Vietnam as that Government can maintain its independence and as rapidly as the North Vietnamese stop their attempts to subvert it."

The Vietcong and North Vietnamese did not, however, stop their campaign to force the United States out of Vietnam, and, as a result, enthusiasm for the war began to decline. In the first half of 1964, the handful of dissenters in Congress grew into a vocal band of critics who questioned the optimistic predictions that South Vietnamese forces would soon be able to defeat the Vietcong without additional American forces. Outside the White House press room, where all the news was good, Pentagon officials recognized that Vietnam was bad news for the military, and even worse news for President Johnson, who would face the voters in November in his bid for a full term in the White House. The Republican minority in Congress had loyally supported the president, but Johnson wanted to foreclose any prospect that he might be attacked during the upcoming campaign for sending "American boys" into a protracted war in a country that most voters did not consider vital to the nation's security. The Republicans had successfully made the Korean War an issue in their electoral victory in 1952, and Johnson feared—totally without foundation, as it turned out—that Vietnam might become another Korea.

These political factors cannot be ignored in reviewing the events of August 2, 1964, just three months before the presidential election. On that day, according to administration officials, North Vietnamese gunboats attacked the U.S. destroyer *Maddox,* which was conducting "a routine patrol" in the Gulf of Tonkin, off the coast of North Vietnam. The next day, Johnson ordered the navy to take retaliatory action against North Vietnamese naval vessels and onshore supporting facilities. On August 4, the news media reported a second attack on two American destroyers. Denouncing the North Vietnamese attacks as an "outrage," Johnson told a national television audience that the American response would be "limited and fitting." He also praised his Republican opponent in the presidential race, Arizona senator Barry Goldwater, for having "expressed his support for the statement that I am making to you tonight." Whatever slim chance Goldwater had of returning the White House to Republican control sank in the Gulf of Tonkin.

With this political victory in hand, Johnson met with congressional leaders and requested a resolution stating the nation's "determination to take all necessary measures in support of freedom and in defense of peace in southeast Asia." His formal message to Congress on August 5 assured its members that the United States "intends no rashness, and seeks no wider war." The Tonkin Gulf Resolution, as it became known, authorized the president, as commander in chief, to take "all necessary measures to repel any armed attack against the forces of the United States and to prevent further aggression." Presumably, "all necessary measures" might include the use of nuclear weapons (which advisers with more rashness than Johnson later proposed) and an unlimited number of American troops. Congress, of course, could cut off funds for military action if majorities in both chambers thought Johnson's measures went too far. But the "outrage" at the North Vietnamese attacks in the Gulf of Tonkin persuaded lawmakers to give the president a blank check for escalating the war.

Both the Senate and House leaders pushed the Tonkin Gulf Resolution with great dispatch and little debate. The Senate passed it on August 6 with only two dissenting votes, cast by Democrats Wayne Morse of Oregon and Ernest Gruening of Alaska. One of the Senate's most respected members, J. William Fulbright of Arkansas, said the facts of the attack "are clear." The House gave its approval the next day with a vote of 416 to 0. Those votes, as we now know, were based on "facts" that were anything but clear. On August 6, just before the Senate vote, Secretary of Defense McNamara had assured Congress that the destroyer *Maddox* was on a "routine patrol in international waters." In fact, the ship was close to the North Vietnamese coast, supporting South Vietnamese commando attacks on the North, which Johnson had secretly authorized the previous February. Hearings before the Senate Foreign Relations Committee in 1968 uncovered this cable from the commander of the *Maddox* on August 4, 1964: "Review of action makes many recorded contacts and torpedoes fired appear doubtful. Freak weather effects and over-eager sonarman may have accounted for many reports. No actual visual sightings by *Maddox*. Suggest complete evaluation before any further action."

Four years after Congress gave President Johnson a blank check for the Vietnam War, the stated justification turned out to be fraudulent. By then, more than 500,000 American troops were bogged down in the quagmire from which more than 50,000 returned in body bags. Johnson broke his 1964 promise of "no wider war" and suffered the consequence, in 1968, by abandoning his quest for a second full term in the White House. It may be facetious to blame an "over-eager sonarman" for the political and military debacle that Johnson bequeathed to his Republican successor, Richard M. Nixon, who narrowly defeated Vice President Hubert H. Humphrey in the 1968 presidential election. But the real blame lay with Congress, whose members were overeager in accepting, without question, the Johnson administration's "facts" about the Tonkin Gulf incident.

Unlike the previous undeclared war, in Korea, the Vietnam War provoked a flood of legal challenges to various actions of the Johnson and Nixon administrations. More than a dozen cases resulted in judicial decisions, ranging from summary dismissal to lengthy opinions that wrestled with the "delicate balance" of legislative and executive powers during wartime. A summary of the most important cases shows the varying responses of federal judges to a task that few relished, some evaded, and others tackled with a recognition that the Constitution is, as the document states, "the supreme law of the land." The judicial backdrop to the Vietnam War cases is the "political question" doctrine, which offers judges the temping option of declaring that disputes over the exercise of legislative or executive powers—particularly conflicts between the two branches of government—are "political" in nature and are consequently unsuited for judicial resolution. This doctrine, in fact, is entirely judge-made and has no textual foundation in the Constitution. Significantly, the Supreme Court in 1962 emphatically rejected the "political question" doctrine in ruling that state legislative apportionment—which resulted in rural voters having much greater weight than urban voters—raised constitutional issues of "equal protection" that federal courts had jurisdiction to decide. But the "one person, one vote" case of *Baker v. Carr* dealt with domestic political issues, not with the wartime powers of Congress and the president, making that ruling easier to ignore or distinguish as a precedent in the Vietnam War cases.

In one of the first cases to reach the federal courts, army private Robert Luftig sued Defense Secretary McNamara in 1966 to block the orders that would ship him to Vietnam, claiming that he could not be forced to serve in an undeclared war. Federal judge Alexander Holtzoff dismissed the case of *Luftig v. McNamara* without even a hearing, ruling in a brief opinion that presidential power to dispatch troops anywhere in the world "is obviously a political question that is outside of the judicial function." The federal appeals court in the District of Columbia stated, also in a brief opinion, that it required "no discussion or citation to authority" to uphold Holtzoff's decision.

Two years later, as public support for the Vietnam War began slipping, another federal judge gave more attention to the "political question" doctrine, in a case filed against President Johnson by

Lawrence Velvel, a University of Kansas law professor. According to Velvel, Johnson had exceeded his constitutional powers in committing troops to an undeclared war. District Judge George Templar followed Holtzoff in dismissing Velvel's suit, holding that the president was empowered as commander in chief to protect "the interests of the country and to carry on such activities in managing our concerns with foreign nations." In his opinion in *Velvel v. Johnson*, Templar stressed that whether "the executive or legislative branches of the government have seen fit to carry on a limited military action without a formal declaration of war by the legislative branch is a matter resting solely within the discretion of those duly elected representatives of the people." Describing the Vietnam War as a "limited military action" strained credulity, but it served Templar's claim that a formal declaration of war "might bring on an international conflagration which our political leaders are carefully seeking to avoid." In effect, Templar was painting the war as a bonfire, rather than the raging forest fire it had become in 1968.

Indeed, several of the Vietnam War cases resulted in significant judicial rulings that, for all practical purposes, read the "declaration of war" clause out of the Constitution. In 1972, District Judge Dudley Bonzal dismissed a suit filed by William Meyers against President Nixon for continuing an undeclared war. Bonzal held that Meyers lacked "standing" as a taxpayer to challenge Nixon's actions. Except in cases dealing with government expenditures for religious purposes, judges routinely dismissed suits based on taxpayer standing, on the grounds that the burden on an individual taxpayer to support a government program—even one as costly as the Vietnam War—was too insignificant to create the "injury" required to confer standing. In *Meyers v. Nixon*, however, Judge Bonzal went beyond the standing issue to assert that, although there had been "no formal declaration of war" in Vietnam, "the evidence of congressional action through appropriations and extensions of the Selective Service Act . . . is sufficient to imply authorization or ratification of the military action in question and to satisfy the requirements of the declaration-of-war clause." In reading into these legislative measures the functional equivalent of a formal declaration of war, Bonzal offered a judicial interpretation that stretched the Constitution beyond the original intent of the Framers.

During the Korean War, as we noted, Justice Robert Jackson had described, in his concurring opinion in *Youngstown Sheet & Tube Co. v. Sawyer,* a "twilight zone" in which Congress and the president acted together—that is, they shared the war powers. Challenges to the Vietnam War gave federal judges the opportunity to apply Jackson's concept, once again stretching the Constitution's wording and intent. Ruling in 1972 on another taxpayer suit, this one brought against Defense Secretary Melvin Laird, two members of a panel of three district judges, sitting in Philadelphia, held in *Atlee v. Laird* that "the Constitution commits the entire foreign policy power of this country to the executive and legislative branches. Because the Constitution does not itemize all possible prerogatives in this field it is a difficult task of interpretation to state categorically that the authority to perform a particular act resides solely in either the executive or the legislature." Judge Arlin Adams, writing for the *Atlee* majority, followed Judge Bonzal in the *Meyers* case in his interpretation of the declaration-of-war clause. "Implicit in this constitutional provision," Adams wrote, "may be congressional authority to take steps short of a formal declaration of war, equivalent to an authorization." Adams stopped short, however, of deciding whether Congress had, in fact, acted to give such an authorization to the president. Presumably, the question of whether it had done so would fall within the court's responsibility to determine the facts and rule on the merits of the case. But Adams invoked the "political question" doctrine to evade the issue.

Disagreeing with Adams, Chief District Judge Joseph Lord wrote, in his dissenting opinion, that the *Atlee* plaintiffs had "a right to a federal forum to adjudicate their claims on the merits." Lord read Jackson's opinion in *Youngstown* as permitting judicial inquiry in "twilight zone" cases. When another branch of government, executive or legislative, "exceeds its constitutional authority in its actions our system of separation of powers with its checks and balances dictates that a court proceed to the merits of the controversy," Lord observed. Unlike Judge Templar in the *Velvel* case, Lord did not consider the Vietnam War a "limited military action" but, in fact, a full-scale war. "When nations contend with force under the authority of their respective governments with the scope of troop commitment and casualties here," he said, "the conflict must be considered war or the word has lost all meaning." Because the declaration-of-war clause limits presidential power, Lord added, courts can decide "whether the executive branch has exceeded its constitutional power." Writing in dissent, Lord declined to decide whether Nixon had unlawfully committed troops to an undeclared war.

Because the rulings in these Vietnam War cases rejected the standing of individual taxpayers to challenge presidential actions, the judges could evade the constitutional issues they raised. But the lawsuits left unresolved whether members of Congress had standing to mount legal challenges to presidential acts, particularly when Congress had voted to limit or deny the president's power to continue military action in the face of congressional opposition. This issue arose in 1973, after Congress had repealed the Tonkin Gulf Resolution, in December 1970, and after President Nixon had pledged to withdraw troops from Vietnam. Nixon had promised voters in 1968 that he would carry out a "secret plan" to end the war if they put him in the White House. That plan involved preliminary negotiations with North Vietnam, brokered by its major backer, the Soviet Union. Secretary of State Henry Kissinger met secretly with North Vietnam's foreign minister, Le Duc Tho, hammering out the details of a face-saving U.S. withdrawal from Vietnam; the negotiations led to the signing of the Paris Peace Accord, on January 27, 1973.

Before Kissinger and Tho, who later shared the Nobel Peace Prize, concluded their efforts, American forces in Vietnam had been scaled back; by February 1972, only 150,000 troops remained. However, the war had already spilled over the Vietnamese borders into Laos and Cambodia, which had served as sanctuaries for Vietcong and North Vietnamese forces. In the spring of 1970, after a secret bombing campaign from the air, the invasion of Cambodia by

American ground troops provoked an outpouring of protest. Students launched strikes that closed hundreds of high schools and colleges around the country, and the public was shocked when National Guard troops fired on a demonstration at Kent State University, in Ohio, killing four students. Congress responded to the protests, and its own anger at having been left in the dark about the Cambodian invasion, by firing its most potent weapon at President Nixon, the power of the purse. On June 29, 1973, Congress passed legislation that forbid the expenditure of all funds for military actions in Cambodia, Laos, and Vietnam, effective on August 15.

Some members of Congress, however, argued that permitting any further hostilities—even for six weeks—conflicted with earlier resolutions to cease all military operations in Southeast Asia. Representative Robert Drinan, a Massachusetts Democrat who was also a Jesuit priest and former dean of Boston College Law School, filed a suit against Nixon; he was joined by three other members of Congress and a member of the air force. Drinan asked federal judge Joseph L. Tauro to enjoin the president from authorizing any further military action. The suit was largely symbolic, since it was unlikely that Tauro would act before August 15, but it reflected the outrage of many members of Congress over the continued bombing of Cambodia. Retreating to the "political question" doctrine in refusing to issue the injunction Drinan had sought, Judge Tauro wrote, in *Drinan v. Nixon,* that conflicts between Congress and the president over military action in Southeast Asia had not gone "beyond the boundaries of traditional dispute and disagreement, which are the prerogatives of these two independent branches, so as to reach the point of clear and resolute conflict that would warrant judicial intervention." But Tauro also substantially limited the scope of that doctrine. Entering the "twilight zone" of executive and legislative power sharing, he stated that "should it be apparent that the political branches themselves are clearly and resolutely in opposition as to the military policy to be followed by the United States, such a conflict could no longer be regarded as a political question, but would rise to the posture of a serious constitutional issue requiring resolution by the judicial branch."

With the Vietnam War finally winding down in 1973, federal judges began to reassert their independent role as arbiters of constitutional disputes between the executive and legislative branches of government. A turning point came in *Mitchell v. Laird*, a case filed in 1973 by Representative Parren Mitchell, a Maryland Democrat, and twelve other House members. Their complaint, brought against Defense Secretary Laird, President Nixon, and other government officials, alleged that the United States had been engaged for seven years in an unlawful war, without congressional approval. Mitchell and his colleagues sought an injunction to prevent the government from "prosecuting the war in Indochina unless, within 60 days from such order, the Congress shall have explicitly, intentionally and discretely authorized a continuation of the war." After a federal judge in the District of Columbia dismissed their complaint, the plaintiffs filed an appeal with the federal circuit court, which affirmed the lower-court dismissal of the suit. However, Circuit Judge Charles Wyzanski, ruling that presidential authority to continue the war raised a justiciable issue, found no bar in the "political question" doctrine to a court "facing up to the question as to whether because of the war's duration and magnitude the President is or was without power to continue the war without Congressional approval."

Judge Wyzanski brushed aside the argument that Congress had authorized the war by voting to appropriate funds for military action. "This court," he wrote, "cannot be unmindful of what every schoolboy knows: that in voting to appropriate money or draft men a Congressman is not necessarily approving of the continuation of a war no matter how specifically the appropriation or draft act refers to that war. A Congressman wholly opposed to the war's commencement and continuation might vote for the military appropriations and for the draft measures because he was unwilling to abandon without support men already fighting." Yet the constitutional "twilight zone" did not provide adequate light to conclude that Nixon had deliberately acted in defiance of congressional directives to with-draw from Vietnam. Only with evidence of "clear abuse amounting to bad faith" should the courts order the president to cease military actions, and Wyzanski did not find such evidence in the *Mitchell* case.

Finally, just three weeks before the August 15 deadline for ending all military operations in Cambodia, a federal judge issued the first injunction against the government, on July 25, 1973. Representative Elizabeth Holtzman, a New York City Democrat, had voted against the resolution setting the deadline, arguing that even one more day of bombing Cambodia was too much. She filed two suits, one against Defense Secretary Elliot Richardson and the other against his successor, James Schlesinger, seeking orders that would end all ground combat and air missions in Cambodia. District Judge Orrin Judd cited the *Youngstown* decision for support in ruling that "the question of the balance of constitutional authority to declare war, as between the executive and legislative branches, is not a political question." Having cleared this judicial underbrush, Judd boldly marched into the constitutional "twilight zone." Congress, he said, had never authorized the bombing campaign in Cambodia, and had passed leg-islation, on June 26, 1973, cutting off all funds to continue the bom-bardment. Nixon had promptly vetoed this measure, and Congress enacted the August 15 deadline after failing to override his veto by the necessary two-thirds margin in both chambers. Reading into this record an "implied grant of power" to continue the bombing, Judd reasoned, would in effect require the president to muster "a vote of only one-third plus one of either House in order to conduct a war."

Judd issued the injunction against further funding of the Cam-bodian bombing the plaintiffs had sought, but his order never took effect. He postponed its effective date until government lawyers could ask the Second Circuit Court of Appeals for a stay of his order, pending a hearing in the case on August 13. Meanwhile, the American Civil Liberties Union, which represented Holtzman, asked Supreme Court Justice Thurgood Marshall, in his capacity as circuit justice, to vacate the stay. Each justice is assigned to handle emer-gency appeals from one or more circuits, most often in last-minute death penalty cases, and Marshall dealt with those from the Second Circuit, in New York. In a brief order, he denied the ACLU's stay application but also noted his personal view that Nixon had exceeded his authority in bombing Cambodia. Under Supreme Court rules, if a circuit justice denies a stay of a judicial order, any other justice can grant one, pending review by the full Court. The ACLU promptly asked Justice William O. Douglas to reverse Marshall's denial, knowing that Douglas had already made clear his view that the Vietnam War was unlawful from the beginning. Sure enough, Douglas vacated the stay on August 3, only to be overruled by his colleagues the next day. Behind this frantic judicial scrambling lay the Court's reluctance to face head-on the constitutional issues of the Vietnam War. Under the Court's informal but long-standing "rule of four," it takes the votes of four justices to hear an appeal from a lower state or federal court. Douglas had consistently voted to grant review in Vietnam cases but had never been able to garner more than three of the necessary four votes. Justice Marshall sided with Douglas in virtually every civil rights and criminal case, as did Hugo Black and William Brennan, but none of his liberal colleagues joined Douglas in a dissent from the Court's denial of review in the Vietnam cases; surprisingly, only Potter Stewart and John Marshall Harlan, both placed on the Court by Republican presidents, ever voted with Douglas on this issue.

The *Holtzman v. Richardson* case returned to the Second Circuit, which promptly ordered Judge Judd to lift his never-enforced injunction and to dismiss the case. Two members of the three-judge panel, applying the "political question" doctrine, held that a "fair reading" of the record showed that Congress had at least tacitly approved the bombing of Cambodia until the August 15 deadline. The sole dissenter, Judge James Oakes, read the record differently. "I fail to see," he wrote, "where the Congress ever authorized the continuation of the bombing in Cambodia after the cease-fire in Vietnam, the withdrawal of our forces there, and the return of our prisoners of war to our shores."

Although a handful of federal judges finally mustered the courage to enter the constitutional "twilight zone" where Congress and the president confronted each other during the Vietnam War, most of the judges took a hands-off position. And the Supreme Court refused to venture even one step into this murky territory, abdicating its power to apply the Constitution as "the supreme law of the land." The Court's reluctance to grant a hearing in even one of these cases brings to mind the admonition by Chief Justice John Marshall, who wrote, in the seminal case of *Marbury v. Madison* (1803), that "it is emphatically the duty and province of the judicial department to say what the law is." The "law" of the Constitution is clear: Only Congress has the power to "declare war," whether by formal declaration or by an "explicit and intentional" prior authorization to the president for the commitment of forces to actual or imminent hostilities. As we have seen, the Framers made explicit statements that presidents could initiate military action only to repel direct attacks on American soil or to protect American citizens and their property in foreign nations or on the high seas.

But Congress, as we have also seen, abdicated its duty to control the president during the Vietnam War. Only during the last phase of that war, after the Paris Peace Accord had been signed and the troops were coming home, did Congress take a small, tentative step into the "twilight zone," by enacting the War Powers Resolution in 1973. This step turned into a stumble, as the legislative effort to hold presidents accountable to Congress proved largely ineffective. The self-congratulation that members showered on themselves in 1973 for passing the War Powers Resolution is embarrassing to read in retrospect. The measure was badly drafted, replete with loopholes, and has been simply ignored by every president—seven in number, from Richard Nixon to George W. Bush—since its enactment.

Congress labored on the resolution for three years. The House passed the first version, by a vote of 289 to 39, in 1970, stating its recognition that the president "in certain extraordinary and emergency circumstances has the authority to defend the United States and its citizens without specific prior authorization by the Congress." This broad, vague language did not, in fact, go beyond the "reprisal" and "repelling attacks" doctrines of the Framers. Needless to say, lawyers make a living by arguing over words like "extraordinary," "emergency," and "defend." Does the term "defend" apply only to "defensive" military actions, or can it be stretched to cover "offensive" actions that are claimed to "defend" the nation's interests, as defined by the president? The 1970 bill also required the president to consult with Congress "whenever feasible" before engaging in armed conflict. The term "feasible" is a lawyer's dream, with half a dozen dictionary definitions. Presidents were also required to report to Congress on the circumstances that provoked military actions, the legislative or treaty provisions that authorized them, the reasons for not seeking congressional approval before the actions, and estimates of their duration and scope. Significantly, the House provided no penalties for noncompliance with the resolution. This bill was all carrot and no stick.

The Senate took no action on the 1970 House resolution, nor on a similar version the House passed the following year. The measure seemed likely to founder until Democrats, who controlled both chambers of Congress, smelled the blood of a wounded president. In June 1972, five burglars, carrying wiretapping equipment, were caught inside Democratic Party offices in the Watergate complex in Washington. One of the burglars worked as security officer for the Nixon reelection committee; another had an address book with the name of the assistant to Nixon's special counsel. Although a White House spokesman dismissed the break-in as a "third-rate" burglary, the prospect of jail time prompted one of the burglars to finger the White House officials who had sent them on their ill-fated spying mission. The trail led to the Oval Office, where Nixon had secretly recorded conversations and telephone calls implicating him in efforts to pay the burglars for perjured testimony. Watergate became a first-rate scandal, leading to televised Senate hearings, Nixon's being named by a grand jury as an "unindicted co-conspirator" with his indicted top aides, and more than a dozen House resolutions calling for his impeachment.

In the midst of this political storm, the War Powers Resolution sailed through Congress in 1973 with hardly a ripple of dissent. But even with Nixon sinking rapidly in public support, Congress passed up the chance to snatch away his ability to launch another Cambodian invasion. Its members were mindful that refusing to provide future presidents with a military life preserver for real emergencies might endanger American lives and the nation's security. In any event, the War Powers Resolution was superfluous, because presidents had always possessed the right to respond to such emergencies with defensive measures. In truth, most members of Congress recognized that presidents from Franklin Roosevelt to Richard Nixon had exercised the war-making power with little regard for Congress, and without significant protest from that body. Passing a bill that placed minimal constraints on presidents was unlikely to alter the "subtle shifts" in "the centers of real power" about which Justice Jackson had spoken in his *Youngstown* opinion. Despite Nixon's weakening grasp on his office, Congress was no longer a "real power" in controlling American foreign policy or military actions.

The drafters of the War Powers Resolution stated, in the preamble, that "it is the purpose of this resolution to fulfill the intent of the Framers." But the Framers of 1787, who fully expected the first president to be the former commander in chief of the Continental Army, did not intend to give George Washington the authority to send forces into combat without prior congressional approval, even for a period of sixty or ninety days. The resolution's requirement that the president "consult" with Congress "in every possible instance" before taking military action leaves the nature of the consultation up to the White House. Obviously, presidents cannot "consult" with every member of Congress, but there are dozens of members of the House and Senate committees on foreign relations, military affairs, and intelligence, as well as the majority and minority leaders of each chamber. The resolution does not specify which members should be consulted and what information they should receive.

The resolution also directs the president to "report" to Congress when troops are dispatched "into hostilities or into situations where imminent involvement in hostilities is clearly indicated by the circumstances." Again, the timing and nature of the reports, and to which members or committees they should be submitted, are undefined. A central provision of the resolution, supposedly the most stringent constraint on unilateral presidential war making, is the time limit on military action without explicit congressional approval. Whenever the president orders troops into "hostilities," they must be withdrawn within sixty days unless Congress approves the action before that time expires, although the deadline may be extended for another thirty days if the president determines that extra time is needed to "protect and remove" the troops from zones of active "hostilities." But because the sixty- to ninety-day clock does not start ticking until the president submits the "report" to Congress, the timepiece has rarely started ticking. In fact, the clock's hands have moved just once, after Gerald Ford reported to Congress in May 1975 about the rescue of the U.S. merchant ship *Mayagüez*, and its crew, from capture by Cambodian forces. By the time his report reached Congress, the military action was over and the sixty-day deadline for withdrawing troops was never reached.

The *Mayagüez* incident, in which forty-one U.S. troops were killed in the rescue of thirty-nine crew members, provides an early illustration of the inherent weakness of the War Powers Resolution. Although President Ford reported the military action to Congress, neither the document he provided nor the rescue mission itself relied for authorization on the resolution; he claimed, instead, to have ordered the operation "pursuant to the President's constitutional Executive power and his authority as Commander-in-Chief of the United States Armed Forces." Indeed, Ford's statement echoed the "inherent" executive powers argument the Supreme Court had emphatically rejected in the *Youngstown* case in 1952. The president's executive powers, of course, are limited by the Constitution to his duty to "take care that the laws be faithfully executed." In the *Mayagüez* incident, Ford did not "faithfully" execute the law, expressed in the War Powers Resolution, requiring him to "consult" with Congress before dispatching troops into the hostilities that ended up costing more lives than were saved by the ill-fated operation. Whether such consultation—perhaps exposing Ford to advice that he pursue diplomatic avenues for releasing the captured crew members—would have stayed his hand is a matter of conjecture. But certainly he failed to follow the course set out in the War Powers Resolution, and consequently neglected to perform his constitutional duties.

Gerald Ford became the first president, but not the last, to evade or ignore the consultation and reporting provisions of the War Powers Resolution. A full review of the military actions that followed the *Mayagüez* incident would unduly expand this chapter, but a brief discussion of the most significant episodes underscores the pattern of White House disregard for the measure's provisions.

President Jimmy Carter, who succeeded Ford in 1977, faced a crisis near the end of his single term in office. In November 1979, Iranian militants broke through the gates of the U.S. embassy in Tehran and took more than fifty Americans hostage, holding them in captivity for more than a year. Efforts to obtain their release through diplomatic channels failed, and Carter responded to growing criticism of his inability to resolve the hostage crisis peacefully by secretly ordering a rescue mission. He dispatched eight helicopters to a remote area near Tehran, given the code name of Desert One, to await orders to swoop into the embassy and rescue the hostages. The Desert One operation became a military disaster. After two helicopters malfunctioned and never reached the staging area, and a third broke down with hydraulic problems, Carter ordered the mission canceled. On their return to U.S. vessels, one helicopter collided with a supporting cargo plane, killing eight troops.

President Carter's compliance with the War Powers Resolution was minimal. He "consulted" with just one member of Congress, Senate Majority Leader Robert Byrd of West Virginia, only hours before launching the abortive mission. Carter discussed with Byrd various options to secure the hostages' release but did not disclose the imminent rescue operation. Reflecting on the Desert One debacle in his memoirs, Carter regretted his failure to inform Byrd of his plans: "His advice would have been valuable to me then—and also twenty-four hours later." Carter also rejected the advice of his secretary of state, Cyrus Vance, who had urged him to continue diplomatic efforts to release the hostages. Vance, who learned of the mission only after it had failed, was so outraged at having been kept in the dark that he resigned in protest. Carter followed Ford in submitting a report to Congress that relied on his "executive powers" and his role as commander in chief.

The loss of American lives in the *Mayagüez* and Desert One rescue missions paled in comparison with the deaths of U.S. marines in Lebanon, during the administration of Ronald Reagan. On the night of October 23, 1983, a truck loaded with explosives rammed into the marine compound in Beirut, killing 241 troops who were sleeping in their barracks. The public shock over the terrorist attack was followed by congressional demands that Reagan withdraw troops in Lebanon, which he did in the spring of 1984. Supposedly the troops had been sent to Lebanon to protect U.S. lives and property during the civil war between pro-Western forces and insurgent groups funded by the Syrian government. In reality, the conflict in Lebanon was an extension of the long-standing battle between Israel and the Arab states over demands for Palestinian autonomy. American support for Israel had fueled resentment among the Lebanese, who sided with the Palestinians.

Reagan, who had dispatched the marines to Lebanon without reporting to Congress under the War Powers Resolution, later explained—in language borrowed from Ford—that he acted pursuant to his "constitutional authority with respect to the conduct of foreign relations and as Commander-in-Chief of the United States Armed Forces." Because Reagan's failure to submit a formal report on the Lebanese deployment avoided the sixty-day deadline under the resolution for withdrawing the troops, Congress responded with legislation that started the clock ticking on August 29, 1983. But Congress also extended the deadline to eighteen months. Although he praised Congress for its "cooperation" in giving him more time, Reagan stated his view that in setting time limits for the deployment of troops, of whatever duration, Congress had encroached on his powers as commander in chief. What might have happened, in Congress or the courts, if the Lebanon deadline had passed without troop withdrawal can only be conjectured. But the deadly episode showed that Congress was more than willing to overlook the president's evasion of the War Power Resolution's reporting provisions.

What is more, Reagan initiated another military action that was begun without any consultation with Congress. On October 25, 1983, just two days after the marine barracks in Beirut was blown up, American troops invaded the tiny Caribbean nation of Grenada. Unlike Lebanon, located in a region of strategic importance to Washington's political and economic interests, Grenada was a poor country that produced nothing of value to the United States. But it did have an insurgent movement with ideological ties to Cuba. After rebel forces killed Prime Minister Maurice Bishop and took control of the Grenadian government, Reagan sent 1,900 army and Marine Corps troops into Grenada, where they quickly subdued the rebels and restored the pro-American government. By any standards, the Grenada operation was a snap, almost as easy as invading Martha's Vineyard. Although the ostensible purpose was to protect the lives of some one thousand American residents and tourists, Reagan claimed that Grenada was "a Soviet-Cuban colony, being readied as a major military bastion to export terror and undermine democracy" in the Caribbean, a classic in presidential hyperbole. His report to Congress dusted off the statement that he acted under his powers "with respect to the conduct of foreign relations and as Commander-in-Chief of the United States Armed Forces." This time, the House responded with legislation that started the sixty-day clock, with an additional thirty days to remove the troops. Before the Senate could act, however, Reagan announced that all troops would be withdrawn by December 23, averting another possible confrontation over the War Powers Resolution.

Ousting the rebel government in Grenada took only a few days in 1983 and a relative handful of American troops. Ousting the regime of General Manuel Noriega in Panama took about a month in 1989 and some eleven thousand troops, who joined thirteen thousand already serving in the Canal Zone. President George H. W. Bush, who succeeded Reagan in 1989, justified this military intervention—dubbed Operation Just Cause by the Pentagon—on three grounds. First, Bush claimed that sporadic assaults on American citizens in Panama by pro-Noriega forces created an "imminent danger" to their safety. Second, the United States acted to restore the elected government of President Guillermo Endara, whom Noreiga had removed from office. And third, Noriega had protected, and profited from, drug cartels that shipped vast quantities of cocaine from Panama into the United States. Noriega had been indicted by a federal grand jury in Florida, and Bush sought to bring him "to justice in the United States."

Noriega's forces quickly melted into the population, and he surrendered to American authorities on January 3, 1990. Flown in chains to Florida, he was tried and convicted on numerous drug charges and sentenced to a long term in federal prison. President Bush won plaudits for removing a thug in uniform; the House passed a resolution praising him for having acted "decisively" in Panama. But this popular intervention raised doubts about setting a precedent for future military campaigns to depose "evil" regimes and their leaders. In the resolution commending Bush, the House emphasized its commitment to "the principle of non-intervention in the internal affairs of other countries." The president had not claimed that Noriega's regime posed any military threat to the United States, and the thirteen thousand troops stationed in the Canal Zone had ample force to protect American citizens in Panama. The actual reasons for deposing Noriega were his protection of drug dealers, and his anti-American rhetoric, neither of which—however deplorable or disturbing—provided grounds for sending troops to arrest him. The State Department's legal adviser at the time, Abraham Sofaer, later stated that the United States "does not accept the notion that a state is entitled to use force to overthrow the dictator of another state." Those words, of course, apply equally to overthrowing a dictator in Panama in 1989 and doing so in Iraq in 2003. Stripping away the false claims that Saddam Hussein's regime possessed "weapons of mass destruction" and collaborated with al Queda terrorists reveals that the second President Bush offered no more justification for deposing Hussein than his father had provided for deposing Noriega.

From its enactment by Congress in 1973 until the Panama operation in 1989, the War Powers Resolution failed to curb the unilateral military actions of four presidents, from Gerald Ford through George H. W. Bush. The rapid growth of the imperial presidency following the Allied victory in World War II, along with the vast expansion of American corporate interests into every corner of the non-Communist world, was accompanied by the establishment of a global network of military bases. From these bases, and from those in the United States, troops could be dispatched anywhere America's "vital" security interests—as defined by the president—were threatened by insurgencies, by political unrest, or simply by foreign leaders whose policies raised the president's ire. Undeterred by the toothless War Powers Resolution, presidents ordered military actions that constituted acts of war, relying for authority on claims of "inherent" powers that federal judges proved unwilling to challenge. As Justice Jackson had predicted in his *Youngstown* opinion, the "real center" of power over war making had shifted from Congress to the White House. Fifty years after the Japanese attack on Pearl Harbor, the United States launched the greatest military assault on another country since that "day of infamy." As we shall see, the Gulf War of 1991, and the invasions of Afghanistan in 2001 and Iraq in 2003, were funded by the same blank checks that Congress had handed out to a parade of chief executives, who cashed them in a dozen countries into which U.S. troops marched with imperial force.

11

"WE WERE GOING TO WAR":

From the Gulf War to Afghanistan

Vietnam had left a bad taste in the mouths of the American public—one that lingered after the last troops departed from that devastated country in 1975. But over the next fifteen years, the sudden collapse of the Soviet Union and the American "victories" in Grenada and Panama emboldened the advocates of the "new world order" that would, in reality, be imposed according to American orders. The end of the Cold War left the United States as the "Number One Nation" in both military and economic power, eager to flex its muscles and push any weakling countries into the sand. And the sands of the Middle East, which covered the vast oil deposits upon which the United States depended for its factories, homes, and gas-guzzling cars, became the next target of America's imperial planners.

It is not simply hyperbole to suggest that President George H. W. Bush launched the Gulf War in 1991 to restore his sagging political fortunes, in addition to his determination to secure access to Middle Eastern oil. Less than two years after he took office, in January 1989, Bush had dropped substantially in public support, along with the Dow Jones average. Going to war has always given a boost to a

president's stock, and Bush found a ready target for military intervention in the Middle East. The United States had supported Saddam
Hussein's rise to power in Iraq, but his invasion of neighboring
Kuwait, on August 2, 1990, threatened the region's stability. More
important, the Iraqi thrust into Kuwait struck terror in the royal
dynasty in Saudi Arabia, whose oil reserves dwarfed those of any
other nation. The Saudi regime had close ties to President Bush, himself an oil millionaire. In fact, Saudi officials and royal family members had pumped millions of dollars into Bush's presidential
campaign, in return for the billions of dollars the U.S. government
had provided in military and economic aid.

The United States had remained silent when the Iraqis crushed an
incipient rebellion by the Kurdish minority in the country's northern
region, killing thousands of Kurds with poison gas and reducing
hundreds of villages to rubble. But the brutal repression of the Kurds
did not threaten American access to Iraq's oil fields. The invasion of
Kuwait, however, did threaten access to oil supplies in that country
and in Saudi Arabia. The fact that Hussein both looked and acted
like a power-mad dictator helped to build the case for coming to the
aid of Kuwait, whose government was hardly a model of democracy.

Two articles in the *Washington Post* illustrate the political factors
that pushed the Bush administration to expel the Iraqis from Kuwait.
On October 16, 1990, a front-page story was headed: "Poll Shows
Plunge in Public Confidence: Bush's Rating Plummets." A dozen days
later, the *Post* reported: "Some observers in his own party worry that
the president will be forced to initiate combat to prevent further ero-
sion of his support at home." Although the decision to force the Iraqis
out of Kuwait was made on October 30, shortly before the Democrats
gained seats in the midterm congressional elections, the electoral setback for the Republicans sealed the plan. Bush began by doubling the
military force in the Gulf region, to some 500,000 troops. Elizabeth
Drew, an experienced Washington reporter for the *New Yorker*,
wrote that Bush's top strategist, John Sununu, "was telling people
that a short successful war would be pure political gold for the
President and would guarantee his re-election" in 1992.

The United Nations had imposed economic sanctions against Iraq on August 7, five days after the invasion of Kuwait, but there was no way to measure their effectiveness before the Security Council responded to American pressure, on November 29, 1990, by adopting a resolution that "authorized" member states to use "all necessary means" to secure Iraq's compliance with prior UN demands that it withdraw from Kuwait. President Bush cited the UN resolution in justifying the deployment of U.S. troops to the Gulf region, but he failed to comply with the provisions of the War Powers Resolution. Senate majority leader George Mitchell and House Speaker Tom Foley, both Democrats, had selected a bipartisan group of lawmakers as a "consultation" committee to meet with the president. Although Bush met with the group on October 30, he did not inform its members of his deployment of additional troops to the Gulf or his decision to engage the Iraqis in combat whenever he decided to issue the orders. Thus the "consultation" was a sham: Bush pretended to listen, but his mind was already made up to begin the Gulf War.

In January 1991, with polls showing the public closely divided on military intervention in Kuwait, members of Congress debated the president's request for authorization to commit troops to combat. Largely split along party lines, Congress reflected the public mood in narrowly passing the Authorization for Use of Military Force Against Iraq Resolution. The House approved the measure by a vote of 250 to 183, and the Senate by the closer vote of 52 to 47. With this blank check in his pocket, Bush sent the "go" order to military commanders on January 15, launching operation Desert Storm with a ferocious aerial bombardment of the Iraqi capital, Baghdad. Captivated by televised scenes of laser-guided "smart bombs" hitting their targets with sniperlike precision, the public shifted from close division over the war to flag-waving support, with polls showing almost 85 percent approval of Bush's decision to force the Iraqis from Kuwait. Later reports indicated that perhaps 40 percent of the "smart bombs" missed their targets, many of them hitting Iraqi homes and hospitals. The Pentagon—refusing to release videos of the damage inflicted by thousands of conventional munitions dropped from B-52 bombers,

which inflicted thousands of civilian casualties—claimed to be uncon-
cerned about the number of Iraqis injured or killed by American bombs.
"To tell you the truth, we're really not focusing on this question," a
senior official told the *Boston Globe*.

Combat operations in the Gulf War ended on February 28, 1991,
with Hussein still in power. In fact, the war had been designed to
weaken his grip on Iraq, not to depose him. U.S. officials wanted to
retain Iraq as a counterweight to Iran, whose government was controlled by stridently anti-American Islamic fundamentalists. The
Bush administration, refusing to support the Kurdish rebellion against
Iraqi repression, feared that autonomy or independence for the
Kurds might encourage other anti-Hussein groups in Iraq to revolt,
endangering the flow of oil from Iraq and upsetting the delicate balance of power in the Middle East. As the *New York Times* reported
on March 26, "President Bush has decided to let President Saddam
Hussein put down rebellions in his country without American intervention rather than risk the splintering of Iraq, according to official
statements and private briefings today."

Despite his decision to let Hussein off the hook, Bush declared
Operation Desert Storm a great success. "The specter of Vietnam has
been buried forever in the desert sands of the Arabian peninsula," he
boasted. But secure in the knowledge that neither Congress nor
the courts would likely impose sanctions for their unilateral actions,
none of the presidents who succeeded Nixon were deterred, by the
defeat in Vietnam, from attacking other Third World countries.

Unlike the Vietnam War, which provoked more than a dozen lawsuits challenging the constitutionality of both congressional and
presidential actions, the Gulf War produced only one significant
judicial test of Bush's decision to commit troops to combat. On
November 20, 1990, Representative Ronald Dellums, a California
Democrat, joined by fifty-three other Democratic House members,
filed a suit against Bush in the federal district court in Washington.
Dellums and his colleagues sought an injunction to block the president from initiating any offensive military operations in the Gulf

unless he first obtained authorization from Congress. The complaint in *Dellums v. Bush* was based on the Constitution's delegation of war powers to Congress; it did not rely on the War Powers Resolution. On December 13, Judge Harold H. Greene denied the injunctive relief that Dellums had requested, holding that the suit was not "ripe" for judicial decision because the president had not issued any orders that would place troops in combat. The "ripeness" doctrine can be invoked by judges when defendants have not yet taken any allegedly unlawful steps, even if plaintiffs claim they are preparing to do so. This judge-made doctrine stems from the long-standing federal practice of avoiding what are called "advisory" opinions. Some state courts—Massachusetts is one example—do issue opinions as to whether a law or action meets state constitutional standards, generally at the request of the legislature, governor, or attorney general. Early in its history, however, the Supreme Court declared that federal judges could rule only on suits that presented a real and current "case or controversy."

Although he dismissed the *Dellums* case on ripeness grounds, Judge Greene stepped into the "twilight zone" between Congress and the president, rejecting the government's claim of "inherent" powers over military actions. Greene noted that if the president "had the sole power to determine that any particular offensive military operation, no matter how vast, does not constitute war-making but only an offensive military attack, the congressional power to declare war will be at the mercy of a semantic decision by the Executive. Such an 'interpretation' would evade the plain language of the Constitution, and it cannot stand." Nevertheless, the president's decision to launch Operation Desert Storm, secretly made six weeks before Judge Greene's decision and carried out four weeks after it, did stand.

Apparently Bush read the "plain language" of the Constitution very differently from Judge Greene. When he signed the congressional resolution authorizing military action against Iraq, Bush made this statement: "As I made clear to congressional leaders at the outset, my request for congressional support did not, and my signing this resolution does not, constitute any change in the long-standing positions of the executive branch on either the President's constitutional authority to use the Armed Forces to defend vital U.S. interests or the constitutionality of the War Powers Resolution." Like every president since the resolution became law, Bush disputed its constitutionality as infringing on his "inherent" powers. He later made his position clear in a speech at Princeton University: "Though I felt after studying the question that I had the inherent power to commit our forces to battle after the U.N. resolution, I solicited congressional support before committing our forces to the Gulf War." However weak the "consultation" provision in the War Powers Resolution had proved, at least it imposed a duty on the president that could not be met by "soliciting" congressional support without disclosing his military plans or decisions. With his political back to the wall in the 1992 presidential campaign, as he was slipping behind Bill Clinton in the polls, Bush took a defiant stance toward Congress. Some of his critics asked why his domestic programs lacked the congressional support he enjoyed for the Gulf War, Bush told voters in Texas. "I didn't have to get permission from some old goat in the United States Congress to kick Saddam Hussein out of Kuwait," he said. "That's the reason."

Bush's rhetorical bluster did not save his reelection bid; the "pure political gold" that John Sununu had predicted as the payoff for the Gulf War turned into tarnished brass. Bill Clinton overcame charges of draft dodging during the Vietnam War by assuring voters that he possessed the toughness to act as commander in chief of an armed forces in which he had never served. Taking office in January 1993, Clinton flexed his muscles, beginning with air strikes against Iraq on June 26. He told the public the launching of twenty-three Tomahawk missiles, aimed at the command-and-control facilities of the Iraqi intelligence service in Baghdad, was retaliation for a planned but never consummated plot to assassinate former president Bush during a postwar visit to Kuwait (three of the Tomahawks missed their targets and killed eight civilians in the surrounding area). Before ordering the attack, Clinton failed to consult any members of Congress; he defended his action as an "exercise of our inherent right of self-defense" and as "pursuant to my constitutional authority with respect to the conduct of foreign policy and as Commander in Chief." With these words, Clinton echoed those of the four presidents who preceded him: Ford, Carter, Reagan, and Bush had all claimed the "inherent" right to initiate military action without prior congressional approval.

After the bombing of Baghdad, Clinton ordered troops into ground combat and aerial strikes in several military operations on three continents, in such widely scattered countries as Somalia, Haiti, and Bosnia. The incursions were all purportedly carried out under United Nations auspices, to enforce UN resolutions and to provide "peacekeeping" services. In each case, Clinton failed to comply with the War Powers Resolution; he claimed that he was acting according to his powers as commander in chief, not as a result of congressional approval. His assertions, in fact, provoked a response in the Senate, in 1994, to Clinton's plan to invade Haiti, during the effort to restore its deposed president, Jean-Bertrand Aristide. The UN Security Council had "invited" its members to use "all necessary means" to remove the military warlords who had ousted Aristide. In the resolution the Senate passed, by a unanimous vote of its one hundred members, the chamber stated that the UN measure "does not constitute authorization for the deployment of United States Armed Forces in Haiti under the Constitution of the United States or pursuant to the War Powers Resolution." Clinton told a press conference that he did not need congressional approval to invade Haiti. "Like my predecessors of both parties," he said, "I have not agreed that I was constitutionally mandated" to secure that approval.

Later, Clinton expanded on this statement in responding to questions as to whether he would veto legislation that would force him to secure consent from Congress before taking military action in Haiti and Bosnia. "All I can tell you," he said, "is that I think I have a big responsibility to try to appropriately consult with members of

Congress in both parties, whenever we are in the process of making a decision which might lead to the use of force. I believe that. But I think that, clearly, the Constitution leaves the President, for good and sufficient reasons, the ultimate decision-making authority." He added that "I think it's a mistake to cut those decisions off in advance," and that he was "fundamentally opposed" to legislation that would "improperly limit my ability to perform my constitutional duties as Commander-in-Chief, which may well have unconstitutional provisions." What Clinton did not explain was why or how the exercise of congressional authority over the nation's war-making power might be unconstitutional. As commander in chief, he had the duty to "faithfully" execute the laws enacted by Congress, including those barring or limiting the use of force. If Congress had prohibited Clinton from sending troops to Somalia or Haiti, or bombing targets in Iraq or Bosnia, he could not have defied such legislation without himself violating the Constitution. Congress did not, however, take such drastic steps, leaving Clinton free to send the troops and bomb the targets. Assuming the mantle of the imperial presidency from his predecessors, Clinton proved just as willing as they had been to exercise the "ultimate decision-making power" that Congress had ceded to him.

Presidents inherit the leftover problems that their predecessors fail to resolve, or the tasks that simply require more time or resources to be completed. Franklin D. Roosevelt, for instance, had to deal with the crushing burden of lifting the American people from the economic collapse of the Great Depression, which began during the term of Herbert Hoover. Just a few months after Roosevelt's sudden death thrust him into the presidency, Harry Truman learned about the development of nuclear weapons and made the decision to drop atomic bombs on two Japanese cities. More recently, Bill Clinton inherited from the administration of George H. W. Bush the challenge that has since become the all-consuming issue in both global and domestic politics: international terrorism. The war on terror, which has crossed almost every country's boundaries, is waged against forces that wear no uniforms, swear allegiance to no government, and pay no heed to the "rules of war" that most nations accept, even if they are often broken.

Terrorism, of course, is hardly a new phenomenon. Acts designed to make ordinary people afraid to go about their daily routines of work, travel, and family life have been carried out for centuries. Since the middle of the twentieth century, terrorist groups on both the right and the left have waged campaigns to promote national liberation or destroy capitalism and Communism alike. In the 1960s and 1970s, for example, the Baader-Meinhof Gang in Germany, the Red Brigades in Japan, and the Weather Underground in the United States employed terrorism on behalf of their causes. Some groups, such as the Irish Republican Army, were organized on military lines, with commanders, officers, and troops, and attacked the police and military forces of the "illegitimate" government against which they battled. But the IRA and similar quasi-military groups also used terrorist tactics against civilians, placing bombs on buses and in restaurants and killing suspected or actual collaborators with the enemy. As we have learned in recent years, terrorism is difficult, often impossible, to detect or deter, before a bomb explodes in a crowded marketplace or subway. Because they do not wear uniforms, terrorists can look like anyone, even a pregnant woman or a child. And because their weapons can be strapped around a waist or carried in a shopping bag, only the most stringent and intrusive security measures—employed today with greatest zeal in Israel—can identify a terrorist before the bomb explodes. What makes the security job even harder is that more terrorists are willing to die, along with their victims, as suicide bombers. In short, terrorist attacks can occur virtually anywhere, at any time, and be carried out by any person, of any age, gender, or nationality.

And as we have also learned, governments can and often do employ terrorist methods against their enemies, although no president or prime minister would use that term to describe acts that are normally denied. Despite its formal commitment to the rule of law, the United States had frequently violated its own statutes, and international law as well; for example, the CIA was involved in the

assassination of hundreds—perhaps thousands—of Vietnamese civilians suspected of Vietcong ties. Among the tradecraft of CIA covert
agents were such tools as exploding pens, poisoned drinks, and sab-
otaged airplanes. Thus terrorism has never been the exclusive tactic
of political and religious zealots; government agencies from the CIA
to the Soviet KGB have used various forms of terrorism against their
enemies.

The issue of terrorism that Bill Clinton inherited from George H. W.
Bush had its deepest roots in the Middle East, a region with a long
history of tribal conflict, national rivalries, and religious divisions.
During the first half of the twentieth century, Western nations com-
peted for control of the vast oil reserves in Saudi Arabia and surrounding countries, with the British having the upper hand. The
British also controlled Palestine, which had no oil but had fertile soil
and Mediterranean seaports. With growing demands by the interna-
tional Zionist movement for a Jewish homeland in areas occupied by
Muslim Palestinians, Palestine became a serious problem for the
British. The establishment of Israel as a Jewish state in 1948, under
UN auspices and with quick American recognition, sparked a brief
war in which Israeli forces decisively routed those of surrounding
Arab states, followed by the expulsion from Israel of more than a
million Palestinians, most of whom settled in neighboring Jordan.
Many others moved into dusty, crowded refugee camps in the Gaza
Strip, funded and administered by UN agencies. The anger of many
Palestinians over their forced exile from their ancestral land led to a
resistance movement that spawned a multitude of loosely coordinated
terrorist groups.

There is no real dispute that the Israeli-Palestinian conflict lies
at the core of the terrorist threat that dominates global politics.
Palestinian militants and their sympathizers in Muslim communities
around the world deeply resent what they see as uncritical American
support, both political and military, for Israel. The United States has
poured billions of dollars into the Israeli Defense Forces, supplying
most of the army's hardware. Despite the efforts of President Jimmy

Carter and his successors to push—or, more accurately, to nudge—the Israeli government into recognizing an independent Palestinian state, the majority of Muslims view these efforts as hollow and hypocritical. Only a small minority of Muslims, however, has joined or actively supported the terrorist campaign against the United States, both abroad and in the American homeland. But terrorist groups do not need large numbers of committed members to plan and carry out their attacks; small cells are actually more effective and more resistant to infiltration and detection.

Although the Palestinian issue has become the lightning rod for Muslim radicals, the Islamic fundamentalist movement developed in Muslim countries such as Egypt and Saudi Arabia, whose pro-Western governments were seen as puppets of the United States. The assassination in 1970 of Egypt's president Gamal Abdel Nasser came at the hands of Muslim extremists who advocated a pure Islamic state based on their interpretation of the Koran, which requires the strict application of religious law, known as Sharia. The bombing of the World Trade Center in 1993, in fact, was carried out by followers of an Egyptian fundamentalist leader and Muslim cleric, Sheik Omar Abdul Rahman, who denounced any assimilation of Western modernism by the Arab states.

During the early 1990s, a new terrorist group emerged from the outer fringes of Muslim extremism. Known as al Qaeda, Arabic for "the base," this group was headed by a Saudi exile, Osama bin Laden, whose family owned one of the largest construction firms in Saudi Arabia and had close ties with the Saudi government. Bin Laden had become the black sheep of his family, after he fell under the sway of the most virulent of the anti-American mullahs, the Muslim clerics who denounced the "great Satan" of the United States for supporting Israel and leading the new "crusade" against Islam. As the leader of a terrorist group, bin Laden had several advantages. His family upbringing had exposed him to Western culture, which he understood but also despised as weak, self-centered, and corrupt. Through his wealthy family and its contacts, he knew a great deal about finance, how to raise money and channel it through respectable charitable groups into the coffers of al Qaeda. Bin Laden also understood that conducting a successful terrorist operation required meticulous planning and great patience. Targets might be selected, and teams prepared to attack them, months or even years before the plan was executed. Bin Laden had carefully selected a cadre of lieutenants with skills in communications, finance, munitions, and engineering. His operatives had access to cell phones, computers, credit cards, and "safe houses" around the world. In reality, al Qaeda rivaled in resources and sophistication the Operations Directorate of the CIA, which carried out covert operations that utilized the tactics and tools of terrorist groups.

Both in conventional and unconventional warfare, successful operations depend on the element of surprise. Not only surprise but shock followed the devastating bombings in 1998 of the American embassies in Kenya and Tanzania, which killed more than two hundred people. These attacks had all the earmarks of an al Qaeda operation, and President Clinton responded by ordering the U.S. military to fire sixty-six cruise missiles into suspected al Qaeda training camps in Afghanistan, where intelligence officials believed that bin Laden was meeting with his lieutenants. He proved an elusive target, however, and the missile attack did little damage to his camps. The CIA had been pursuing bin Laden since 1996, after the agency's director, George Tenet, decided that al Qaeda posed a major terrorist threat to the United States, particularly to American facilities and citizens in foreign countries. But the craggy mountains and deep valleys in the Afghan regions on the Pakistan border gave bin Laden shelter, and his frequent and sudden moves, often at night, made him hard to track and harder to grab. CIA officials were frustrated that, following revelations about the summary executions of suspected Vietcong sympathizers during the Vietnam War, President Gerald Ford had signed an order banning American involvement in assassinations. Tenet rebuffed proposals to ambush and kill bin Laden because doing so would violate the law. All that CIA agents could do was try to seize him and turn him over to law enforcement officials;

if bin Laden resisted and was killed, so much the better. But every plan to grab the terrorist leader failed.

How the world might look today if a cruise missile had blown up bin Laden, or if a U.S. Special Forces team had snatched him, is impossible to say. But the world looks much different today from what it did on the morning of September 11, 2001. On that bright, sunny day, two hijacked domestic airliners smashed into the north and south towers of the World Trade Center, in lower Manhattan. A third hijacked plane crashed into the west wing of the Pentagon, just across the Potomac River from the nation's capital. A fourth plane, whose intended target was either the White House or the Capitol building, plunged into a field in Pennsylvania after heroic passengers tried but failed to overcome the hijackers. Everyone on the hijacked planes died in the crashes, along with 2,602 people in the twin towers of the trade center, and 126 more in the Pentagon. The death toll from those carefully coordinated terrorist attacks exceeded that of the most deadly previous surprise assault on American soil, the Japanese bombing of Pearl Harbor, on December 7, 1941.

The event that is now known simply as "9/11" stunned the American people, and the entire world as well. President George W. Bush was visiting a second-grade class in Sarasota, Florida, when his chief of staff, Andrew Card, whispered the news of the World Trade Center attack into his ear. Bush later recalled his first reaction to this shocking report of the terrorist assault: "They had declared war on us, and I made up my mind at that moment that we were going to war." At 9:30 A.M., the president faced a bank of television cameras in the school's media center and made a brief statement. Describing what he called "an apparent terrorist attack" on the World Trade Center, Bush promised that the government would use every resource at its command to track down and locate "those folks who committed this act," adding that "terrorism against our nation will not stand."

Bush left no doubt that America was "going to war" against the terrorists who carried out the assault on the World Trade Center and the Pentagon. Almost immediately, he and his advisers began to explore the military options for a strike against al Qaeda forces in

Afghanistan, where Osama bin Laden had been given sanctuary by the country's Taliban government, led by Muslim fundamentalists who had imposed a rigid Islamic regime. The Taliban had come to power in 1996 after a long and bloody struggle to oust the Soviet troops that had occupied the country since 1979. The high-level strategy sessions in the White House proceeded with the clear understanding that any military response to the 9/11 attacks would not only target al Qaeda strongholds but would attempt to dislodge and replace the Taliban, as payback for its role in harboring bin Laden.

The American response in Afghanistan—whether from the air, on the ground, or both—would certainly, as Bush had said, take the United States into war. Ten years earlier, when Bush's father initiated the Gulf War against Iraq, the president first met with congressional leaders and secured their support for the Authorization for Use of Military Force Against Iraq Resolution, which was adopted by narrow votes in both the House and the Senate. But that was a war against another nation, limited to a specific region, with an end date in mind, the date on which the last Iraqi forces withdrew from Kuwait. In contrast, the war on terror planned by the Bush administration, although directed initially against al Qaeda bases in Afghanistan and the Taliban regime, was conceived, from the beginning, as worldwide in scope and indefinite in duration. In the minds of its planners, this war would not end until every terrorist group that had attacked Americans in the past, up to and including the 9/11 assaults, or might launch attacks in the future, had been destroyed. In this regard, the war on terror might last for years or even decades, or even become a perpetual war, given the deep-rooted hostility toward the United States, not only on the part of Muslim fundamentalists like Osama bin Laden but among other groups that resented American domination of the world economy and political system. So long as the American empire remained intact, then, the war on terror would continue.

The 9/11 attacks created abrupt, far-reaching changes in the nation's political and military situation—changes that would, in turn, raise significant constitutional issues. Not since 1941 had

Congress exercised its constitutional power to declare war on another country. From Korea in 1950 through the Gulf War in 1991, Congress had allowed presidents—sometimes eagerly and sometimes with grave reservations—to commit forces on the basis of resolutions that constituted functional declarations of war. Rather than limiting the president's war-making powers, as its sponsors intended, the War Powers Resolution of 1973 actually expanded them by failing to include any enforcement provisions. As we have observed, presidents could—and most often did—ignore the resolution's consultation and reporting provisions, or comply in the most perfunctory manner.

The day after the 9/11 attacks, President Bush met with congressional leaders, telling them of his decision to retaliate against al Qaeda in Afghanistan but also advising them that the broader war on terror would continue indefinitely. The Senate's majority leader, Tom Daschle, a South Dakota Democrat, pledged bipartisan support for Bush's decision. As the president was preparing a nationally televised address to Congress and the public, Daschle urged him to choose his words carefully. "War is a powerful word," Daschle said. Senator Robert Byrd, the eighty-three-year-old West Virginia Democrat who had dealt with ten presidents, bluntly told Bush that he could easily obtain a supporting resolution from Congress but would not receive the blank check that President Johnson had been given in the 1964 Tonkin Gulf Resolution. Despite this warning from the Senate's patriarch, Bush sent Congress a proposed resolution that would have authorized him to use all "necessary" military force "to deter and pre-empt any future acts of terrorism or aggression against the United States." Disturbed by the sweeping language, congressional negotiators finally persuaded the president to accept a resolution that limited him to retaliating only against those nations, organizations, or persons responsible for the 9/11 attacks. Bush signed the congressional resolution into law on September 18, 2001, just seven days after the attacks.

Less than three weeks later, on October 7, American forces launched aerial and ground operations in Afghanistan, driving the

Taliban from power within weeks of the first assault. However, despite massive air strikes on the caves in the mountainous Tora Bora region, where bin Laden sought cover, and forays into that area by American and Afghan troops, bin Laden eluded capture. More than three years later, although several of his top lieutenants have been arrested or killed, the terrorist leader remained at large. Although Bush vowed to continue the hunt for bin Laden, placing a $25 million price on his head, the president made clear that the invasion of Afghanistan was merely a prelude to his primary goal, one that had become almost an obsession for Bush and the advocates of "preemptive war." Even before the regime change in Afghanistan, Bush focused the massive resources of the imperial presidency on a bigger target, Saddam Hussein.

12

"WE WILL NOT HESITATE TO ACT ALONE":

The American Colossus in the Age

of Preemptive War

Recounting, in some detail, the planning stages of the invasion of Iraq in 2003 sheds a great deal of light on a process in which the American people are most often left in the dark. Investigative reporters like Bob Woodward, in his book *Plan of Attack*, have produced almost daily accounts of the discussions that shaped and finalized the invasion plans. In this chapter, the much briefer narrative of these events focuses on the disastrous consequences of the administration's allowing its enthusiasm for a preemptive war to drown out warnings about the aftermath of the quick victory President George W. Bush anticipated. As we have learned from the continuing insurgency in Iraq, mistaken assumptions about the eagerness of the "liberated" Iraqis to welcome the U.S. occupation of their country, and to set aside tribal and religious divisions, have weakened both the presidency and the nation's dominant role in world affairs.

As we noted in the previous chapter, the invasion of Afghanistan was merely a warm-up for the bigger war that President Bush had, from his first day in office, intended to wage. On September 15, 2001, four days after the 9/11 attacks, Bush met with his top advisers at the Camp David retreat in Maryland. The group included CIA Director George Tenet, Secretary of Defense Donald Rumsfeld, and Secretary of State Colin Powell, along with the president's national security adviser, Condoleezza Rice. Tenet brought along the deputy director, John McLaughlin, and the CIA's counterterrorism chief, Cofer Black; Rumsfeld was accompanied by his deputy secretary, Paul Wolfowitz. At first the discussion centered on the various options to retaliate against al Qaeda and the Taliban, but later turned to an issue brought up by Rice. Looking beyond Afghanistan, she asked, should the president consider military action against Iraq? Everyone in the room shared a visceral hatred of Iraq's brutal dictator, Saddam Hussein, no one more than Bush himself. The memory of the abortive Iraqi plot to assassinate his father, which prompted Bill Clinton to fire twenty-three cruise missiles at Baghdad in 1993, still rankled the president. Because of recent intelligence reports that Iraq had evaded UN resolutions requiring it to destroy all stocks of weapons of mass destruction, including chemical and biological weapons, several participants at the meeting considered the decision to leave Hussein in power a serious mistake. There were also reports that Iraq had not abandoned its efforts to develop nuclear weapons, another violation of UN resolutions.

Rice had raised the prospect of using military force to depose Hussein out of concern that Iraq might have assisted al Qaeda in the 9/11 attacks. Just four days after those attacks, there was no credible evidence of such Iraqi support, but the possibility could not be dismissed. Paul Wolfowitz had long been a vocal advocate of ousting Hussein by any means possible, including American support for opposition groups that might foment a rebellion, dissident officers in the Iraqi army who might stage a coup, or covert operations that might target Hussein in a fatal "accident" like a helicopter crash. What Wolfowitz feared was that Afghanistan might become a mountainous version of the Vietnam swamps, forcing U.S. troops to fight on terrain that enemy forces knew much better. On the other hand, Iraq was flat; the major targets—including Hussein's many palaces—were in big, well-mapped cities, and his repressive regime had alienated a majority of the Iraqi people. To Wolfowitz, there was also a probability, somewhere between 10 and 50 percent, that Iraq had aided the 9/11 attackers. Even if bin Laden was killed and al Qaeda crippled, he argued, Hussein might find or create new terrorist groups. In a worst-case scenario, terrorists might gain access to Iraq's weapons of mass destruction.

Wolfowitz was not a recent convert to military action against Iraq, nor was he alone, at the Camp David meeting, in pressing this option. More than three years earlier, in January 1998, he and Rumsfeld, along with several other future Bush administration officials, had signed a letter to President Clinton, urging him to adopt a strategy that "should aim, above all, at the removal of Saddam Hussein's regime from power." The communication had been sent on the letterhead of the Project for a New American Century, a group made up largely of so-called neoconservatives, many of them—like Wolfowitz—former Democrats who held liberal views on domestic issues but had become hawkish on foreign policy, rejecting the dovish approach of Democrats like Senator Ted Kennedy. Unlike his deputy, Don Rumsfeld was a lifelong Republican, elected to the House from Illinois in 1962 at the age of thirty; he later served as chief of staff to President Gerald Ford and for two years as Ford's defense secretary, a post he also filled for George W. Bush. The amalgam of "neocons" and "old cons" in the Project for a New American Century believed that America should fill the post–Cold War vacuum with a muscular presence, unafraid to intervene anywhere in the world to advance the country's political and economic interests.

The interventionist position that led Wolfowitz to press, in 1998, for a military effort to depose Hussein, and to renew the proposal after the 9/11 attacks, had roots going back to 1992, when Wolfowitz served in the first Bush administration as undersecretary of defense for policy. Dick Cheney, who became vice president in the administration of George W. Bush, had served in the elder Bush's cabinet as secretary of defense. Even more of a foreign policy hawk than Rumsfeld, Cheney had delegated to Wolfowitz the task of drafting the Defense Planning Guidance, a document that would outline America's mission in the post–Cold War world.

The strategic program that Wolfowitz prepared, and Cheney signed, envisioned a world in which the United States would have no rivals for political, economic, and military supremacy. More important, the nation would allow no competitors to emerge, whether singly or as a bloc. And, in fact, in the early 1990s there were no potential rivals. The Soviet Union, now Russia, had destroyed its domestic economy in its futile attempt to match the United States in military hardware and troops. Russia had shrunk in size and population, as breakaway republics such as Belarus gained their independence. Within its new borders, Russia faced a terrorist problem of its own, as insurgent groups in Chechnya and other areas launched national liberation movements and threatened civil society by bombing subways in Moscow. Japan, for several decades the world's second-largest economy, struggled with recurrent financial crises and had only a tiny, self-defense military force. China, whose aging Communist leaders had ceded their power to a younger generation of pragmatists, had a booming economy and a huge standing army but no desire to challenge American dominance. In short, the United States had become the new world Colossus, capable of "deterring potential competitors from even aspiring to a larger regional and global role," as Wolfowitz had urged.

In light of such unchallenged supremacy, the Defense Planning Guidance argued, the United States could take unilateral actions — including the use of military power to avert any use, by potential enemy states, of nuclear, biological, or chemical weapons, "even in conflicts that otherwise do not directly engage U.S. interests." In other words, the United States would become the world's police officer, with a roving warrant to arrest rogue nations that possessed or were developing weapons of mass destruction. Of course, almost every country larger than Liechtenstein has at least the capability of developing WMDs, even if they are not stocked in its arsenal. As of 2005, nine nations have nuclear weapons, a dozen have biological weapons, and seventeen have chemical weapons. The number of countries capable of producing biological and chemical weapons, which can be manufactured with relative ease, is much greater. The United States, as we know, has long had all three types of WMDs.

The new, and disturbing, element in the policy Wolfowitz outlined in 1992 was that of preemptive military action by the United States. The DPG document included no precise standards for determining when to preempt a potential threat: How to measure the seriousness of a threat, and what—if any—conditions must be present to engage in preemptive action, were questions that Wolfowitz did not examine. Rather, he used vague terms, most likely to avoid setting standards that presidents might be held to by critics. "We will retain the preeminent responsibility for addressing selectively those wrongs which threaten not only our interests but those of our allies or friends, or which could seriously unsettle international relations," Wolfowitz said. Without being put on notice of what kinds of "wrongs" might trigger a preemptive action, other countries were expected to have "the sense that the world order is ultimately backed by the U.S." The bottom line of this new policy was that "the United States should be postured to act independently when collective action cannot be orchestrated." Those words, of course, became the foundation of President Bush's decision in 2003 to invade Iraq.

In 1992, Wolfowitz and Cheney submitted the Defense Planning Guidance to President George H. W. Bush, who was locked in a tight reelection battle with Bill Clinton. The document's hawkish tone horrified Bush, who had ordered the Desert Storm campaign against Iraq but preferred not to be viewed as eager to engage in more wars. Wolfowitz toned down the document, but when he returned to the Defense Department, in the administration of Bush's son, the preemptive doctrine appeared in the National Security Strategy, an updated version of a document released in September 2002. Reflecting the impact of the 9/11 attacks and the war on terror, the revised document pulled no punches. "We will not hesitate to act alone, if necessary, to exercise our right of self-defense by preemptively acting against such terrorists," it stated. President Bush announced the new strategy in a graduation speech at West Point on June 1, 2002. "The war on terror will not be won on the defensive," he said. "We must take the battle to the enemy [and] be ready for preemptive action when necessary."

Even before the public unveiling of what became known as the Bush Doctrine, the president had decided that it was "necessary" to invade Iraq and depose Hussein. The president was fully prepared to "go it alone" in this operation, but several of his key advisers, including Secretary of State Colin Powell, urged him, first, to seek supporting resolutions from both Congress and the United Nations. The international body had imposed a number of conditions on Hussein for the lifting of sanctions against Iraq; the most important was his agreement to allow UN inspectors to search the country and verify that it was no longer stockpiling or producing WMDs. Although the Iraqis made it difficult for the inspectors to carry out their task, the UN teams reported finding no evidence that Iraq was hiding or producing any of the prohibited arms. Even so, the Bush administration, particularly Cheney, repeatedly expressed doubts that the inspectors were searching hard enough. The vice president stated flatly his conviction that Iraq was concealing the weapons. The drumbeat of official skepticism from the White House was designed to prepare the public for the war that was already in the planning stages. All that remained to be settled was its timing.

The real question about the invasion was not whether to launch the assault but when. George W. Bush had made the decision to depose Saddam Hussein more than a year before he gave the go-ahead to open fire on Iraq, on March 19, 2003. In fact, planning for the war started just a few months after American forces had launched the air and ground assault on Afghanistan. Senator Bob Graham, a Florida Democrat and former chair of the Senate Intelligence Committee, recounted, in his book *Intelligence Matters*, a meeting in February 2002 with General Tommy Franks, who directed the Afghan operation. Franks told Graham that "his men and resources were being moved to Iraq, where he felt that our intelligence was shoddy. This admission came almost fourteen months before the beginning of combat operations in Iraq and only five months after the commencement of combat in Afghanistan." Although Franks's comment about "shoddy" intelligence on Iraq, as later revelations showed, was prescient, his reservations failed to slow the momentum in the Bush administration for the invasion.

Even with the toppling of the Taliban regime in Afghanistan, American forces could not quickly mount a much greater operation in Iraq. A full-scale military invasion takes substantial preparation. Much of the process is logistical: Troops must be trained and deployed; planes and ships stationed and supplied; contingency plans revised as the military situation changes. Pentagon staffers, both civilian and uniformed, spent thousands of hours planning the invasion, work that normally is shrouded in secrecy. In the case of this operation, however, military officials made no secret of their plans, and in fact shared them with the news media, just five months after Franks confided the strategy to Graham. "President George W. Bush and his advisors are reviewing plans for a massive, full-scale military conquest of Iraq that would require five ground force divisions numbering 200,000, two Marine Corps divisions, and fifteen wings of U.S. fighter and bombers," United Press International reported on July 10, 2002, eight months before the war began.

Pentagon officials would not have revealed such detailed information without approval from the White House. They did so, quite clearly, because the Bush administration—with the president calling the shots—felt compelled to flex its military muscles publicly, in order to cover up the weakness of its case for invading a country that posed no imminent threat to the United States. The Bush Doctrine of preemptive war rested on claims that nations like Iraq constituted so serious a danger to world peace that only "regime change" would eliminate their capacity to create international havoc. In reality, this doctrine had little difference from the practice of killing the town bully to "eliminate" a menace to law-abiding citizens. Such vigilante executions, more common in American history than most people realize, have no sanction in law but are rarely punished. In the same way, deposing or even killing a despised ruler, simply because the leaders of "law-abiding" nations consider him a threat to his neighbors, his region, or even the world community, has no sanction in international law. For this reason, the Bush administration needed to persuade skeptics—both at home and abroad—that Hussein represented a "clear and present danger" to other countries, and not only in the Gulf region.

Indeed, Bush had made no secret of his determination to depose Hussein. "I do firmly believe that the world will be safer and more peaceful if there's a regime change in that government," he stated in July 2002. Polls showed that a majority of the American public agreed with Bush on this issue. But two obstacles stood in his path. One was the Constitution, whose Framers had placed the power to declare war in the hands of Congress and had limited the president, as commander in chief of the armed forces, to using the nation's military forces—without prior congressional approval—only for defensive "reprisals" against invasions by hostile nations. This hurdle President Bush could easily clear, because Congress had long ago abdicated its war-declaring power to his predecessors, from Harry Truman through Bill Clinton. There was little doubt that Congress would grant Bush the authorization to launch an invasion of Iraq, just as it had already given him one to pursue "regime change" in Afghanistan, in which American forces toppled the Taliban in reprisal for harboring the al Qaeda network of Osama bin Laden.

Where Bush confronted a more serious obstacle was in facing a highly skeptical international community. The leaders of three countries in particular—President Vladimir Putin of Russia, President Jacques Chirac of France, and Chancellor Gerhard Schröder of Germany—voiced their opposition to a preemptive invasion of Iraq. Two weeks after the 9/11 attacks, Bush had called Putin to ask for Russia's aid in preparing the attack on Afghanistan. "We are going to support you in the war on terror," Putin had assured the president, offering to use his influence to obtain basing rights for U.S. troops and planes in the former Soviet states of Central Asia. Nevertheless, Putin was not supportive of Bush's plan to depose Hussein. Chirac and Schröder, both facing vocal domestic resistance to the "cowboy" president and his "gun-slinger" foreign policy, were openly critical of Washington's war plans. None of these leaders had the slightest desire to contribute troops to the military coalition against Iraq that Bush—at least in public—was promoting, in large measure because of cautionary words from Secretary of State Powell. While the former chairman of the Joint Chiefs of Staff recognized that U.S. forces could easily defeat the Iraqi army, Powell also knew that a go-it-alone assault would probably turn the nation's allies into adversaries.

Loyally and effectively, Powell had marshaled the backing of Russia, Pakistan, and several Central Asian states for the Afghan operation; the secretary of state was helped by the fact that most of these countries—Russia in particular—were themselves threatened by domestic terrorist groups, many with ties to al Qaeda. But forging a political and military coalition to participate in an American-led invasion of Iraq was a far more difficult job. Over the summer and fall of 2002, Powell undertook the delicate task of persuading Bush to consider the dangers of a unilateral invasion. On August 5, 2002, Powell met with the president, along with National Security Adviser Rice, and laid out his concerns. First, he told Bush, any effort to produce a regime change in the Middle East might prompt militant Islamic groups to retaliate by undermining or even overthrowing friendly governments such as those in Egypt, Jordan, and Saudi Arabia, plunging the region into chaos. Second, even a quick victory and the departure or death of Hussein would probably require a lengthy (and costly) military occupation of Iraq, because separatist groups—particularly the Kurdish minority—would seek independence, and warring political and religious factions would try to dominate any post-Saddam government. And as Powell also told Bush, invading Iraq might have disastrous consequences for the world economy, reducing or even shutting off Iraq's oil production and driving up already high oil prices.

Powell's concern about oil reflected its crucial role not only in fueling the American economy but in sustaining the nation's far-flung empire. As we have seen, access to dependable supplies of oil, and protection of the worldwide petroleum shipping routes, had driven American foreign policy since the beginning of World War II. The United States had spent billions of dollars in economic and military aid to prop up the repressive regimes in Saudi Arabia and other oil-rich Middle Eastern states. Jeopardizing the stability of the region by invading Iraq might well cost the United States far more than the benefits of deposing Hussein. The Bush administration, however, could not admit that oil was a factor in its war planning. Indeed, Secretary of Defense Rumsfeld bristled when he was asked by reporters in November 2002 about this issue. "It has nothing to do with oil, literally nothing to do with oil," he said.

Denying something twice in one breath often sounds more like an admission. Others with experience in the politics of oil spoke more candidly. Anthony H. Cordesman, senior analyst at the Center for Strategic and International Studies, a Washington think tank whose advisory board included Henry Kissinger and James Schlesinger, a former defense secretary and CIA director, dismissed Rumsfeld's denial. "Regardless of whether we say so publicly," Cordesman replied, "we will go to war, because Saddam sits at the center of a region with 60 percent of all the world's oil reserves." Iraq, in fact—with 113 billion barrels of proven oil reserves—was second only to Saudi Arabia and controlled 11 percent of the world total. Two weeks after Rumsfeld's firm words, a leading industry journal, *Alexander's Gas and Oil Connections*, reported that Bush administration officials were meeting with exiled Iraqi opposition leaders to "recommend to an interim government ways of restoring the petroleum sector following a military attack in order to increase oil exports to partially pay for a possible U.S. military occupation government—further fueling the view that controlling Iraqi oil is at the heart of the Bush campaign to replace Hussein with a more compliant regime."

In light of the long-standing personal and political connections that George W. Bush, Vice President Cheney, and other top administration officials had to the oil industry, the conclusion that "oil drives everything" is hard to dismiss. But the decision to invade Iraq reflected broader geopolitical interests—in particular, the ability of the United States to dominate the flow of capital and goods around the world. In this view, deposing Hussein would send a message to the leaders of other "disruptive" nations that they might share his fate. Charles Freeman, ambassador to Saudi Arabia in the first Bush administration, spoke of the "hawks" in the second who believed "you have to control resources in order to have access to them. They are taken with the idea that the end of the Cold War left the United States able to impose its will globally—and that those with the ability to shape events with power have the duty to do so. It's ideology."

This is the ideology of empire, which links power with duty. Conceptions of that "duty" have often incorporated a religious mission into the mercenary interests of imperial designs. Columbus had a mandate from Queen Isabella to Christianize the "Indians" as well as to plunder their gold and enslave them. "Let us in the name of the Holy Trinity go on sending all the slaves that can be sold," Columbus wrote of the Arawak natives he shipped from Hispaniola to Spain. George W. Bush is far removed from Columbus in time and purpose, but, more than any other president, he has infused his foreign policies with evangelical religiosity, often speaking of America's mission to "rid the world of evil" and to promote "God-given values" around the world. The ability of the United States to "shape events" added to that mission a license to depose "evil" leaders such as Saddam Hussein.

For more than a year before the invasion began, and while war preparations were being developed, the Bush administration mounted a public offensive against Iraq, with two goals. The first, and easier one, was to rally the American public behind the president, who had portrayed the assault on Afghanistan as the first skirmish in the long-range "war on terror." In the aftermath of 9/11, fears of even more deadly attacks overcame any doubts that such a war had become a necessity, particularly because Osama bin Laden had eluded capture. Riding high in his role as commander in chief, Bush could rely on domestic support for the next battle in the war on terror. The second, and more difficult, goal of the administration's campaign was to lay out the case for invading Iraq while the hunt for bin

Laden was still going on. Why begin another war so quickly, and why begin that war against Iraq?

Answering those questions required more than simply asserting that Hussein was an "evil" dictator, a claim that hardly anyone disputed. Following this logic, however, an equally persuasive case could be made for deposing several other "evil" dictators, including Kim Jong Il of North Korea, whose pursuit of nuclear weapons posed a "clear and present danger" to world peace. By any measure, Kim ruled his people with greater brutality than Hussein. "I loathe Kim Jong Il," Bush told the journalist Bob Woodward. "I've got a visceral reaction to this guy, because he is starving his people." Then why not invade North Korea and topple Kim? "I'm not foolish," Bush assured Woodward. "They tell me, we don't need to move too fast, because the financial burdens on people will be so immense if we try to—if this guy were to topple." But toppling Hussein would impose severe financial burdens on the American economy, particularly if Powell's concerns about a lengthy occupation and disruptions in the oil supply were correct. North Korea, of course, does not produce oil, nor does it have the strategic importance of Iraq.

Since the White House understood that invading Iraq simply because Hussein was a brutal dictator would bring down a chorus of domestic and international condemnation, the Bush administration based its case for military action on two additional arguments, both related to the fear, raised by the 9/11 attacks, of even more serious terrorist acts. The first, and by far the more threatening claim, was that Iraq possessed weapons of mass destruction, including chemical, biological, and nuclear armaments. What gave this claim credibility was the undeniable fact that, in the 1980s, Iraq had killed thousands of its Kurdish minority with poison gas. There was also clear evidence, from that period, that Iraq had the technological know-how to produce biological weapons and that Baghdad had been pursuing a nuclear weapons program. After the Gulf War in 1991 had driven the Iraqi army from Kuwait, however, the United Nations demanded that Iraq destroy its stockpiles of chemical weapons and stop all programs for developing biological and nuclear weapons. The United Nations backed up its demands with economic sanctions and dispatched inspectors to monitor compliance. Hussein complained loudly about the "indignity" of UN inspections, and Iraqi officials dragged their feet in allowing inspection teams to visit sites—including military bases, factories, and laboratories—that might be used for producing or storing the banned materials. Despite the Iraqi obstructionism, UN inspectors found no clear evidence of WMD storage, production, or development over a period of several years. In fact, in February 2001, just one month after President Bush took office, Powell declared that Hussein "has not developed any significant capability with respect to weapons of mass destruction. He is unable to project conventional power against his neighbors."

Nine months after Powell's statement, Richard Perle, a top Pentagon adviser, contradicted him. Perle stated flatly in November 2001 that Iraq "has weapons of mass destruction." He made no bones of his desire to launch an invasion of Iraq. "The lesser risk is in pre-emption," he added. "We've got to stop wishing away the problem." If Powell was confident in asserting that Iraq had no "significant" WMD capability as of February 2001, what prompted Perle and other administration officials to claim later that year that it did? The obvious answer lies in the 9/11 attacks and the decision to depose Hussein. Claiming that Iraq had weapons of mass destruction offered a justification for Perle's advocacy of a preemptive invasion to prevent the WMDs from being used against Iraq's neighbors.

Perle's statement did not make a big media splash. But a later speech by Vice President Cheney hit the headlines. "Cheney Says Peril of a Nuclear Iraq Justifies Attack," reported the *New York Times* in a front-page story on August 27, 2002. Speaking to a Veterans of Foreign Wars convention, Cheney took the hardest line yet of any Bush administration official. "There is no doubt that Saddam Hussein now has weapons of mass destruction," the vice president said. "There is no doubt that he is amassing them to use against our friends, against our allies and against us." Cheney all but declared war on Iraq. Confronted by a "murderous dictator" whose scientists were rushing to produce nuclear weapons, the United

States faced "as grave a threat as can be imagined," he warned. "The risks of inaction are far greater than the risk of action," he concluded. A month after Cheney's hard-line speech, Rumsfeld testified before the House Armed Services Committee. "We do know that the Iraq regime has chemical and biological weapons," he stated.

The administration's claims finally reached the top in October 2002, when the president echoed Rumsfeld in telling the press that Iraq "possesses and produces chemical and biological weapons." Raising another specter in laying the groundwork for the coming invasion, Bush asserted that Iraq "is seeking nuclear weapons." While stumping around the country that month for Republican congressional candidates, the chief executive repeated, at least fifteen times, his certainty that Iraq had WMDs.

With every House seat and one-third of the Senate at stake in the November elections, Bush had carefully timed his invasion campaign. On October 2, he submitted to Congress a proposed resolution, authorizing him to employ military force against Iraq. The resolution included sweeping claims of the president's constitutional power, as commander in chief, "to take action in order to deter and prevent acts of international terrorism against the United States, as Congress recognized in the joint resolution on Authorization for Use of Military Force," in 1991, when Congress had given Bush's father the green light to drive the Iraqi army from Kuwait. Once again, Congress was being asked to authorize the president to begin a war, without a formal declaration. Whether such an authorization met the constitutional standard had become a moot point, since Congress had long ago abdicated its war-declaring power to the executive branch.

Although congressional leaders balked at resting the new Iraq resolution on the earlier authorization, the final version provided Bush with all the leeway he claimed as commander in chief. The resolution cited as justification for its blank-check grant of power all three of the president's repeated charges against the Iraqi regime, including the "brutal repression of its civilian population," its "capability and willingness to use weapons of mass destruction against other nations and its own people," and its role in "supporting and harboring terrorist organizations." The House approved the resolution by a vote of 296 to 133, and the Senate followed with the even greater margin of 77 to 23. Virtually all the House dissenters were Democrats who held safe seats and thus faced little risk of electoral reprisal, while only a single Senate Republican, Lincoln Chafee of Rhode Island, opposed the resolution, which President Bush signed on October 16, 2002.

With the blank check in his pocket, Bush moved ahead with invasion preparations. Over the next five months, the president went through the steps of seeking UN approval of an international coalition under the command of American generals, a move that would require a Security Council resolution. Because of the vocal opposition of the French, who hold a veto power in the council, Bush knew that the proposal was doomed to failure. Nonetheless, he dispatched Secretary of State Powell to Manhattan on February 5, 2003. Swallowing his words of two years earlier, the secretary of state loyally joined the line of march. In what can only be called a charade, Powell appeared before the UN General Assembly, ostensibly to make a final appeal for approval of the coming invasion. The highlights of his show-and-tell presentation were aerial surveillance photographs of supposed chemical weapons facilities. "Our conservative estimate," Powell stated, "is that Iraq today has a stockpile of between 100 and 500 tons of chemical weapons agent. That is enough agent to fill 16,000 battlefield rockets." When Powell left the United Nations without a supporting resolution, no one was surprised. The sole remaining source of support for Bush was from what he called the "coalition of the willing," a patchwork of nations from Bulgaria to Australia. Only the British offered any substantial commitment of troops, although Prime Minister Tony Blair had to rely on backing from Conservative members of Parliament to overcome the vehement opposition from within his Labor Party.

As war plans reached their final stages, only the Constitution stood in Bush's path. With the aid of compliant federal judges, he easily brushed aside the minor irritant of a lawsuit, filed in February 2003, by six Democratic House members, including John Conyers,

Jr., of Michigan, Dennis Kucinich of Ohio, and Jesse Jackson, Jr., of Chicago. They were joined by several active-duty soldiers and army reservists, who claimed they faced duty in a war that Congress had not declared and sought protection from official retaliation by filing as "Does." Their lawyer, John Bonifaz, argued in *Doe v. Bush* that the president "is not a king" and "does not have the power to wage war against another country absent a declaration of war by Congress." On February 24, the suit came before Judge Joseph L. Tauro in Boston, who had relied on the "political question" doctrine thirty years earlier, in dismissing a suit brought by members of Congress against the Nixon administration's bombing of Cambodia. Tauro again relied on this doctrine in dismissing the *Doe* case. The plaintiffs filed an appeal with the federal circuit court, which affirmed Tauro's ruling on March 13. Unlike Tauro, the appellate judges cited the "ripeness" doctrine in turning aside the latest challenge to presidential war powers. Admitting that the war-power issue "is a somber and weighty one," the judicial panel agreed that the case "is not fit now for judicial review" because "questions remain about whether there will be a war, and, if so, under what conditions." Bush answered the first question just six days later, when he ordered the air strikes and ground assault that began the war.

While U.S. tanks sped across the desert sands of southern Iraq toward Baghdad, the American public followed their progress from the turrets, as "embedded" journalists offered a televised, exuberant travelogue, complete with waving Iraqis on the roadsides. With victory seemingly a matter of weeks or even days ahead, congressional opposition to the war melted away like the Iraqi army. Two days after the invasion began, only eleven House members voted against a resolution expressing the "unequivocal support and appreciation of the Nation to the President as Commander-in-Chief for his firm leadership and decisive action in the conduct of military operations in Iraq as part of the on-going Global War on Terrorism." Before the tanks reached the outskirts of Baghdad, Saddam Hussein had vanished, eluding capture until December 23, when American troops dragged him, disheveled and hungry, from an underground "dog-hole" near his hometown of Tikrit, in northern Iraq.

From the start of the military operation, Bush exulted in the success of his mission to depose Hussein and deliver "freedom" to the Iraqi people. He scored a major publicity coup on May 1, 2003, when he took the controls of a navy jet and landed on the aircraft carrier *Abraham Lincoln,* conveniently sitting thirty miles off the Pacific Coast from San Diego. Shedding his flight suit, Bush thanked the troops under a banner that boasted MISSION ACCOMPLISHED. "The liberation of Iraq," he said, "is a crucial advance in the campaign against terror. We've removed an ally of al Qaeda and cut off a source of terrorist funding."

What followed Bush's victory speech, of course, can best be described as the defeat of "Mission Impossible." The waving crowds of Iraqis turned into mobs of looters, and sporadic resistance by Hussein's loyalists developed into a sustained, well-organized insurgent movement against the forces imposing an occupation regime on the "liberated" country. Even the return of "self-rule" to Iraq, on June 30, 2004, was a charade. Handpicked by U.S. officials, the interim Iraqi government remained dependent on protection, by American troops, from frequent—and often successful—assassination efforts. As late as September 2004, Bush refused to put a deadline on ending the military occupation, with forecasts running into a decade or longer.

Not only did Hussein quickly vanish after American tanks rolled across the Iraqi border, but the Bush administration's pretext for the invasion quickly vanished as well. On March 22, 2003, three days after the war began, General Tommy Franks—who had confessed to "shoddy" prewar intelligence a year earlier—professed "no doubt" that Iraq possessed weapons of mass destruction. "As this operation continues," he said, "those weapons will be identified, found, along with the people who produced them and guard them." Two months later, however, no such weapons had been located, and National Security Adviser Condoleezza Rice took a more guarded stance. "U.S.

officials never expected that we were going to open garages and find
weapons of mass destruction," she stated on May 12. A less guarded
admission came on May 30 from Marine Corps lieutenant general
James Conway, who headed the military teams searching for banned
weapons. "We've been to virtually every ammo supply point between
the Kuwaiti border and Baghdad," he said, "but they're simply not
there. We were simply wrong."

Conway's teams found no WMDs in the southern part of Iraq.
But searchers in the north came up with a find that gave Bush a
chance to crow. He relied on the discovery of two large trailers containing laboratory equipment. The CIA had released a White Paper
to the media on May 28, describing the trailers as "Iraqi Mobile
Biological Warfare Agent Production Plants" and stating they were
"the strongest evidence to date that Iraq was hiding a biological
warfare program." The report admitted, however, that inspectors
had found no trace in the trailers of biological agents that could be
used to produce weapons. Bush skipped over the small print. "We
found the weapons of mass destruction," he stated flatly. But journalists read the CIA report more carefully and soon poked holes in
the claims.

Secretary of State Powell, who in his UN speech in February 2003
had displayed surveillance photographs of other supposed biological
warfare facilities, ate crow a year later, blaming faulty CIA intelligence. His UN presentation, Powell said in May 2004, "was based
on the best information that the CIA made available to me." But he
had since discovered that "the sourcing was inaccurate and wrong
and in some cases deliberately misleading. And for that, I am disap-
pointed and I regret it." Bush, however, professed no regrets about
his repeated claims that Iraq possessed WMDs.

The most authoritative report on weapons of mass destruction
came from David Kay, the chief U.S. weapons inspector and head of
the Iraq Survey Group. "I'm personally convinced," he said, "that
there were not large stockpiles of newly produced weapons of mass
destruction. We don't find the people, the documents or the physical

plants that you would expect to find if the production was going on. I think they gradually reduced stockpiles during the 1990s."

Perhaps the most telling—and chilling—admission on this key issue was made by Paul Wolfowitz, a leading architect of the preemptive war doctrine. "For bureaucratic reasons we settled on one issue, weapons of mass destruction, because it was the one reason everyone could agree on," he later said, without a trace of regret.

The second major justification for the invasion, based on claims of Iraqi collaboration with al Qaeda, also vanished under close scrutiny. As late as January 2004, Vice President Cheney doggedly insisted the Bush administration had "overwhelming evidence there was a connection between al Qaeda and the Iraqi government." Six months later, however, the blue-ribbon presidential commission on the 9/11 attacks, headed by former New Jersey governor Thomas Kean, concluded that its exhaustive investigation had discovered no evidence of any "collaborative relationship" between Iraq and al Qaeda. The commission's staff report on this issue, based on a thorough review of CIA and Pentagon records, also found "no credible evidence that Iraq and al Qaeda cooperated in attacks against the United States." What the CIA did have credible evidence to support, however, was that Saudi Arabian officials had provided funds for at least two of the 9/11 hijackers, according to former Senate Intelligence Committee chair Bob Graham. But this evidence, Graham said in September 2004, had been withheld from the 9/11 commission on orders from the White House, which later dismissed Graham's allegations as a partisan attack on Bush. Whether evidence of a Saudi connection to al Qaeda might have prevented the 9/11 attacks remains an unanswered question. But the question of whether the Bush administration knew that Iraq had not collaborated with al Qaeda in those attacks, and thus misled the American public, appears to have been answered by the 9/11 commission report.

It is tempting to pin the blame for misleading the American public—and the rest of the world—on the Bush administration, from the president on down the bureaucratic ladder. But there is plenty of blame to spread. The news media reported, uncritically, the claims by the White House that it had evidence that Iraq possessed stockpiles of banned weapons and that Iraq was harboring al Qaeda operatives. Belatedly, but to their credit, both the *New York Times* and the *Washington Post* published self-critical reviews of their prewar reporting, in which administration claims received front-page coverage, with little or no challenge to their credibility. But these postmortems of flawed journalism came too late to undo the damage to the media's own credibility. The press had failed to apply the chastening lessons of the Vietnam War; during its early years, most reporters simply retyped the daily handouts from the army's press room in Saigon, rarely venturing into combat zones until the death toll of U.S. troops had risen into the thousands.

A greater share of blame, however, falls on Congress, which failed to hold the Bush administration to account for its misleading claims about Iraqi WMDs and complicity in the 9/11 attacks. Unlike the media, Congress has the power to call officials before its committees and grill them about their actions and statements. But like the media, Congress neglected to exercise its investigative and oversight responsibilities until the damage had been done. Most often, administration officials received kid-glove treatment from committee members of both parties and departed with profuse thanks for having appeared. Defense Secretary Rumsfeld, for example, told the House Armed Services Committee in September 2002 that Iraq possessed biological and chemical weapons, without being asked to produce the intelligence reports on which he based this claim.

Perhaps the sharpest commentary on the failure to probe the credibility of administration claims came from Senator Robert Byrd, who had warned President Bush of the pitfalls of invading Iraq. On October 17, 2003, seven months after the invasion, Byrd spoke to an almost-deserted Senate chamber; he titled his remarks "The Emperor Has No Clothes." He aimed his first rhetorical volley at the Bush administration. "We were told that we were threatened by weapons of mass destruction in Iraq," he said, "but they have not yet been seen. We were led to believe that Saddam Hussein was connected to the attacks on the Twin Towers and the Pentagon, but no evidence has ever been produced." Critics of the war, Byrd noted, "have had our patriotism questioned. Those who dared to expose the nakedness of the Administration's policies in Iraq have been subjected to scorn. Having misled the American people and stampeded them to war, this Administration must now attempt to sustain a policy predicated on falsehoods." But the Senate's longest-serving member did not spare his colleagues. "The time has come," he chided, "for the sheep-like political correctness which has cowed members of this Senate to come to an end." Byrd walked past rows of empty seats as he left the chamber, and tucked the folded pages of his speech into his pocket. The time had not come, however, for the American people to heed his cautionary words: On November 2, 2004, the majority of voters ignored the evidence of "falsehoods" about Iraq and returned President Bush to the White House.

13

"THE CONSTITUTION IS JUST A PIECE OF PAPER":

Empire vs. Democracy

From its first pages, this book has placed the events it recounts against the backdrop of the Constitution, from its framing in 1787 to the present. Most of these events, including five declared wars and scores of undeclared wars and military incursions into other nations, took place outside the United States, in places as close as Mexico and as remote as Afghanistan. As we have seen, the Constitution has not stood firm as a barrier against presidential disregard of its command that only Congress has the power to declare war, and of the Framers' clear intention that, without prior congressional sanction, presidents can send troops into combat only to "repel invasions" and to protect American citizens and property. In this final chapter, we return from foreign wars to equally important battles over the Constitution's protection of citizens against their own government. The federal courts have, most often, turned aside challenges to presidential actions at home—for example, upholding the prison terms of World War I dissenters for "seditious" speech and the mass internment of Japanese Americans during World War II. But there have been exceptions to this pattern of judicial evasion and timidity. The

Civil War cases of John Merryman and Lambdin Milligan established the principle that the Constitution "is a law for rulers and people, equally in war and peace, and covers with the shield of its protection all classes of men, at all times, and under all circumstances." But the Supreme Court simply ignored or brushed aside this principle in the sedition and internment cases.

Previous chapters have looked at wars, both declared and undeclared, in which more than one million Americans lost their lives. That is the greatest price anyone can pay for serving his or her country, willingly or not. But other Americans, some of whom refused to fight in what they considered "imperialist" wars, have suffered in prison or have been condemned as cowards or even traitors to their country. And the government, in recent years, has tightened the legal screws on dissenters and suspected terrorists. This chapter will look at those efforts, and at the perhaps surprising rebuke to them by the Supreme Court, which has belatedly returned to the *Milligan* principle that the "great exigencies of government" cannot excuse congressional or presidential disregard of constitutional protections. The Court has not yet ruled, however, on some of the most ominous threats to the rights of Americans to voice their opinions without censorship, to protect their privacy against invasion, even to worship in churches or mosques without surveillance.

As noted in chapter 12, the quick dismissal of the lawsuit brought against President Bush by Democratic House members demonstrated that the Constitution would not block the invasion of Iraq. But it did at least slow down the administration's invasion of constitutional rights in pursuit of alleged terrorists, both at home and abroad. In fact, the war on terror has inflicted severe damage to the Bill of Rights, although the Supreme Court has recently curbed the most sweeping claims of "inherent" presidential power to declare anyone—including U.S. citizens—to be "enemy combatants" with no recourse to judicial review of their indefinite detention. Nevertheless, the Bush administration did not shrink from asserting powers that no earlier president had dared to claim.

The first salvo in the assault on the Bill of Rights landed in

Congress even before the smoke had cleared from the 9/11 attacks. At the direction of Attorney General John Ashcroft, Justice Department lawyers had drafted a 342-page bill with the cumbersome title Uniting and Strengthening America by Providing Appropriate Tools Required to Intercept and Obstruct Terrorism Act of 2001, which produced the catchy acronym USA Patriot Act. Cobbled together from existing statutes, amendments to them, and new provisions, the Patriot Act was rushed by the Republican leadership in both chambers of Congress to quick votes with perfunctory hearings and no committee reports. Hardly any members had a chance to read, let alone to digest and debate, this massive bill before its enactment, by the huge margin of 356 to 66 in the House, and with only one dissenter—Democrat Russell Feingold of Wisconsin—in the Senate. Even Senator Robert Byrd, who later deplored the "cowed" manner in which his colleagues had authorized Bush to invade Iraq, voted for the Patriot Act. Bush signed the law on October 26, 2001, handing a beaming Ashcroft one of the souvenir pens.

Before casting the solitary negative vote, Feingold issued this warning: "Preserving our freedom is one of the main reasons that we are now engaged in this new war on terrorism. We will lose that war without firing a shot if we sacrifice the liberties of the American people." The Patriot Act has eroded those liberties in dozens of provisions, some of which set forth brand-new federal crimes. The most extreme—and chilling—new crime is that of "domestic terrorism," which extends far beyond acts of violence to include any "acts dangerous to human life that are a violation of the criminal laws . . . [if such acts] . . . appear to be intended . . . to influence the policy of a government by intimidation or coercion" and are conducted "primarily within the territorial jurisdiction of the United States." Such a sweeping definition of "terrorism" can subject virtually any act of civil disobedience to prosecution; for example, Greenpeace activists who tried to block Japanese whaling ships from entering U.S. territorial waters could be charged with attempting to intimidate the Japanese government. Protesters who face arrest for violating local "trespass" or "disorderly conduct" laws can now be charged with "domestic terrorism" and sentenced to lengthy terms in federal prison. It is not inconceivable that demonstrators who sit down and block traffic on Pennsylvania Avenue, in Washington, to protest the war in Iraq—or a future war—would be prosecuted for committing acts "dangerous to human life." Dismissing the prospect of such prosecutions as far-fetched overlooks the government's penchant for stifling legitimate criticism during wartime, which goes as far back as the Sedition Act prosecutions during World War I.

Another dangerous provision of the Patriot Act makes it a crime to lend "material support" to any terrorist organization designated as such by federal officials, who have complete discretion in deciding which groups have "terrorist" aims. The term "material support" is broadly defined to include any "physical asset," "personnel," "training," or "expert advice and assistance." What is disturbing is that this provision does not require proof that a person charged with this crime intended to further any terrorist activities. Suppose, for example, that someone with computer expertise volunteered to help an organization—none of whose members had been charged with committing terrorist acts—set up and maintain its Web site. This is not a hypothetical example; it is exactly what a University of Idaho graduate student did for the Islamic Assembly of North America, whose Web site was open to postings, by anyone who sought permission to use it, without censorship of their contents. Sami Al-Hussayen, a citizen of Saudi Arabia with a student visa, was charged in 2003 by federal prosecutors with providing "expert advice and assistance" to a terrorist organization. Surprisingly, in what can be viewed as a popular backlash to the excesses of the Patriot Act, a jury in conservative Idaho acquitted Al-Hussayen in June 2004 of the Patriot Act charges. John Steger, a jury member, said of the Web site postings: "Ninety-five percent of it was fine, and the stuff that was inflammatory, by the First Amendment, he had the right to do that."

The Bush administration, however, vowed to continue Patriot Act prosecutions. A month after Al-Hussayen's acquittal, the Justice Department released a twenty-nine-page report to Congress, noting that "terrorist investigations" had resulted in charges against 310 people, with 179 convictions or guilty pleas. "The Patriot Act is al Qaeda's worst nightmare when it comes to disrupting and disabling their operations here in America," boasted John Ashcroft. But critics responded that many of these prosecutions were for crimes that included child pornography and the kidnapping of an eighty-four-year-old woman. Anthony Romero, legal director of the American Civil Liberties Union, said the nonterrorist cases showed that "the Patriot Act went too far too fast and gave law enforcement officials too much power that had nothing to do with terrorism." Most of the 310 cases, Romero added, involved immigration cases in which drag-net sweeps of heavily Islamic communities pulled in suspects who had overstayed student and tourist visas. Representative John Conyers, Jr., the ranking Democrat on the House Judiciary Committee, whose Detroit constituents include thousands of Arab Americans, charged that, considering the Justice Department's "consistent record of exaggerating their record about terrorism, this entire report is suspect."

During the first year after Congress passed the Patriot Act, federal agents interrogated more than eight thousand people from Arabic and Southeast Asian countries, and detained several hundred, often for months, refusing to release their names or allow them to contact family members or lawyers. This form of racial profiling raised disturbing echoes of the mass detention of Japanese Americans during World War II, which the Supreme Court upheld in 1943 and 1944 in the *Hirabayashi* and *Korematsu* cases. On a smaller scale, but with a similar basis in race and nationality, the roundup of Arabic and other Muslim terrorist suspects bore out the prediction of Justice Robert Jackson in his *Korematsu* dissent that the Supreme Court's validation of mass detention on grounds of race or nationality—he might have added religion as well—"lies about like a loaded weapon, ready for the hand of any authority that can bring forward a plausible claim of an urgent need."

No one disputes that protecting the nation against terrorist attacks has become an urgent need. Considering, however, that only a handful of those detained in the recent terrorist sweeps were later charged with anything more than immigration offenses, the question remains whether the Bush administration fired this "loaded weapon" without a plausible reason. One indication of the government's trigger-happy approach came in a speech by Ashcroft in October 2001, in which he vowed to use "aggressive arrest and detention tactics in the war on terror." The attorney general sounded like a Wild West marshal. "Let the terrorists among us be warned," he said. "If you overstay your visa—even by one day—we will arrest you. If you violate a local law, you will be put in jail and kept in custody as long as possible. We will use every available statute. We will seek every prosecutorial advantage. We will use all our weapons within the law and under the Constitution to protect life and enhance security for America." Apparently Ashcroft viewed the Constitution not as a guarantee of individual rights but as a license to lock up suspected terrorists for "as long as possible," with no regard for the due process clause of the Fifth Amendment.

It may seem an exaggeration to compare Ashcroft to such predecessors as Torquemada, who presided over the Spanish Inquisition and subjected that nation's Jews to the most painful forms of torture if they refused to renounce their faith and convert to Christianity. But the parallels between the horrors of the fifteenth century and the Bush administration's harsh treatment of suspected "enemy combatants" are striking. Much like Torquemada, Ashcroft presided over a supposedly "legal" process under which people suspected of adhering to "subversive" doctrines were summarily arrested and, in secret proceedings, grilled about their beliefs and activities. To be sure, the penalty for those who failed the Ashcroft Inquisition was not death but deportation. It is also fair, however, to note that Justice Department officials later admitted that federal jail guards had abused some prisoners with beatings and death threats.

But the treatment of prisoners in federal jails, most of whom were later released without being charged, paled in comparison to the mental and physical abuse inflicted on those who had been seized by U.S. troops during the war in Afghanistan and later in Iraq. Hundreds of actual and suspected al Qaeda and Taliban fighters, along with many civilians, found themselves bundled onto military planes, hooded and shackled, and transported to a military detention center at the U.S. naval base in Guantánamo Bay, at the eastern end of Cuba. As we saw earlier, the United States had forced the Cubans to grant a perpetual lease for this base as a condition of American recognition of Cuba's independence. More than six hundred prisoners, of some forty-four nationalities, including citizens of Australia and Britain, were held as "enemy combatants" at the infamous Camp X-Ray on the Guantánamo base. Many Americans were shocked by photographs of prisoners confined outdoors in steel-mesh cages, exposed to searing heat, forced by shackles to crawl on their knees, their heads covered by hoods or helmets that blocked out all light. U.S. officials defended these conditions as necessary to prevent the prisoners from attacking guards or communicating with one another. Defense Secretary Rumsfeld called them "hardened criminals willing to kill themselves and others for their cause," while Vice President Cheney described them as "the worst of a very bad lot. They are very dangerous."

The Camp X-Ray inmates no doubt included some hardened al Qaeda and Taliban fighters, but others quite obviously posed no threat to anyone, and many had been simply bystanders or innocent villagers when they were grabbed by American troops in Afghanistan. The release of three Afghani men, after eleven months of detention at Camp X-Ray, revealed that mistakes had been made. David Rhodes, a *New York Times* reporter, described one prisoner, who said he was 105 years old: "Babbling at times like a child, the partially deaf, shriveled old man was unable to answer simple questions." Rhodes described another, who said he was ninety, as a "wizened old man with a cane" who had been arrested when U.S. troops raided his village. Despite these belatedly admitted mistakes, U.S. officials claimed that harsh conditions and forceful interrogation techniques were necessary to extract information from al Qaeda members who might have knowledge of future terrorist attacks or the whereabouts of Osama bin Laden and key lieutenants who remained at large.

There is little question that the president's war powers as commander in chief allow him to authorize military officials to detain "enemy combatants" and subject them to interrogation. But there is also little question that presidents and their subordinates are bound by the provisions of international laws and treaties that provide for humane treatment of people captured on the battlefield or in theaters of war. The key issue here is whether the alleged al Qaeda and Taliban fighters were, in fact, entitled to be treated as prisoners of war and accorded the protections of the Geneva Conventions, a treaty the United States ratified in 1949. Under these stipulations, captured members of a "regular" army or supporting militia must be allowed to communicate with family members and representatives of their governments, and brought before a "competent tribunal" to determine their legal status if "any doubt" is raised about that status. The Bush administration flatly refused to abide by the Geneva Conventions in detaining the Camp X-Ray prisoners, simply asserting that al Qaeda and Taliban prisoners were not "regular" military troops. Thus the prisoners could be held indefinitely, without access to family or legal counsel, and with no recourse to challenge their detention in federal courts. In effect, much like President Lincoln during the Civil War, Bush suspended the writ of habeas corpus for as long as he—or his successors—determined that the war on terror was being fought.

In making this decision, Bush relied for legal advice on White House counsel Alberto Gonzales, a close friend and confidant from the president's years as governor of Texas; Bush later named Gonzales to replace John Ashcroft as attorney general in his second term. In January 2002, shortly after the first batch of prisoners arrived at the Guantánamo base, Gonzales drafted a memorandum to Bush, backing the president's decision not to treat the Camp X-Ray inmates as prisoners of war under the Geneva Conventions. In his memo, Gonzales made three main points. First, he said, giving the detainees POW status would increase the danger of "vague" charges being leveled against American military personnel for such violations of the Conventions as "outrages upon personal dignity" and "inhuman treatment" of prisoners. Second, Gonzales wrote, "it is difficult to predict the needs and circumstances that could arise in the course of the war on terrorism" ("needs" that presumably included forceful methods of interrogation). And third, Gonzales worried about possible charges against military personnel under the War Crimes statute, Section 2441 of the federal criminal code. This law includes violations of the Geneva Conventions as criminal offenses. "It is difficult to predict the motives of prosecutors and independent counsels who may in the future decide to pursue unwarranted charges based on Section 2441," Gonzales wrote to Bush. "Your determination would create a reasonable basis in law that Section 2441 does not apply, which would provide a solid defense to any future prosecutions."

Conceding that his hard-line position had opponents within the administration, Gonzales told Bush that Secretary of State Colin Powell "has requested that you reconsider" the decision to withhold POW status from Camp X-Ray inmates. Powell was concerned, as Gonzales put it, that "our position would likely provoke widespread condemnation among our allies and in some domestic quarters, even if we make clear that we will comply with the core humanitarian principles of the treaty as a matter of policy." Gonzales urged Bush to reject Powell's cautionary stance. "On balance, I believe the arguments for reconsideration and reversal are unpersuasive." Bush heeded his White House counsel, although Powell's prophecy turned out to be correct. The United States endured "widespread condemnation" for its treatment of the Guantánamo prisoners, both at home and abroad, particularly after worldwide outrage erupted in early 2004 over the humiliation, torture, and murder of Iraqis by American military personnel at the notorious Abu Ghraib prison.

The connection between the "inhuman" treatment of Camp X-Ray inmates at Guantánamo Bay and the torture and murder of Abu Ghraib prisoners in Iraq reveals the perils of an imperial presidency that treats the Constitution with disdain, even contempt. That connection ran from the Justice Department to the White House, through another memorandum, written in August 2002 by Jay Bybee, who then headed the Office of Legal Counsel under Attorney General Ashcroft. Bybee had been delegated to prepare a legal analysis of the Geneva Convention Against Torture and Other Cruel, Inhuman, and Degrading Treatment or Punishment, a treaty ratified by the Senate in 1949, with the binding force of U.S. law. His task was to provide a legal definition of "torture" that would set parameters for military and CIA interrogators at Camp X-Ray who were charged with extracting information from suspected al Qaeda and Taliban prisoners. Sitting in his air-conditioned office in Washington, just blocks from the White House but more than a thousand miles from the sweltering human cages at Camp X-Ray, Bybee drafted a memo for Bush that was Orwellian in both style and substance. Although the dictionary definition of "torture" is "the inflicting of severe mental or physical pain to force information or confession," Bybee wrote his own definition, under which the infliction of severe mental pain "not intended to have lasting effects" would not be classified as torture. In other words, the infliction of "temporary" mental pain—produced by threats of death, for example—would be an acceptable interrogation technique. So would the infliction of severe physical pain, unless the interrogators intended to cause "serious physical injury such as death or organ failure." According to Bybee's definition, beating a prisoner into unconsciousness, or breaking bones, would also be acceptable. Only acts "intended" to cause the prisoner's death, or beatings "intended" to cause a kidney or spleen to burst, according to Bybee's definition, would subject the interrogator to possible charges under military or federal law. In his memo Bybee explained to Bush that his purpose was to "negate any claims that certain interrogation methods violate the statute" making torture a crime. He was, in effect, preparing a brief for lawyers defending U.S. soldiers or CIA agents charged with torturing prisoners.

It is, of course, impossible to link Bybee's memo—and its virtual invitation to employ interrogation techniques not "intended" to maim or kill prisoners—with the subsequent revelations that such brutal methods were actually used in Afghanistan and at Camp X-Ray. But the document certainly reflected the Bush administration's attitude that suspected terrorists could be abused with impunity. In December 2002, shortly after the memo reached the White House, a front-page story in the *Washington Post* reported the cynical comment of an official who supervised the treatment of prisoners in Afghanistan: "If you don't violate someone's human rights some of the time, you probably aren't doing your job." The *Post* article described some of the tactics used on prisoners at Bagram Air Base, in Afghanistan: "Those who refuse to cooperate inside this secret CIA interrogation center are sometimes kept standing or kneeling for hours, in black hoods or spray-painted goggles. . . . At times, they are held in awkward, painful positions and deprived of sleep with a 24-hour bombardment of lights—subject to what are known as 'stress and duress' techniques." These practices, also used at Camp X-Ray, pass muster under the Bybee definition of torture.

Later media reports detailed far more brutal treatment of prisoners, including over a dozen deaths in Afghanistan and at the infamous Abu Ghraib prison in Iraq. Not until early 2004, when the American public saw the graphic photographs of U.S. troops grinning and giving thumbs-up approval of the sexual humiliation of Abu Ghraib prisoners—and over dead bodies as well—did the Bush administration take any steps to deal with the kinds of torture and "cruel, inhuman, and degrading treatment" of prisoners the United States was bound under the Geneva Conventions to avoid and prevent. Only the media revelations and public outrage prompted Defense Secretary Rumsfeld to name a four-member commission, headed by one of his predecessors and a close friend, James Schlesinger, to investigate the Abu Ghraib scandal. Rumsfeld escaped unscathed in the commission's report, although one member, Tillie Fowler, a former Republican House member from Florida, pointed her finger directly at him. "We found fundamental failures throughout all levels of command," she said, "from the soldiers on the ground to Central Command [in Iraq] and to the Pentagon. These failures of leadership helped to set the conditions which allowed the abusive practices to take place." Despite denying any knowledge of the Abu Ghraib torture and murders, Runsfeld sounded contrite. "These events occurred on my watch," he told the Senate Armed Services Committee in May 2004. "As secretary of defense, I am accountable for them and I take full responsibility." President Bush, however, resisted calls for Rumsfeld's scalp and professed full confidence in his loyal subordinate.

Whatever its effect on the troops and the CIA agents who tortured suspected terrorists, the Bybee memo is a chilling reminder that some government officials share the view of John J. McCloy, who served as assistant secretary of war under President Franklin Roosevelt and supported the mass internment of Japanese Americans during World War II. "The Constitution is just a piece of paper," he said contemptuously. In one sense, McCloy was correct. Unless those in power respect and enforce the Constitution, its provisions are just "paper protections," as James Madison said in pressing for the Bill of Rights in 1789. Jay Bybee also escaped unscathed before his memo reached the front pages. In 2003, Bush named him to the Court of Appeals for the Ninth Circuit, in which post he wrapped himself in black robes and refused to discuss his torture memo. One colleague on the court, however, described Bybee as unrepentant in sanctioning any treatment of suspected terrorists short of "death or organ failure." The real failure in this episode, it seems clear, was the Bush administration's effort to evade its legal duty to uphold the provisions of the Geneva Conventions, which it viewed as just a piece of paper that could be tossed into the wastebasket.

Nevertheless, the Bybee memo may have had the unintended effect of stiffening the backbone of the Supreme Court. The memo, along with revelations about the Abu Ghraib torture scandal, hit the front pages while the justices were considering three cases that challenged the government's power to detain, indefinitely and without recourse to family members, lawyers, or the federal courts, those whom the White House identified as "enemy combatants." Ruling in June 2004, the Court firmly rejected the Bush administration's claims of "inherent" presidential power to hold anyone—U.S. citizens and foreign nationals alike—without some kind of meaningful, neutral judicial review of their detention. The Court's decisions in these cases delivered the sharpest blow to the imperial presidency since its *Youngstown Sheet & Tube* ruling, in 1952, stating that Harry Truman had no "inherent" power as commander in chief to seize the nation's steel mills.

The legal questions in the enemy combatant cases, of course, involved more serious constitutional issues than the property rights of steel mill owners. More than two centuries ago, in the *Federalist Papers*, Alexander Hamilton acutely noted that, for the government to confiscate someone's property without trial "must at once convey the alarm of tyranny throughout the whole nation but confinement of the person, by secretly hurrying him to jail, where his sufferings are unknown or forgotten, is a less public, less striking, and *therefore a more dangerous engine* of arbitrary government." The Constitution's Framers, as we have seen, erected a barrier against detention without judicial recourse in providing that "the Writ of Habeas Corpus shall not be suspended, unless when in cases of rebellion or invasion the public safety may require it." However much the "public safety" is endangered by threats of terrorism, at home or abroad, even suspected terrorists cannot be held indefinitely and incommunicado, without violating the suspension clause. That was the argument made before the Supreme Court by lawyers for the supposed "enemy combatants," who had been imprisoned for more than two years at Guantánamo Bay in Cuba and in navy brigs in the United States. Attorneys for the Bush administration argued, in response, that federal judges had no authority even to consider writs of habeas corpus when the president had designated someone as an enemy combatant. It would be hard to imagine a sharper conflict between judicial and executive powers—and more serious consequences to prisoners who might never emerge from their cages and cells if President Bush had won this battle with the courts.

Two of the "enemy combatant" cases involved American citizens, Yaser Esam Hamdi and Jose Padilla, with similar claims to habeas corpus protection but with very different circumstances. Hamdi was born in 1980 in Louisiana to parents from Saudi Arabia; his father worked in the oil fields. The Fourteenth Amendment confers citizenship on "all persons born or naturalized in the United States," regardless of their parents' nationality. Hamdi returned to Saudi Arabia as a child and most likely never thought about his citizenship until he was seized in Afghanistan as a suspected Taliban fighter and shipped to Guantánamo Bay. Once his American birth and citizenship came to light, Hamdi was transferred to a Navy brig in Virginia. Padilla, in contrast, was born and grew up in Chicago, before he converted to Islam and supposedly joined al Qaeda; he received training in Pakistan and Afghanistan before returning to Chicago in 2002. Federal agents grabbed Padilla when he got off the plane, and Attorney General Ashcroft promptly called a news conference to announce that Padilla had plans to set off a "dirty bomb" that would scatter radioactive debris across an American city. Dubbed by the press as the "dirty bomber," Padilla was hustled to the Navy brig in Norfolk, Virginia, and later transferred to one in Charleston, South Carolina. The third "enemy combatant" case involved more than six hundred prisoners at Camp X-Ray, none of whom—after Hamdi was shipped to the Virginia naval brig—held U.S. citizenship.

After months of detention, Yaser Hamdi became the first "enemy combatant" to drag the Bush administration into federal court, through a habeas corpus petition filed on behalf of his father against Defense Secretary Rumsfeld. District Judge Robert Doumar, named to the bench by President Reagan, appointed a federal defender, Frank Dunham, Jr., to represent Hamdi, although government lawyers refused to allow Dunham to meet with his client. At the first hearing before Judge Doumar, he asked the Justice Department's lawyer, Gregory Garre, to explain the government's decision to detain Hamdi without charges or access to counsel. Garre handed Doumar a two-page affidavit by Michael Mobbs, identified as a "special advisor to the undersecretary of defense for policy." Mobbs had never met Hamdi, but his affidavit claimed that a "review" of government records convinced him that Hamdi had been "seized while fighting with the Taliban in Afghanistan." Hamdi had supposedly turned over a Kalashnikov rifle when he was captured by troops of the American-backed Northern Alliance. Judge Doumar noted that every statement in the Mobbs affidavit was hearsay, based on unidentified sources and with no supporting documentation. "I'm challenging everything in the Mobbs declaration," Doumar told Garre. "Indeed, a close inspection of the declaration reveals that [it] never claims that Hamdi was fighting for the Taliban, nor that he was a member of the Taliban." Garre replied that revealing the records Mobbs had relied on might endanger government agents or compromise intelligence sources. Nonetheless, Doumar ordered the government to turn over the records for his inspection. With the courtroom temperature rising, Garre declined to comply. "The present detention is lawful," he doggedly insisted. Doumar had one final question: "So the Constitution doesn't apply to Mr. Hamdi?" Garre had no answer.

After that judicial standoff, Frank Dunham—still refused access to his client—filed an appeal with the Fourth Circuit, reputedly the most conservative federal court of appeals in the country. A three-judge panel answered Doumar's question with a firm "no." The claims in the Mobbs affidavit, the appellate judges said, "if accurate, are sufficient to confirm that Hamdi's detention conforms with a legitimate exercise of the war powers given to the executive." But the judges declined to look behind the affidavit, simply taking the government's word that Hamdi was "affiliated" with the Taliban. John Ashcroft praised the "ask-no-questions" ruling as "an important victory for the president's ability to protect the American people in times of war." The attorney general said nothing about protecting the constitutional rights of "enemy combatants" like Hamdi, whose Taliban affiliation remained unproven and untested in court.

When Hamdi's appeal from the Fourth Circuit reached the Supreme Court, along with similar appeals from Jose Padilla and the Camp X-Ray inmates, government lawyers repeated their claim that Bush had the "inherent" power as commander in chief to detain any person, anywhere in the world and for any period, whom he designated as an enemy combatant. The attorneys made three further arguments. The first was that Congress had, in fact, given Bush the right to detain suspected terrorists when it passed the Authorization for Use of Military Force Resolution in September 2001, allowing the president "to use all necessary and appropriate force against those nations, organizations, or persons he determines" had any role in planning, carrying out, or aiding the 9/11 attacks on the World Trade Center and the Pentagon. The second argument, limited to Padilla's case, was that he had filed his habeas corpus petition in the wrong court and against the wrong individual. Padilla had filed his petition in the District of Columbia, against Defense Secretary Rumsfeld. He should have brought his suit in federal court in South Carolina, where he was confined, against the warden of the Charleston naval brig, the person holding him in custody. Although such jurisdictional questions torment first-year law students, they offer an easy out to judges who would rather not decide a case on its merits. The third argument, also based on jurisdiction, relied on the hairsplitting claim that federal judges could not rule on the habeas petitions of the Camp X-Ray inmates, because the Guantánamo naval base, they claimed, was actually on Cuban territory, outside the reach of federal courts.

Lawyers for the prisoners in all three cases disputed the claim that Congress had authorized the president to go beyond the use of military force in Afghanistan, certainly not to detain anyone for an indefinite period. They pointed the justices to the federal habeas corpus law, which gives courts jurisdiction over "any person who claims to be held in custody in violation of the Constitution or laws or treaties of the United States." The term "any person" would cover foreign nationals as well as American citizens, lawyers for the Camp X-Ray inmates argued; if the Guantánamo naval base was not within U.S. jurisdiction, they added, it would be a "lawless" territory. Presumably, inmates could be tortured or even murdered with impunity. Padilla's lawyer told the justices that Rumsfeld was a proper defendant because he had decided where Padilla would be held, and the naval brig warden acted under his command.

It took the justices three months to weigh these conflicting arguments and write opinions in the three cases. When the Court issued its rulings in June 2004, reporters quickly skimmed through more than one hundred pages of opinions, crammed with footnotes and citations to dozens of prior cases. They found their lead in Justice Sandra Day O'Connor's opinion in *Hamdi v. Rumsfeld,* in which she declared that "a state of war is not a blank check for the president when it comes to the rights of the Nation's citizens." The bottom line of the Court's ruling was that the Constitution afforded Hamdi a right to challenge his detention "before a neutral decision-maker." But these words left undecided the crucial questions of who that decision-maker might be, and what kind of proceedings Hamdi would be entitled to in pursuing that challenge.

In fact, the justices were sharply divided over the first issue addressed in O'Connor's opinion, the validity of Hamdi's detention in the first place. On this question, only Chief Justice William Rehnquist and Justices Anthony Kennedy and Steven Breyer joined this part of her opinion, holding that the congressional Authorization for Use of Military Force had granted President Bush sufficient leeway to detain suspected "enemy combatants" seized in Afghanistan, even American citizens, such as Hamdi. "Because detention to prevent a combatant's return to the battlefield is a fundamental incident of waging war, in permitting the use of 'necessary and appropriate force,' Congress has clearly and unmistakably authorized detention in the narrow circumstances considered here," O'Connor wrote. But her conclusion was not at all clear to the four justices who dissented on this issue. Not surprisingly, two of the Court's most liberal members, David Souter and Ruth Bader Ginsburg, disagreed with O'Connor. The Use of Force resolution "never so much as uses the word detention, and there is no reason to think Congress might have perceived any need to augment Executive power to deal with dangerous citizens within the United States," Souter wrote for himself and Ginsburg. Souter also cited the "cautionary example" of the *Korematsu* case, noting that President Roosevelt in that case and Bush in *Hamdi* had invoked "the same presidential power" as commander in chief. The Court had upheld FDR's authority, ratified by Congress, to detain Japanese American citizens for an indefinite period, but Souter and Ginsburg found no such ratification in the Use of Force resolution on which the Bush administration relied.

More surprisingly, one of the most conservative justices, Antonin Scalia, issued a pointed dissent that was joined by the Court's most stalwart liberal, John Paul Stevens. It made no difference, Scalia argued, whether the Use of Force resolution could be read broadly enough to infer congressional approval of Hamdi's detention. No American citizens, Scalia asserted, can be detained any longer than it would take to file charges against them, no matter what crimes they are accused of committing. Hamdi, of course, had not been charged with any criminal offense, compounding the deprivation of his due process rights. Unless he was charged with treason or some other crime, Scalia wrote, Hamdi should be promptly released from custody. Citing the Civil War case of *Ex parte Milligan,* the justice noted that Congress had not suspended the writ of habeas corpus, that federal courts were functioning, and that President Bush had no "inherent" power to detain citizens without charges or access to counsel.

Despite their lack of agreement on the president's authority to detain Hamdi, eight justices rejected the Bush administration's claim that "enemy combatants" had no access to judicial review of their detention; Clarence Thomas stood alone in dissenting from this holding. His agreement that Congress had authorized President Bush to detain "enemy combatants" had provided O'Connor with the necessary majority on this issue, but Thomas disagreed with his fellow conservative, Justice Scalia, that government lawyers should either bring criminal charges against Hamdi or release him from custody. President Bush's determination that Hamdi was an enemy combatant, Thomas wrote, "should not be subjected to judicial second-guessing." Thomas, in effect, would allow the president to detain American citizens suspected of committing or aiding terrorist acts for the rest of their lives.

None of his colleagues shared Thomas's complete deference to executive power during wartime. Writing for a plurality of four, O'Connor held that "a citizen-detainee seeking to challenge his classification as an enemy combatant must receive notice of the factual basis for his classification, and a fair opportunity to rebut the Government's factual assertions before a neutral decision-maker." In other words, Judge Doumar had correctly ruled that the Mobbs affidavit, by itself, lacked enough supporting evidence to decide whether Hamdi's detention was lawful. Significantly, O'Connor quoted from Justice Frank Murphy's 1944 dissent in the *Korematsu* case, in which he argued that "the military claim must subject itself to the judicial process of having its reasonableness determined and its conflicts with other interests reconciled." O'Connor was saying, in effect, that the majority decision in *Korematsu*, upholding the wartime internment of Japanese Americans, was no longer a precedent the Court would follow.

The Court's decision that Hamdi was entitled to judicial review of the legality of his detention, however, did not free him from military custody. At the first hearing in Hamdi's case, Judge Doumar had asked the Justice Department lawyer how long the government could detain him: "A year? Two years? Ten years? A lifetime? How long?" The answer, it turned out, was three years. In September 2004, bowing to the Supreme Court's ruling, the Bush administration grudgingly released Hamdi from the navy brig. To gain his freedom, Hamdi agreed to return to Saudi Arabia and to renounce his American citizenship. "He has always thought of himself as a Saudi citizen," said his lawyer, Frank Dunham, "and he wasn't willing to spend another day in jail over it." After his return to Saudi Arabia, Hamdi expressed no bitterness at his treatment and simply said, "I am an innocent person." Whether he was innocent of any terrorist acts, of course, was a question the Bush administration had refused to permit a court to decide.

The Court's ruling in Yaser Hamdi's case would seemingly apply to Jose Padilla as well. Both were American citizens, held without charges. Surprisingly, however, the Supreme Court gave the government a short-term victory in agreeing that Padilla had filed his habeas petition in the wrong court and against the wrong defendant. His lawyers were free to file another petition, in South Carolina, against the navy brig's warden, which they promptly did. Ruling in February 2005, federal district judge Henry F. Floyd, who had been named to the bench by President Bush in 2003, dealt the government another judicial rebuke. Following the *Hamdi* ruling, Floyd held that "the President has no power, neither express nor implied, neither constitutional nor statutory, to hold Petitioner as an enemy combatant." He ordered that Padilla be released from custody within forty-five days, although he noted that government lawyers could still bring criminal charges against Padilla in the federal courts.

The Court's ruling in the *Hamdi* case left open the issue of whether the suspected al Qaeda terrorists and Taliban fighters held at Guantánamo Bay, none of them American citizens, had the same right to challenge their detention in federal courts. In an even greater rebuff to the Bush administration, six justices agreed that they did, in a case brought by two Australians and twelve Kuwaitis, *Rasul v. Bush*. Justice John Paul Stevens, who had joined Scalia's concurrence in *Hamdi*, wrote for the majority, rejecting the government's claim that the Guantánamo naval base was not American territory, in which case federal judges would lack jurisdiction. Stevens said the Camp X-Ray inmates "are not nationals of countries at war with the United States, and they deny that they have engaged in or plotted acts of aggression against this country; they have never been afforded access to any tribunal, much less charged with and convicted of wrong-doing; and for more than two years they have been imprisoned in territory over which the United States exercises exclusive jurisdiction and control." Stevens left undecided the question of what kind of tribunal, military or civilian, might decide the inmates' challenges to their detention, but he made clear that such proceedings must, at a minimum, provide counsel, notice of charges and evidence, and opportunity to rebut that evidence. In a concurring opinion, Justice Anthony Kennedy stressed the need for prompt resolution of these cases. "Perhaps, where detainees are taken from a zone of hostilities," he wrote, "detention without proceedings or trial would be justified by military necessity for a matter of weeks; but as the period of detention stretches from months to years, the case for continued detention to meet military exigencies becomes weaker."

Justice Scalia, whose *Hamdi* opinion had blasted the detention without trial of American citizens and had showed little deference to Bush as commander in chief, wrote a blistering dissent in *Rasul,* which Chief Justice Rehnquist and Justice Thomas joined. Scalia displayed no similar concern for the rights of noncitizens; he would have handed Bush the "blank check" that Justice O'Connor had refused to sign for the Court. "The Commander-in-Chief and his subordinates," Scalia wrote, "had every reason to expect that the internment of combatants at Guantánamo Bay would not have the consequence of bringing the cumbersome machinery of our domestic courts into military affairs." In his characteristic hyperbole, Scalia accused the majority of "judicial adventurism of the worst sort."

In truth, what the Court's majorities had shown in both the *Hamdi* and *Rasul* cases was not "judicial adventurism" but judicial adherence to the Constitution's command that "no person" can be deprived of liberty without due process of law. This guarantee applies equally to a person charged with a minor crime like shoplifting, or one suspected of complicity in the most devastating and deadly terrorist attack in American history. But the Court's rebuke in these cases to the Bush administration's disdain for due process has not been matched by judicial adherence to another of the Constitution's declarations, that only Congress has the power to commit the nation to war. The imperial presidency suffered a setback in the *Hamdi* and *Rasul* cases, imposed by justices who took seriously yet a third command of the Constitution, that its provisions are the "supreme law of the land" and cannot be disregarded by any official, even the president. Whether the Court will someday depose the imperial presidency, and return the Constitution's war powers to their rightful place, in Congress, remains to be seen. In the end, however, only the American people have the power—through their voices and their votes—to answer the questions posed in this book's introduction: "Why and how do we go to war?" As the voters showed in 2004, these are questions that a slight majority of citizens would rather leave in the hands of a commander in chief than decide for themselves. In the book's conclusion, we will explore some of the factors that may influence the future course of the American empire and the imperial presidency at its helm.

CONCLUSION

As we noted in chapter 13, only the collective voices and votes of the American people can provide answers to the questions posed in this book: How and why do we go to war? In the conclusion, we look both to recent and more distant events to explain the emergence of the imperial presidency and to speculate—because that is all we can do—about possible scenarios that might further expand presidential war powers, or return those powers to their constitutional home in Congress, as the Framers intended. In any case, events that cannot now be foreseen will shape the course of America's role in world affairs.

We can begin with the most recent significant event. The victory of President George W. Bush in the 2004 election represented, as well, a victory for the Bush Doctrine of preemptive war, which led to the America invasion of Iraq in 2003. There were sharp differences between Bush and his Democratic challenger, Senator John Kerry, over the invasion of Iraq and a wide range of other foreign policy issues. In campaign debates and speeches, the focus was on the question of which candidate was better qualified to serve as commander in chief. Significantly, neither Bush nor Kerry said anything, during the campaign, about the role of Congress in deciding questions of war and peace. And neither candidate uttered a word about the constitutional issues raised by the invasion of Iraq or the global war on terror, which both men promised to wage with every resource at the president's command.

There should be nothing surprising about the fact that presidential candidates hardly ever discuss issues of "institutional competence" or even the checks and balances between the branches of government. Quite understandably, voters are more concerned about the candidates themselves than about abstract principles like the proper allocation of governmental authority. Although Bush and Kerry differed over the invasion of Iraq and how best to wage the war on terror, neither candidate suggested that whoever served as president should not make the decision to send troops into combat. In this sense, Bush and Kerry shared an imperial vision of presidential power, despite their lack of agreement over the exercise of the executive function. Bush's go-it-alone policy of unilateral intervention in Iraq had the same purpose as Kerry's proposal for multilateral action: removal of Saddam Hussein from power. It was on the means of attaining this shared goal that the two candidates differed.

As Bush noted with great effect during the campaign, Kerry had voted with the bipartisan Senate majority to authorize military action to bring about regime change in Iraq. At no point, before or during the campaign, did Kerry argue that only a congressional declaration of war could authorize military action against Iraq. Kerry would simply have taken a different route to Baghdad, one that proceeded through the United Nations in New York rather than directly from the White House. This is not a cynical view that Bush and Kerry would both have launched a war at the same time and with the same array of military forces. Most likely, Kerry would have pursued every diplomatic option to persuade Hussein to reopen the gates for UN weapons inspectors. Whether such efforts might have succeeded is, of course, impossible to say. Most knowledgeable observers have expressed doubts that Hussein, even knowing that inspectors would find no weapons of mass destruction, would have bowed to pressure from the United States and allowed something analogous to rummaging through his bedroom drawers. In this respect, Hussein's paranoia and megalomania blocked any rational assessment of the risks and rewards of cooperating with outside inspectors, including the Americans who drove his army out of Kuwait in 1991. It is possible, however unlikely, that Kerry's after-the-fact advocacy of "coalition building" and diplomacy might have succeeded in avoiding war. To put it another way: What might have happened if Colin Powell—whose positions on Iraq were closer to Kerry's than to Bush's—had been president rather than secretary of state, without Dick Cheney as vice president and Donald Rumsfeld as defense secretary?

This kind of "what-if" speculation has a broader point than Bush's decision to invade Iraq. Who occupies the Oval Office has a significant effect on presidential decisions about war and peace. Some former presidents—including such political opposites as William McKinley and Jimmy Carter—only reluctantly sent troops into countries like Cuba and Iran. Others, most notably in the nation's early years, took military action only in the emergency situations contemplated by the Framers, in the absence of congressional declarations of war. But even the most pacific in temperament and patient in responding to foreign threats have engaged in acts of war without congressional sanction.

Perhaps the major conclusion of this book is that the presidency as an office and institution has become more important than the presidents themselves. In this respect, the imperatives of the American empire, since the end of World War II, have, in effect, forced presidents to don the uniform of commander in chief and take unilateral military action to protect those imperial interests. It bears repeating that every president since Harry Truman has cited America's "vital interests" as justification for military intervention, in wars from Korea to Iraq. Those vital interests are rooted in the demands of corporate and financial institutions for access to resources and markets. Even countries with few essential resources, such as Korea in 1950, assumed geopolitical significance because of their location in regions, such as Asia, with vast resources and potential markets.

Korea and Vietnam, whose very different wars spanned the quarter century from 1950 to 1975, both embroiled the United States in military conflict against the backdrop of the Cold War struggle, between the Western "democracies" and the Communist "police states." There were, in fact, clear distinctions between the political and personal liberties possessed by people on either side of the Cold War. Even during the height of repression under Senator Joseph McCarthy's anti-Communist crusade, in the late 1940s and early 1950s, American citizens enjoyed much greater protection of their right to criticize the government than those in the Soviet Union and its satellites, and in China, before and after the Communist revolution in 1949. But the Cold War itself, however much it stemmed from ideological disparities over the rights of citizens and state power, was deeply rooted in the combined economic, political, and military interests of two rival empires, one based on "state capitalism" and the other on "state socialism." Even before World War II, the free-market system and laissez-faire capitalism had become nothing more than myths, as outmoded as mom-and-pop stores in the Wal-Mart age.

After 1945, the American empire became a reality, anchored in conglomerates with global reach and protected by U.S. military bases around the world, which have at their disposal an arsenal of nuclear and conventional weapons. What is more, the empire is headed and staffed by a network of corporate leaders and government officials who move back and forth across the Beltway that surrounds Washington. Regardless of which party occupies the White House, those who control the nation's political and economic institutions agree that presidents should be able to deploy military force to meet challenges to the vital interests of the United States. The "revolving door" policy has marked the system ever since President Franklin Roosevelt invited business leaders to manage wartime agencies. Thus corporate CEOs take government jobs in the departments responsible for monitoring the very industries the tycoons headed; later, under another administration, perhaps, the recruits to Washington return to their former corporate lairs, where the businesses they now run benefit from the (de)regulating they recently oversaw.

In his farewell address in 1961, President Eisenhower warned the people about the growing influence of the military-industrial complex, but the alarm bells went unheeded by Congress and future presidents. Eisenhower himself had named Charles E. Wilson of General Motors to head the Defense Department; Wilson became famous for saying "What's good for General Motors is good for the country." In addition, the defense secretaries who followed Wilson include Robert McNamara, who ran the Ford Motor Company; James Schlesinger, a director of Seven Seas Petroleum and the investment firm of Lehman Brothers; and Donald Rumsfeld, former CEO of both the worldwide Searle pharmaceutical firm and the General Instrument Corporation, a major defense contractor. The point of this listing, which could be greatly expanded to include other defense and foreign policy positions, is that presidents call upon members of the military-industrial complex, men and women with vested interests in the American empire, to plan and carry out the unilateral, interventionist policies of the imperial presidency.

This leads to a further point. Ever since World War II, presidents have commanded a huge defense bureaucracy, which far outstrips, in size and budget, the meager resources available to Congress. In 2004, for example, the Defense Department had 636,000 civilian employees and directed a military establishment of 2.3 million troops and support staff, with a total budget of $360 billion. (By comparison, the entire gross domestic product of Russia in 2002— the most recent numbers—was just $347 billion.) The Pentagon building itself houses 23,000 employees, with another 17,000 in various CIA facilities around the world. The recently established Department of Homeland Security has 180,000 employees. Put together, more than 3 million people work in defense-related agencies, from army privates to the secretary of defense. In contrast, Congress has a total budget of $3.6 billion and a total workforce of

30,000. Both figures are roughly 1 percent of those for the defense establishment. Moreover, the Senate and House committees with jurisdiction over defense and foreign policy have, between them, just a small fraction of the congressional budget and staff.

This huge disparity in the funding and staffing of the Defense Department and Congress helps to explain why the executive branch has been able to impose its will on Congress over the war-making powers. There are other factors as well. Franklin Roosevelt, the first imperial president, was also the first to make effective use of modern communications; his "Fireside Chats" with the American people, broadcast over the radio, brought FDR's voice into millions of living rooms. Later presidents—most notably John Kennedy, Ronald Reagan, and Bill Clinton—used television to full advantage. The major networks air presidential speeches and press conferences, and nightly news programs feature reports from White House correspondents and sound bites of presidential statements. The ability of presidents to command the airwaves should not be underestimated in explaining the triumph of the imperial presidency over Congress. During the 2004 congressional session, with Republicans controlling both chambers, the chairs of the House and Senate defense-related committees were experienced, respected legislators: Duncan Hunter and Henry Hyde chaired the House armed services and foreign affairs committees, John Warner and Richard Lugar chaired the Senate armed services and foreign relations committees. But hardly anyone outside the Beltway could identify these legislators, who between them have served in Congress for more than one hundred years.

Presidents have long enjoyed, and employ to the hilt, what Teddy Roosevelt called the "bully pulpit" of the Oval Office. The audience for presidential State of the Union speeches and even for televised press conferences far exceeds the small number of viewers who follow congressional floor debates or committee hearings on C-SPAN, or see the snippets of these proceedings on network news. Even when a committee grills a top administration official, such as the secretary of defense or state, it is generally those officials whose statements get the biggest share of television coverage and newspaper headlines.

But the disparate funding, staffing, and media coverage only partly explains why, since the late 1940s, Congress has virtually abdicated its constitutional war powers to the imperial presidency. During this period, presidents from Harry Truman to George W. Bush have seized the initiative in taking unilateral military action. This pattern has created both momentum and precedent, to which Congress has responded with blank-check authorizations. Presidents who contemplate military intervention abroad, in Grenada, Iraq, or anywhere else, are certainly aware that neither Congress nor the courts blocked any of their predecessors from taking action. Members of Congress, as well, realize that none of their predecessors took steps to hinder presidential war making. The few exceptions are striking for their ineffectiveness. For example, Congress voted in 1970 to cut off funding for bombing Cambodia, but the explosives had already been dropped. In fact, members of Congress are reluctant, for obvious political reasons, to criticize or vote against a military operation that has already begun, with planes in the air and troops on the ground. Even when presidents ask Congress for prior authorization to use military force, the momentum for action has generally built up enough steam that dissenters—particularly within the president's own party—are unwilling to stand in front of the train. For instance, we observed that only 133 House members and 23 in the Senate, almost all Democrats, voted in 2002 against the resolution authorizing George W. Bush to invade Iraq. The precedents for blank-check authorization go back to the Tonkin Gulf Resolution in 1964, when Congress granted Lyndon Johnson the power to use "all necessary force" in Vietnam; similar resolutions were enacted for the Gulf War in 1991 and the invasion of Afghanistan in 2001. It is reasonable to conclude, as Senator Robert Byrd said of his colleagues after the Iraq invasion in 2003, that virtually all members of Congress have become "cowed" by presidents who know they can disregard the Constitution with impunity. The precedents for unilateral presidential war making have also cowed the federal courts, whose members have been consistently unwilling to block the use of force. Unlike members of Congress, federal judges are insulated by lifetime tenure from reprisals at the voting booth. But judges are also conscious that barring a president from sending troops abroad, or ruling that troops in combat must be withdrawn, would likely precipitate a constitutional and political crisis. In this respect, what judges call "prudential" factors weigh more heavily than the clear wording of the Constitution, and the clear intent of its Framers, that only Congress has the power to declare war. Considering the conservative dominance of the federal judiciary, with more than two-thirds of its members named by Republican presidents, it is simply not realistic to expect that judges will do what Congress has been unwilling to do, in reversing the precedent and momentum of presidential war making.

Given these factors, is it realistic to expect *any* reversal of the precedent and momentum? In one sense, it can be argued that Congress has not completely abdicated its sole power to declare war. A formal declaration of war, of course, provides as much of a blank check to the commander in chief as the "authorizations" for military action in Vietnam, Kuwait, Afghanistan, and Iraq. Franklin Roosevelt was no more constrained by Congress in deploying troops during World War II than George W. Bush has been in Iraq. We can view these latter-day authorizations as functional equivalents of formal declarations of war, with the same constitutional sanction and significance. One could argue that only constitutional literalists could quibble over what seems to many people a purely semantic difference between "declaring" and "authorizing" war. The result is the same: Presidents may use "all necessary force" to accomplish their objectives. But in my view, absent a sudden attack on American soil by troops or planes—or even nuclear missiles—of a foreign state, a military response to any other provocation should await the deliberations of Congress, and debate over a formal declaration of war. Such a policy would still allow presidents to take the kind of emergency actions the Framers contemplated, for limited periods of time and only to protect American lives.

One might also argue that the ineffective War Powers Resolution should be updated and amended, to preclude the kind of "quick and easy" military invasions that President Reagan launched against Grenada in 1983 and the first President Bush conducted in Panama in 1989. Both actions ended before the sixty-day clock had expired, rendering the provisions of the resolution moot. There have been suggestions to shorten the clock to twenty days, or to require presidents to secure congressional funding before initiating any military action, or to require federal judges to decide cases brought by any member of Congress that challenge presidential war making. However well intentioned, such proposals, it strikes me, represent tinkering with a badly damaged system.

In my view, there is just one realistic prospect for ending the subversion of the Constitution and returning the war-making power to Congress, where it was placed by the Framers and where it belongs. And that prospect, however slim and remote it may seem today, depends largely on the political process. It may seem trite and simplistic to some, but the iron grip of the president on every aspect of foreign policy will loosen only when Congress reasserts its constitutional powers. The near-term likelihood of that reassertion is slim, to say the least. In the 2004 elections, the voters not only gave President Bush a popular-vote majority of 3.6 million but increased the Republican margins in both the House and the Senate, solidifying the already tight control of the conservatives in both chambers. Bush exulted after the election that "I earned political capital in the campaign, and I intend to spend it." He listed among his second-term priorities "fighting and winning the war on terror." For their part, congressional Democrats not only lost seats in 2004 but lost the debate over the course of American foreign policy.

During Bush's second term, national security planners in both the White House and the Pentagon are expected to rely for guidance on the Bush Doctrine of preemptive war, which allows the president to send troops into any country, and even to overthrow governments, on whatever pretext he offers. Never before has the planet faced a worldwide "marshal" with such a massive arsenal at his disposal and with no institution, domestic or international, willing or able to restrain him. The Wild West metaphor is not far-fetched. Much like Sheriff Will Kane in the 1952 film *High Noon,* Bush has postured himself for shootouts with such "outlaw" countries as Iran and North Korea, while members of Congress, much like the cowering townspeople in the film, voice their concerns about unilateral action but refuse to block the president from the showdown that could endanger world peace. The political cartoons portraying Bush as a trigger-happy cowboy express in simple visual terms what many pundits use jargon-loaded paragraphs to explain. In essence, the preemptive war doctrine confers on the president a warrant to "act independently" to punish any country whose actions "seriously unsettle international relations," as Paul Wolfowitz, one of the doctrine's architects, stated its basic postulates.

As far as domestic political factors go, there is little chance of reversing the momentum of the imperial presidency during Bush's second term. But there are always unforeseen events that might constrain his actions, or those of his successors. In the near term, if the American occupation of Iraq continues to exact a high price in deaths and deficits, public opinion might turn against the president, as it did against Lyndon Johnson during the Vietnam War. But Johnson, a fellow Texan, did not have Bush's swagger and evangelical certitude about the rightness of his actions. And with the departure from the cabinet of Secretary of State Colin Powell, a self-described "reluctant warrior," and his replacement by Condoleezza Rice, Bush's second-term circle of advisers lacks any cautionary voices. And like Congress, the international community has no real leverage over American foreign policy. The United Nations did not dissuade Bush from invading Iraq, nor could it deter him from launching further interventions.

Given the unlikelihood of change in the near future, those who wish to return the war power to Congress must adopt a long-range strategy, one based on the slow, incremental grassroots activism that marked the civil rights movement in its struggle against Jim Crow laws. Decades of patient, often tedious, and sometimes dangerous organizing laid the groundwork for such victories as the Supreme Court's *Brown v. Board of Education* decision in 1954 and congressional passage of the Civil Rights Act ten years later. Not even a brilliant legal strategist like Thurgood Marshall, or a charismatic leader such as Martin Luther King, Jr., could have single-handedly produced those momentous events. Any movement to curb the powers of the imperial presidency cannot wait for or depend upon another Marshall or King. Its success must depend on the American people, coming together in the kinds of town meeting gatherings that sparked the colonists to rebel against the imperial rule of King George III.

Perhaps we should look back for guidance to James Madison, whose patient work produced the Constitution, whose provisions form the bedrock of this nation. When that document was sent to the states for ratification, with the outcome still uncertain, Madison voiced his apprehension to George Washington. "The country must finally decide," he said, "the sense of which is as yet wholly unknown." To provide answers to the fateful questions of how and why we go to war, the country must finally decide.

NOTES

Note to Readers

The quotations in these notes are cited to the most accessible source I have used, although most quotations are available in multiple sources. Citations include all quoted material from the first few words listed in the note to the end of quotations from the speaker or author. I have listed works of special interest and importance, along with cited sources, in the Suggested Readings and Sources. Particularly in the last two chapters, I have cited quotations to Web sites from which they were obtained; again, multiple sources are available for most quotations. Sources for most quotations can also be located through keyword searches on such search engines as Google and Yahoo; for example, Senator Albert Beveridge's quote "The Philippines are ours forever" can be located through "beveridge philippines forever."

A final note about quotations from judicial opinions: Because there are several "reporters" of opinions, and because pagination varies among them, I have cited quotations by the reporter edition and the first page of the opinion. For U.S. Supreme Court opinions, the official reporter is *United States Reports* (abbreviated as U.S.), which is cited by volume number, first page of the opinion, and year of decision; for example, *Marbury v. Madison,* 5 U.S. 137 (1803). Unofficial (and commercial) reporters of Supreme Court opinions include *Lawyers' Edition* and *Supreme Court Reporter,* each with different pagination. Supreme Court opinions can be accessed on the Internet through the Court's own Web site (www.supremecourtus.gov) and through www.findlaw.com. Again, keyword searches on Google or Yahoo can locate most quotations from court decisions; for example, Chief Justice Marshall's famous statement in *Marbury v. Madison* that "it is emphatically the province and duty of the judicial department to say what the law is" can be located through "marshall province duty judicial." Readers should keep in mind that Google and Yahoo have made trips to the library to find sources for quoted material (or virtually any fact or subject) almost unnecessary; a few clicks on the keyboard will usually do the trick.

1: In the Beginning

12 "its sovereignty": Peter Irons, *A People's History of the Supreme Court*, 18.

13 "take into consideration": Charles Mee, *The Genius of the People*, 8.
"the situation": ibid., 10.

14 "a due supremacy": ibid., 68–69.

15 "the Articles": James Madison, *Notes of Debates in the Federal Convention of 1787*, 30.

16 "to legislate": ibid., 44.

18 "antecedent": W. Taylor Reveley III, *War Power of the President and Congress*, 160.

19 "punctually to observe": ibid., 56.
"that a national Executive": Madison, 30.

20 "peace and war": Louis Fisher, *Presidential War Power*, 4.
"was for vesting": id.
"making peace and war": David Grey Adler and Larry N. George, *The Constitution and the Making of American Foreign Policy*, 196.
"executive powers": id.
"The legislature": id.
"proceedings were": Reveley, 82.
"was for vesting": id.

21 "never expected": Madison, 476.
"leaving to the Executive": Fisher, 6.
"the executive": ibid., 7.
"was for clogging": id.
"the Framers": 119 *Congressional Record* S14141 (1973).

22 "Congress must": Francis D. Wormuth and Edwin B. Firmage, *To Chain the Dog of War*, 37.

24 "subject to such orders": ibid., 107.

25 "the commander in chief": id.
"shall, by virtue": Edward Keynes, *Undeclared War*, 52.
"In almost": Abraham Sofaer, *War, Foreign Affairs, and Constitutional Powers*, 49.

26 "would amount": Edward M. Earle, *The Federalist*, 448.
"those who are": James Madison, *The Writings of James Madison*, vol. 6, 148.

2: *"Not Only War But Public War"*

31 "repel force by force": David Grey Adler and Larry N. George, eds., *The Constitution and the Making of American Foreign Policy*, 261.
"such of the armed": ibid., 269.
32 "friendly and impartial": John C. Fitzpatrick, ed., *The Writings of George Washington*, 416.
33 "if one citizen": Louis Fisher, *Presidential War Power*, 20.
"the *organ*": id.
34 "In no part": ibid., 21.
"the wisdom,": ibid., 21–22.
36 "Every contention by force": *Bas v. Tingy*, 4 U.S. 37 (1800).
37 "to recommend": Fisher, 17.
"now in a state": ibid., 18.
38 "to any port or place": *Little v. Barreme*, 6 U.S. 169 (1804).
40 "that every syllable": *United States v. Smith*, 27 Federal Cases 1192 (Cir. Ct. N.Y. 1806).
42 "unauthorized by the Constitution": Fisher, 25.
"To have awaited": ibid., 27.

3: *"A War Unjust and Unnecessary"*

47 "indignities and injuries": Louis Fisher, *Presidential War Power*, 28.
49 "whenever the United States": *Martin v. Mott*, 25 U.S. 19 (1827).
52 "shall be incorporated": *American Insurance Co. v. 356 Bales of Cotton*, 26 U.S. 511 (1828).
55 "ought to be acknowledged": Fisher, 30.
"It will always": id.
56 "insultingly refused": id.
"pecuniary consideration": id.
"another revolution": id.
57 "to confer authority": ibid., 31.
"Mexico has passed the boundary": ibid., 32.
"The president has announced": id.
"I do not see": id.
58 "our object was": ibid., 33–34.
"unnecessary and improper": ibid., 34.
"it was clear": id.

59   "a war unnecessarily": id.
      "Allow the President": id.
60   "subject to the sovereignty": *Fleming v. Page,* 50 U.S. 603 (1850).
62   "California and the fine bay": Fisher, 30.
63   "mischievous" and "blacks and persons": ibid., 35.
      "the lives or property": *Durand v. Holland,* 8 Federal Cases (Cir. Ct.
      S.D.N.Y. 1860) 1123.
64   "is limited to": Fisher, 36.
      "Without the authority": ibid., 37.

4: "The Great Exigencies of Government"

67   "a covenant with death": Peter Irons, *A People's History of the
      Supreme Court,* 153.
68   "bought and sold": *Dred Scott v. Sandford,* 60 U.S. 393 (1857).
      "The *Dred Scott*": Philip van Doren Stern, ed., *The Life and Writings of
      Abraham Lincoln,* 399.
      "warfare on the Supreme Court": Don Fehrenbacher, *Slavery, Law, and
      Politics,* 260.
69   "the power vested": Irons, 182.
70   "whether strictly legal": Louis Fisher, *Presidential War Power,* 38.
      "approving, legalizing": ibid., 39.
71   "Had the President": *The Prize Cases,* 67 U.S. 635 (1863).
74   "say what the law is": *Marbury v. Madison,* 5 U.S. 137 (1803).
      "It cannot be delegated": *The Prize Cases,* 67 U.S. 635 (1863).
78   "any offense against": *Ex parte Merryman,* 17 Federal Cases 144 (Cir.
      Ct. D.Md.) 1861.
80   "be allowed": Message to Congress in Special Session, July 4, 1861.
81   "inciting insurrection": *Ex parte Milligan,* 71 U.S. 12 (1866).
86   "blank check": *Hamdi v. Rumsfeld,* www.supremecourtus.gov/
      opinions/2003 term.

5: "Remember the Maine"

88   "American factories": Howard Zinn, *A People's History of the United
      States,* 299.
      "In the interests": id.
89   "a crime against": ibid., 300.
      "All the great": id.
      "We have about decided": Louis Fisher, *Presidential War Power,* 42.
90   "I will not mobilize": id.
      "it injuriously affects": id.
      "by an exterior": id.

91   "the people of the Island": ibid., 43.
       "possibly the President": id.
93   "the government of Cuba": Francis D. Wormuth and Edwin B.
       Firmage, *To Chain the Dog of War,* 146–47.
       "There is, of course": Zinn, 312.
       "Proceed at once": Fisher, 44.
94   "instructed him": Zinn, 316.
95   "The Philippines": 56 *Congressional Record* 704–712 (1900).
96   "involved no war": Fisher, 46.
       "reasonable efficiency": ibid., 47.
97   "I took the Canal Zone": ibid., 49.
98   "serious doubt": ibid., 50.
99   "No doubt I could do": id.
100   "I fear we have not": ibid., 51.

6: *"We Must Have No Criticism Now"*

103   "There is such a thing": Howard Zinn, *A People's History of the United
       States,* 361.
       "The war opened": ibid., 362.
       "War is the health": ibid., 359.
104   "A ship carrying": Arthur S. Link, ed., *The Papers of Woodrow Wilson,*
       vol. 33, 134–35.
       "No doubt": Louis Fisher, *Presidential War Power,* 56.
       "The Senate of the United States": James D. Richardson, ed., *A
       Compilation of the Messages and Papers of the Presidents,* vol. 16, 8218.
105   "I am not expecting": Harvey A. DeWeerd, *President Wilson Fights His
       War,* 21.
       "rationalization of the flimsiest sort": Zinn, 361.
107   "the righteous conquest": ibid., 362.
       "Shall we or any other": Richardson, 8735.
108   "The United States assumes": 58 *Congressional Record* 8777 (1919).
       "cut out the heart": Fisher, 71.
       "The initiative": Woodrow Wilson, *Constitutional Government in the
       United States,* 77–78.
112   "We must have": Peter Irons, *A People's History of the Supreme Court,*
       266.
       "there are men": id.
113   "widespread opposition": ibid., 267.
114   "Long Live the Constitution": *Schneck v. United States,* 249 U.S. 47
       (1919).
115   "man's destiny is to fight": ibid., 270.
       "Doesn't this squashy": id.
117   "The Constitution": *Ex parte Milligan,* 71 U.S. 12 (1866).

118   "disloyal, scurrilous": *Abrams v. United States,* 250 U.S. 616 (1919).
119   "directed to inciting": *Brandenburg v. Ohio,* 395 U.S. 444 (1969).

7: *"The Sole Organ of the Nation"*

122   "shall be used": 69 *Congressional Record* 6684 (1928).
       "no money appropriated": 47 Statutes 439 (1932).
123   *Panama Refining Co. v. Ryan,* 293 U.S. 388 (1935).
       A. L. A. Schechter Poultry Co. v. United States, 295 U.S. 495 (1935).
124   "if the President finds": *United States v. Curtiss-Wright Corp.,* 299 U.S.
       304 (1936).
128   "upon the outbreak": 49 Statutes 1081 (1935).
       "the people of the United States": *Public Papers and Addresses of
       Franklin D. Roosevelt,* 192 (1937, vol. 6).
129   "would require Congressional action": Charles C. Tansill, *Back Door
       to War,* 591.
       "shall first certify": 54 Statutes 681, sec. 14 (1940).
       "to use all constitutional": *Opinions of the Attorney General* 484–86,
       vol. 39 (1940).
       "we will not participate": *Public Papers and Addresses of Franklin D.
       Roosevelt,* 495 (1940, vol. 9).
       "your boys": ibid., 517.

8: *"The Very Brink of Constitutional Power"*

Note: To avoid excessive citation, readers should note that all quotations in the
account of the Japanese American internment cases, between pages 133 and 140,
are drawn from chapter 27 in Peter Irons, *A People's History of the Supreme
Court.* That chapter, in turn, is based upon the fuller treatment of the cases in
Peter Irons, *Justice at War: The Story of the Japanese American Internment
Cases.*

141   "We have no occasion": *Hirabayashi v. United States,* 320 U.S. 81
       (1943).
144   "prevent incidents": Irons, *A People's History of the Supreme Court,*
       359.
145   "But hardships": *Korematsu v. United States,* 323 U.S. 214 (1944).
       "the underlying": *Ex parte Endo,* 323 U.S. 284 (1944).
146   "permitted the same freedoms": Irons, *A People's History of the
       Supreme Court,* 360.
       "grave injustice": *Personal Justice Denied,* Report of the Commission
       on Wartime Relocation and Internment of Citizens, 18.

147 "Since this is not so": Irons, *A People's History of the Supreme Court,* 362.

"The judicial process": ibid., 363.

"a United States citizen": id.

"A man of quiet bravery": ibid., 364.

"race prejudice": *Personal Justice Denied,* 18.

148 "their attachments to Japan": *Hirabayashi v. United States,* 320 U.S. 81 (1943).

"remains on the pages": Irons, *A People's History of the Supreme Court,* 363.

151 "all persons who are subjects": *Ex parte Quirin,* 317 U.S. 1 (1942).

155 "covers with the shield": *Ex parte Milligan,* 71 U.S. 2 (1866).

9: *"A World-Wide American Empire"*

158 "seek no aggrandizement": Howard Zinn, *A People's History of the United States,* 412.

"it is thoroughly": id.

159 "Leadership toward": Peter Irons, *America's Cold War Crusade,* 49.

161 "enormous post-war trade": National Foreign Trade Council, *Proceedings of the National Foreign Trade Convention,* 1945, 46.

"will be a greater market": Junius B. Wood, "How Russia Trades With Us," *Nation's Business,* March 1945, 46.

"Whatever the outcome": Carl Marzani, *We Can Be Friends,* 108.

162 "fill the vacuum": Eugene Lyons, "The U.S. and World Affairs," *Nation's Business,* April 1946, 25.

163 "whole world": 89 *Congressional Record* 2031 (1945).

"Resolved by the House": ibid., 7623.

"through its constitutional": ibid., 7647.

164 "general international organization": Louis Fisher, *Presidential War Power,* 75.

"must have the power": *Department of State Bulletin* 447-48 (1945, vol. 11).

165 "in accordance with": Fisher, 77.

"If we are talking": ibid., 78.

166 "If it is to be contended": 91 *Congressional Record* 7988 (1945).

"entirely within the wisdom": Fisher, 81.

167 "were agreed on": ibid., 82.

168 "that we ought": Irons, 79.

"Great Britain": Zinn, 426.

169 "free peoples": id.

"Unhappily, one imperialist nation": Irons, 105.

171 "in accordance with": *Public Papers of the Presidents,* 1950, 491.

171 "I have ordered": ibid., 492.

"we are not at war": ibid., 1951, 503.

"in the usual": Fisher, 87.

172 "some American action": Dean Acheson, *Present at the Creation,* 408.

"When we agreed": 96 *Congressional Record* 9268 (1951).

173 "without congressional approval": ibid., 9323.

174 "endanger the well-being": *Youngstown Sheet & Tube Co. v. Sawyer,* 343 U.S. 579 (1952).

10: "What Every Schoolboy Knows"

181 "The whole Vietnamese people": Howard Zinn, *A People's History of the United States,* 470.

182 "Communist control": ibid., 471.

"Indochina is immensely wealthy": ibid., 472.

183 "South Vietnam was essentially": id.

"There is going to be": *Public Papers of the Presidents,* 1954, 306.

"the absence of some kind": Louis Fisher, *Presidential War Power,* 104.

184 "dispatch of agents": Zinn, 474.

"Some units" and "I do not feel": id.

185 "to move our forces": Fisher, 115.

186 "outrage": *Public Papers of the Presidents,* 1964, vol. 2, 927.

"determination to take": id.

"intends no rashness": id.

"all necessary measures": 78 Statutes 384 (1964).

187 "are clear": 110 *Congressional Record* 18399 (1964).

"routine patrol": Zinn, 476.

"Review of action": Fisher, 117.

188 "one person, one vote": *Baker v. Carr,* 369 U.S. 186 (1962).

"is obviously a political question": *Luftig v. McNamara,* 252 F.Supp. 819 (D.D.C. 1966). U.S. District Court opinions are reported in the Federal Supplement, abbreviated as F.Supp., prefaced by the volume number and followed by the first page number, the court (abbreviated by district and state), and the year of decision.

189 "the interests of the country": *Velvel v. Johnson,* 287 F.Supp. 846 (D.Kan. 1968).

"no formal declaration": *Meyers v. Nixon,* 339 F.Supp. 1388 (S.D.N.Y. 1972).

191 "When nations contend": *Atlee v. Laird,* 347 F.Supp. 689 (E.D.Pa. 1972).

192 "beyond the boundaries": *Drinan v. Nixon,* 364 F.Supp. 854 (D.Mass. 1973).

193 "facing up to the question": *Mitchell v. Laird,* 488 F.2d 611 (D.C. Cir. 1973).

194 "the question of the balance": *Holtzman v. Richardson*, 361 F.Supp. 544 (E.D.N.Y. 1973).

195 "fair reading": *Holtzman v. Richardson*, 484 F.2d 1307 (2d Cir. 1973).

196 "it is emphatically": *Marbury v. Madison*, 5 U.S. 137 (1803).
"in certain extraordinary": 87 Statutes 555 (1973).

198 "it is the purpose": id.

199 "pursuant to the President's": *Public Papers of the Presidents, 1975*, vol. 1, 670.

200 "His advice": Jimmy Carter, *Keeping Faith*, 514.

201 "constitutional authority": *Public Papers of the Presidents, 1982*, vol. 2, 1238.

202 "a Soviet-Cuban colony": ibid., 1521.
"with respect to the conduct": ibid., 1513.

203 "imminent danger": ibid., 1989, vol. 2, 1722–23.
"does not accept the notion": Fisher, 147.

11: "We Were Going to War"

206 "Some observers": Howard Zinn, *A People's History of the United States*, 594–95.
"was telling people": ibid., 595.

207 "all necessary means": Louis Fisher, *Presidential War Power*, 148.
"Authorization for Use": 105 Statutes 3 (1991).

208 "To tell you": Zinn, 597.
"President Bush has decided": ibid., 599.
"The spectre of Vietnam": ibid., 600.

209 "had the sole power": *Dellums v. Bush*, 752 F.Supp. 1141 (D.D.C. 1990).

210 "Though I felt": *Public Papers of the Presidents, 1991, 497.
"I didn't": ibid., 1992–93, 995.

211 "exercise of our inherent right": 29 *Weekly Compilation of Presidential Documents*, 1993, 1181.
"does not constitute": 140 *Congressional Record* S10415–33 (August 3, 1994).
"Like my predecessors": 30 *Weekly Compilation of Presidential Documents* 1616 (1994).
"All I can tell you": ibid., 2101–2.

217 "They had declared war": Bob Woodward, *Bush at War*, 15.
"an apparent terrorist attack": ibid., 15–16.

219 "War is a powerful word": ibid., 45–46.
"to deter and pre-empt": Rep. Peter DeFazio, "Unilateralism, Preemption and the War Powers Act," www.house.gov/defazio/pf-MorseCenter/102703.

12: "We Will Not Hesitate to Act Alone"

223   "should aim, above all": Rep. Peter DeFazio, "Unilateralism, Preemption and the War Powers Act," www.house.gov/defazio/pf-MorseCenter/102703.

224   "deterring potential competitors": id.
       "even in conflicts": id.

225   "We will retain": id.
       "the sense that the world order": id.
       "We will not hesitate": id.

226   "The war on terror": Bob Woodward, *Plan of Attack,* 132.
       "his men and resources": www.foxnews.com/story/0.2933.131516.00.

227   "President George W. Bush": www.cnn.com/2002/us/07/07/iraq.bush.

228   "I do firmly believe": www.newsmax.com/archives/2002/7/10/174300.
       "We are going to support you": Bob Woodward, *Bush at War,* 118.

230   "It has nothing": www.cbsnews.com/stories/2002/11/15/world/printable529569.
       "Regardless of whether": Anthony H. Cordesman, "Western Security Efforts and the Greater Middle East," www.usinfo.state.gov/journals/itps/0604/ijpc/cordesman.
       "recommend to an interim": *Alexander's Gas & Oil Connections,* vol. 7, issue 23, November 27, 2002.

231   "you have to control": quoted in Robert Dreyfuss, "The Thirty-Year Itch," *Mother Jones,* March/April 2003.
       "Let us in the name": Howard Zinn, *A People's History of the United States,* 14.
       "rid the world of evil": *Washington Post,* Sept. 14, 2001, 1.

232   "I loathe Kim Jong Il": Bob Woodward, *Bush at War,* 340.

233   "has not developed": www.state.gov/secretary/rm/2001/933.
       "has weapons of mass destruction": www.pbs.org/newshour/bb/middle_east/jan-june03/wmd_5-29.
       "There is no doubt": *New York Times,* Aug. 27, 2002, 1.

234   "We do know": www.defenselink.mil/speeches/2002/s20020918-secdef2.
       "possesses and produces": www.whitehouse.gov/news/releases/2000/10/20021007-8.
       "to take action": www.epic-use.org/policywatch/warresolution.
       "brutal repression": www.cbsnews.com/stories/2002/10/10/attack/main525165.

235   "Our conservative": www.washingtonpost.com/wp-srv/nation/transcripts/powelltext_020503.

236   "is a somber": www.lawyersagainstthewar.org/legalarticles/appeal.
       "unequivocal support": www.iraqwatch.org/government/us/legislation/hconres104-032103.

237   "The liberation of Iraq": www.cnn.com/2003/us.05/01/bush.transcript.

237 "no doubt": *Washington Post,* March 22, 2003, 1.
"U.S. officials": www.activeopposition.com/wmd.
238 "We've been to virtually": www.cnn.com/2003/world/meast/05/30.
"the strongest evidence": www.cbsnews.com/stories/2003/08/10/iraq/main567510.
"We found the weapons": *Washington Post,* May 31, 2003, 1.
"was based on": www.slate.msn.com/id/2100684.
"I'm personally convinced": www.cia.gov/cia/public.affairs/speeches/2003/david.kay.10022003.
239 For bureaucratic reasons": www.defenselink.mil/transcripts/2003/tr20030528/depsecdef0222.
"overwhelming evidence": www.house.gov/schakowsky/cheney_link.doc.
"no credible evidence": *The 9/11 Report: The National Commission on Terrorist Attacks Upon the United States,* 36.
240 "We were told": www.byrd.senate.gov/byrd_speeches_2003october.

13: "The Constitution Is Just a Piece of Paper"

243 "is a law for rulers": *Ex parte Milligan,* 71 U.S. 2 (1866).
244 "Preserving our freedom": www.epic.org/privacy/terrorism/usapatriot/feingold.
"acts dangerous": 115 Statues 271 (2001).
245 "Ninety-five percent": Boise (Idaho) *Spokesman-Review,* June 11, 2004, 1.
246 "The Patriot Act is al Qaeda's": www.foxnews.com/story/0,2933,125551,00.
"the Patriot Act went too far": www.aclu.org/safeandfree.
"consistent record": www.house.gov/judiciary_democrats/justicepatriotreptpr71404.
247 "aggressive arrest": www.usmayors.org/uscm/us_mayor_newspaper/documents/11_05_01/ashcroft.
248 "hardened criminals": www.writ.news.findlaw.com/mariner/20021104.
"the worst": www.whitehouse.gov/vicepresident/news-speeches/speeches/vp20020127.
"Babbling at times": *New York Times,* October 1, 2002, A18.
250 "it is difficult": www.lawofwar.org/torture_memos_analysis.
251 "not intended": *Washington Post,* June 9, 2004, 3.
252 "If you don't": Nat Hentoff, *The War on the Bill of Rights and the Gathering Resistance,* 66.
"We found fundamental failures": www.cbsnews.com/stories/2004/10/20/iraq/main650247.
253 "These events occurred": www.cnn.com/2004/allpolitics/05/07/politics.abuse.main.

253 "The Constitution": Peter Irons, *A People's History of the Supreme Court,* 351.

254 "must at once convey": www.worldnewsstand.net/1/federalist/84.

255 "special advisor": Hentoff, 54–58.

256 "I'm challenging everything": ibid., 57.
"if accurate": ibid., 60.
"an important victory": ibid., 59.

257 "any person": 28 U.S. Code, sections 2244–2266; 14 Statutes 385 (1867).

258 "a state of war": *Hamdi v Rumsfeld,* www.supremecourtus.gov/opinions/2003/03-6696.

260 "He has always": www.iht.com/articles/540211.

261 "are not nationals": *Rasul v. Bush,* www.supremecourtus.gov/opinions/2003/03-334.

Conclusion

273 "The country must": Peter Irons, *A People's History of the Supreme Court,* 58.

SUGGESTED READINGS
AND SOURCES

Readers who wish to consult any of the material cited in these notes can find almost all of them in any good college or university library, and in many public libraries. There are extensive bibliographies on war powers issues in the following books, cited below: David Gray Adler and Larry N. George, eds., *The Constitution and the Conduct of American Foreign Policy*; Louis Fisher, *Presidential War Power*; W. Taylor Reveley III, *War Powers of the President and Congress*; Abraham D. Sofaer, *War, Foreign Affairs, and Constitutional Power: The Origins*; Gary M. Stern and Morton H. Halperin, eds., *The U.S. Constitution and the Power to Go to War: Historical and Current Perspectives*; and Francis D. Wormuth and Edwin B. Firmage, *To Chain the Dog of War: The War Power of Congress in History and Law*.

Books Cited

Acheson, Dean, *Present at the Creation: My Years In the State Department* (New York: W. W. Norton, 1969).

Adler, David Gray and Larry N. George, eds., *The Constitution and the Making of American Foreign Policy* (Lawrence: University Press of Kansas, 1996).

Carter, Jimmy, *Keeping Faith: Memoirs of a President* (New York: Harper-Collins, 1982).

DeWeerd, Harvey A., *President Wilson Fights His War: World War I and the American Intervention* (New York: Macmillan, 1968).

Fehrenbacher, Don, *Slavery, Law, and Politics: The Dred Scott Case in Historical Perspective* (New York: Oxford University Press, 1981).

Fisher, Louis, *Presidential War Power* (Lawrence: University Press of Kansas, 1995).

Fitzpatrick, John C., *The Writings of George Washington* (New York: Random House, 1948).

Hentoff, Nat, *The War on the Bill of Rights and the Gathering Resistance* (New York: Seven Stories Press, 2003).

Irons, Peter, *America's Cold War Crusade: Domestic Politics and Foreign Policy, 1942–1948* (Ph.D. dissertation, Boston University, 1973).

———, *Justice at War: The Story of the Japanese American Internment Cases* (New York: Oxford University Press, 1983).

———, *A People's History of the Supreme Court* (New York: Viking Press, 1999).

Keynes, Edward, *Undeclared War: Twilight Zone of Constitutional Power* (University Park: Pennsylvania State University Press, 1982).

Link, Arthur S., ed., *The Papers of Woodrow Wilson* (Princeton, NJ: Princeton University Press, 1974).

Madison, James, *Notes of Debates in the Federal Convention of 1787*, Adrienne Koch, ed. (Athens: Ohio University Press, 1966).

———, *The Writings of James Madison* (New York: Best Books, 2000).

Marzani, Carl, *We Can Be Friends* (New York: Topical Books, 1952).

Mee, Charles, *The Genius of the People* (New York: HarperCollins, 1987).

Reveley, W. Taylor III, *War Power of the President and Congress* (Charlottesville: University Press of Virginia, 1981).

Richardson, James D., ed., *A Compilation of the Messages and Papers of the Presidents* (available online at www.indypublish.com, 2004).

Sofaer, Abraham, *War, Foreign Affairs, and Constitutional Power: The Origins* (Cambridge, MA: Ballinger Publishing, 1976).

Stern, Gary N., and Morton H. Halperin, eds., *The U.S. Constitution and the Power to Go to War: Historical and Current Perspectives* (Westport, CT: Greenwood Press, 1994).

Stern, Philip van Doren, ed., *The Life and Writings of Abraham Lincoln* (New York: Random House, 1940).

Tansill, Charles C., *Back Door to War: The Roosevelt Foreign Policy, 1933–1941* (Westport, CT: Greenwood Press, 1975).

Wilson, Woodrow, *Constitutional Government in the United States* (New York: Best Books, 1961; reprint edition).

Woodward, Bob, *Bush at War* (New York: Simon & Schuster, 2002).

———, *Plan of Attack* (New York: Simon & Schuster Paperbacks, 2004).

Wormuth, Francis D., and Edwin B. Firmage, *To Chain the Dog of War: The War Power of Congress in History and Law* (Dallas, TX: Southern Methodist University Press, 1986).

Zinn, Howard, *A People's History of the United States* (New York: HarperCollins/Perennial Classics, 2001; first published by Harper & Row, 1980; numerous subsequent editions in various formats).

Articles Cited

Lyons, Eugene, "The U.S. and World Affairs," *Nation's Business,* April 1946.
Wood, Junius B., "How Russia Trades With Us," *Nation's Business,* March 1945.

Government Documents Cited

Commission on Wartime Relocation and Internment of Civilians, *Personal Justice Denied* (1983).
Congressional Record
Department of State Bulletin
National Commission on Terrorist Attacks Upon the United States, *The 9/11 Report* (New York: St. Martin's Paperbacks, 2004; also available from the Government Printing Office).
Opinions of the Attorney General
Public Papers of the Presidents
Weekly Compilation of Presidential Documents

Cases Cited

Note: Cases are listed below in chronological order of their decision.
Bas v. Tingy, 4 U.S. 37 (1800)
Marbury v. Madison, 5 U.S. 137 (1803)
Little v. Barreme, 6 U.S. 169 (1804)
United States v. Smith, 27 Fed. Cases 1192 (Cir. Ct. N.Y. 1806)
Martin v. Mott, 25 U.S. 19 (1827)
American Insurance Co. v. 256 Bales of Cotton, 26 U.S. 511 (1828)
Fleming v. Page, 50 U.S. 603 (1850)
Dred Scott v. Sandford, 60 U.S. 393 (1857)
Durand v. Holland, 8 Fed. Cases 1123 (Cir. Ct. S.D.N.Y. 1860)
Ex parte Merryman, 17 Fed. Cases 144 (Cir. Ct. D. Md. 1861)
The Prize Cases, 67 U.S. (635 (1863)
Ex parte Milligan, 71 U.S. 12 (1866)
Schenck v. United States, 249 U.S. 47 (1919)
Abrams v. United States, 250 U.S. 616 (1919)

Panama Refining C. v. Ryan, 293 U.S. 388 (1935)

Schechter Poultry Co. v. United States, 295 U.S. 495 (1935)

United States v. Curtiss-Wright Corp., 299 U.S. 304 (1936)

Ex parte Quirin, 317 U.S. 1 (1942)

Hirabayashi v. United States, 320 U.S. 81 (1943)

Korematsu v. United States, 323 U.S. 214 (1944)

Ex parte Endo, 323 U.S. 284 (1944)

Youngstown Sheet & Tube Co. v. Sawyer, 343 U.S. 579 (1952)

Baker v. Carr, 369 U.S. 186 (1962)

Luftig v. McNamara, 252 F. Supp. 819 (D.D.C. 1966)

Velvel v. Johnson, 287 F. Supp. 846 (D. Kan. 1968)

Brandenburg v. Ohio, 395 U.S. 444 (1969)

Meyers v. Nixon, 339 F. Supp. 1388 (S.D.N.Y. 1972)

Atlee v. Laird, 347 F. Supp. 689 (E.D.Pa. 1972)

Drinan v. Nixon, 364 F. Supp. 854 (D.Mass. 1973)

Mitchell v. Laird, 488 F.2d 611 (D.C. Cir. 1973)

Holtzman v. Richardson, 361 F. Supp. 544 (E.D.N.Y. 1973)

Holtzman v. Richardson, 484 F.2d 1307 (2d. Cir. 1973)

Dellums v. Bush, 752 F. Supp. 1141 (D.D.C. 1990)

Hamdi v. Rumsfeld, U.S. Sup. Ct. 2004 (available on Supreme Court Web site: www.supremecourtus.gov; also on www.findlaw.com)

Rasul v. Bush, U.S. Sup. Ct. 2004 (available on Supreme Court Web site: www.supremecourtus.gov; also on www.findlaw.com)

INDEX

About the Author

A professor of political science at the University of California–San Diego, Peter Irons is the author of numerous books, including *A People's History of the Supreme Court,* and editor and narrator of *May It Please the Court.* His writings have earned him an unprecedented five Silver Gavel awards from the American Bar Association. He is a graduate of Harvard Law School, and is a member of the Supreme Court bar.

THE AMERICAN EMPIRE PROJECT

In an era of unprecedented military strength, leaders of the United States, the global hyperpower, have increasingly embraced imperial ambitions. How did this significant shift in purpose and policy come about? And what lies down the road?

The American Empire Project is a response to the changes that have occurred in America's strategic thinking as well as in its military and economic posture. Empire, long considered an offense against America's democratic heritage, now threatens to define the relationship between our country and the rest of the world. The American Empire Project publishes books that question this development, examine the origins of U.S. imperial aspirations, analyze their ramifications at home and abroad, and discuss alternatives to this dangerous trend.

The project was conceived by Tom Engelhardt and Steve Fraser, editors who are themselves historians and writers. Published by Metropolitan Books, an imprint of Henry Holt and Company, its titles include *Hegemony or Survival* by Noam Chomsky, *The Sorrows of Empire* by Chalmers Johnson, *How to Succeed at Globalization* by El Fisgón, *Crusade* by James Carroll, *Blood and Oil* by Michael Klare, and *Dilemmas of Domination* by Walden Bello.

For more information about the American Empire Project and for a list of forthcoming titles, please visit www.americanempireproject .com.